Securing Democracy:
political parties and democratic consolidation in southern Europe

The new democracies of Mediterranean Europe – Italy, Portugal, Spain and Greece – are generally seen as conforming to the western European model of liberal democracy. But the process of democratization is a gradual one, and each national democracy is moulded by its own political, social, and economic characteristics. In particular, the active role of national political parties is of prime importance.

The contributors to this volume focus on party systems in the three new democracies of Greece, Spain and Portugal since the end of their authoritarian regimes, and on Italy in the post-war period. Combining cross-national chapters with national case-studies, the book provides the first comparative analysis of southern Europe's development through democratic transition towards democratic consolidation. The differing approaches to securing democracy in these countries have broadened the political experience of western Europe, and give insights into the workings of more established democracies which will be of use to students of politics, European studies, and development studies.

The Editor
Geoffrey Pridham is Reader in European Politics, and Director of the Centre for Mediterranean Studies. His previous books include *The New Mediterranean Democracies* and *Political Parties and Coalitional Behaviour in Italy*.

The Centre for Mediterranean Studies (CMS), established at the University of Bristol in October 1987, is an inter-disciplinary research centre focusing on the countries of Mediterranean Europe. It promotes co-operation with universities and institutes in the countries of that region, and receives financial support from the European Commission.

Securing Democracy: political parties and democratic consolidation in southern Europe

Edited by
Geoffrey Pridham

The Centre for Mediterranean Studies, University of Bristol

Routledge
London and New York

First published 1990
by Routledge
11 New Fetter Lane
London EC4P 4EE

Simultaneously published in the USA and Canada
by Routledge
a division of Routledge, Chapman and Hall, Inc.
29 West 35th Street, New York, NY 10001

© 1990 Geoffrey Pridham

Typeset by LaserScript Limited, Mitcham, Surrey

Printed and bound in Great Britain by
Biddles Ltd, Guildford and King's Lynn

British Library Cataloguing in Publication Data
Securing democracy: political parties and democratic consolidation in
southern Europe.
  1. Southern Europe. Political parties
  I. Pridham, Geoffrey
  324.24
  ISBN 0-415-02326-2

Library of Congress Cataloging in Publication Data
Securing democracy : political parties and democratic consolidation in
southern Europe / edited by Geoffrey Pridham.
  p. cm.
"Published for, Centre for Mediterranean Studies, University of Bristol."
Includes bibliographical references.
ISBN 0-415-02326-2
  1. Political parties—Europe, Southern. 2. Europe, Southern—Politics and
government. I. Pridham, Geoffrey, 1942–   . II. University of Bristol.
Centre for Mediterranean Studies.
JN94.A979S43 1990   89-10903
324.24--dc20   CIP

Contents

Contents

vi

Tables

Contributors

Kevin Featherstone is Lecturer in the Department of European Studies at the University of Bradford. He is the co-editor of *Political Change in Greece: Before and After the Colonels* (1987) and of various articles on contemporary Greek politics. His research interests also include the European left, and the European Community. He is the author of *Socialist Parties and European Integration: A Comparative History* (1988).

Richard Gillespie is Lecturer in the Politics of Mediterranean Europe at the University of Warwick. He is the author of *The Spanish Socialist Party: A History of Factionalism* (1989) and several articles on Spanish and southern European politics.

Ken Gladdish is Senior Lecturer in Politics, University of Reading, and has written extensively on west European politics.

David Hine is Official Student (Fellow) in Politics at Christ Church, Oxford University, and has published many articles on constitutional matters and political parties in Italy.

Ulrike Liebert has been research fellow at the European University Institute, Florence. She is author of *Neue Autonomiebewegung und Dezentralisierung in Spanien: Der Fall Andalusien* (1986) and of articles on Spanish and comparative European themes. She is co-editing a book on *Parliaments and Democratic Consolidation in Southern Europe*.

Gianfranco Pasquino is Professor of Political Science at the University of Bologna and Vice-President of the Cattaneo Institute. He has published numerous books and articles on Italian politics, including *Crisi dei Partiti e Governabilita* (1980), and (editor) *Il Sistema Politico Italiano* (1985).

Contributors

Geoffrey Pridham is Reader in European Politics and Director of the Centre for Mediterranean Studies at Bristol University. Among his book publications are (editor) *The New Mediterranean Democracies: Regime Transition in Spain, Greece and Portugal* (1984), (editor), *Coalitional Behaviour in Theory and Practice: An Inductive Model for Western Europe* (1986), and *Political Parties and Coalitional Behaviour in Italy* (1988).

Donald Sassoon is Reader in History at Queen Mary and Westfield College, University of London. He has edited Togliatti's *Gramsci and Other Essays* (1977) and *The Italian Communists Speak for Themselves* (1977), and is the author of *The Strategy of the Italian Communist Party* (1981), *Contemporary Italy* (1986), and numerous articles as well as two reports on television broadcasting systems for the RAI (Italian State TV). He is currently working on the west European left since 1945.

Susannah Verney is a graduate of the School of Slavonic and East European Studies, University of London, and also studied for a year at the University of Thessaloniki in Northern Greece. She is currently preparing a Ph.D. thesis on Greek political parties and the debate on accession to the European Community, 1974–9. She has published several academic articles on contemporary Greek issues.

Preface

This publication is the result of one of the first projects of the Centre for Mediterranean Studies (CMS), established at Bristol University in October 1987, in a series on democratic transition and consolidation in southern Europe. It was also started in conjunction with the Politics and Society in Mediterranean Europe (POSME) group of the Political Studies Association, with a panel at the latter's annual conference at Aberdeen in April 1987 and a further meeting of contributors to discuss revision of work in December 1987, organized by Ken Gladdish at Reading University.

The theme examined in this volume is one neglected in comparative work on the problems of democratic consolidation in southern European countries, yet it is one quite decisive to the outcome of that process. The contributors have followed the comparative framework set out on pp. 26–8.

The editor would like to thank Leonardo Morlino, Yannis Papadopoulos, and Walter Opello for their helpful comments on some of the early drafts.

Geoffrey Pridham
Centre for Mediterranean Studies
University of Bristol

Chapter one

Southern European democracies on the road to consolidation: a comparative assessment of the role of political parties

Geoffrey Pridham

Political parties in liberal democracies

It is now regularly assumed in the growing literature on the new democracies of Mediterranean Europe that they have at last conformed to the type of liberal democracy common throughout western Europe. Thus Schmitter in his introduction to the collective study *Transitions from Authoritarian Rule* comments on the various contributions:

> implicitly, they argue that these countries – Italy some time ago; Portugal, Spain and Greece more recently; and Turkey more ambiguously – have entered into, and can be expected to remain within, the range of institutional variation and patterns of political conflict characteristic of Western Europe as a whole.[1]

Similarly this conclusion is evident in some country studies on these new democracies. For example Opello's *Portugal's Political Development: A Comparative Approach* commences:

> The Portuguese political tradition, although no doubt different in important ways from that of the major powers, is as much West European as is that of France, West Germany or Italy. The inclusion of Portugal within the tradition of comparative scholarship adds one more case to the universe of pluralist democracies and can aid our understanding of the West European political experience generally.[2]

This assumption about the outcome of regime change is tantamount to saying that, transition to democracy having been accomplished, these countries have now embarked on the subsequent process of democratic consolidation or have even moved well towards its achievement. Such an assumption begs, however, a variety of questions. There are, first, different types of liberal democracies in terms of institutional, political, and cultural features, so that testing for the outcome of regime change requires some differentiation. Second, the process of democratic

1

consolidation is rather more complicated and distinctly lengthier than the preceding phase of democratic transition, suggesting in the case of the new democracies of the 1970s that the former phase if only for reasons of time has not yet been completed. Indeed, the other case of Italy is really a classic instance of difficult and lengthy consolidation, taking in the view of many commentators as much as a generation. There is, therefore, a need at least for definitional clarity when broaching the question of regime consolidation in southern Europe.

In general, focusing on political parties and party systems must remain a basic if not the central theme for examining not only the quality of the liberal democracy in question but also its progress towards and achievement of democratic consolidation. As any textbook description of this type of system will emphasize, 'party competition is the hallmark of liberal democracy; it is the device which makes governments responsive to electorates'.[3] Bingham Powell has elaborated:

> Scholars and commentators assert that a strong system of political parties is essential for a strong democracy. The party system shapes citizen participation through the electoral process. The stability of political leadership depends on party activities in the electoral and legislative arenas. The dynamics of the party system may either inhibit or exacerbate turmoil and violence. The strategies and commitments of party leaders can be critical for the support of the democratic regime in time of crisis.[4]

Similarly writing on stability in west European democracies, Sontheimer has noted: 'the stability of the party system is the really decisive factor for the stability of the whole system in all democratic systems, in which political parties play a prevalent role both in the formation of governments and in the development of political will'.[5] In other words, political parties provide a crucial test of exactly how far democracies are pluralist; furthermore they are central to the acquisition of legitimacy by new democracies. Needless to say, it is important to approach the whole question of regime consolidation through an analysis of their party systems and not merely of individual parties in the countries concerned.

In making this hypothesis, there are a variety of objections that cannot pass without mention as they are relevant to our discussion and in any case reflect on the general role of political parties in liberal democracies. In particular, there has been growing scepticism about the impact and hence importance of political parties in western democracies, challenging the previous and widely held view of parties as the central component of these systems.[6] This has occurred in the very same period in which three of our southern European countries embarked on democratization; there have been some similar criticisms of parties in these new systems as elsewhere, for example an emphasis on leader personalities rather than programmes, the lack of internal party democracy. All the same, the debate over change in European party systems, with which this scepticism has been linked, has itself remained inconclusive about the extent and the meaning of such change while identifying its symptoms.[7] The degree of this change has sometimes been exaggerated; it has not really been established whether the scenario is one of party realignment or, more seriously, of a growing detachment from parties as such. Recent surveys of this question have tended to indicate elements of continuity as well as change.[8] But whichever scenario is confirmed, our concern in this volume is with the particular exercise of consolidating new democracies rather than with political performance as such in established democracies, where conceivably the potential for weariness with familiar party actors is much greater.

The other main objection, one parallel to the foregoing, has settled on alternatives to political parties as key actors in liberal democracies. For instance, new social movements, interest groups, and also the media have been highlighted in comparative studies as challenging the traditional role of parties as instruments of popular control and civic orientation.[9] This has for instance been identified as one reason for the instability of the new Spanish party system. According to Antonio Bar

> The limitation of the role of the party system as an active subject in the political system and the consequent presence within the latter of other determining forces of great importance. . . . The King, the armed forces, the police, the bureaucracy and the Church, together with other social groups, have maintained autonomous roles, and their strength has been decisive when it came to determining the functioning of a political system characterised by weak parties, lacking both internal consolidation and stable and solid bonds with their electorates.[10]

But this phenomenon is also nationally variable, as Bar himself points out in the case of Spain: 'this is partly due to the historic conditions under which the transition to democracy took place in Spain, a transition in which a whole set of different forces converged as active elements'.[11] Whether this also holds for democratic consolidation there is however a somewhat different matter, given that new problems have to be faced in this process and the significance of some actors might change.[12]

In any case, political parties remain as effective and significant intermediary structures in liberal democracies, even if collectively they are less dominant in some systems than others. Above all, they are – at least seen conventionally – crucial as political and organizational linkages between state and society, a role it is difficult for some of their challengers (new social movements, the media) to replicate. Moreover, as the growing literature on parties in the new southern European democracies itself strongly suggests, there is an unmistakable (and really obvious) relationship between the consolidation of their party systems and their system consolidation as a whole. Another and rather more hopeful assessment of the Spanish case (1985) concluded that 'Spanish democracy will be strengthened if the political parties consolidate their organisations and extend their influence over other actors in the society.'[13] In fact, a principal reason why southern European democracies have been distinctly more successful at consolidating themselves than their counterparts in Latin America has been precisely the more advanced state of civil society and also of political organizations in the former. According to Schmitter, in explaining this difference: 'another possible "unobtrusive" indicator of the greater strength of civil societies in Southern Europe compared with Latin America can be seen in the parties and factions that have emerged to fill the new spaces for political action'.[14] Clearly, then, the two parallel processes of consolidation – of the party system and of liberal democracy – interact in some way; conceivably this interaction may be either mutually reinforcing and hence positive, or the opposite where democratic consolidation may either be delayed or even self-destruct.

As noted earlier, there are variations in the system of liberal democracy; it is logical that these variations may affect the scope for parties to perform as agents of regime consolidation. Obviously there is a risk in this argument of circular reasoning, for parties themselves usually play a key if not the principal role in defining the type of system, especially its institutional features as set out in the constitution. In some cases the parties may be less influential, notably in Portugal among our countries, for here the military codetermined the Constitution of 1976. Conceivably political parties have a broad preference for a parliamentary model of liberal democracy since this allows them greater control than in a presidential one. (Portugal was commonly seen as a 'semi-presidential' version until the constitutional revision of 1982.) But these questions, however important, are perhaps not so relevant to our theme since they are essentially a matter of democratic transition rather than democratic consolidation, at least in the cases in question. It is assumed, with the completion of transition, that the institutions are settled (in these circumstances, the issue of constitutional revision could be seen as a prolongation of transition) and that they have begun to acquire some autonomy or even 'persuasion', that is the parties have to observe the rules of the game on which they have agreed. We therefore return to the question of the institutional and political opportunities for political parties in the process of regime consolidation. In short, what types of liberal democracies are there in southern Europe?

By and large, these democracies have conformed to the parliamentary model once transition gave way to the business of regime consolidation. Portugal's 'semi-presidential' system effectively moved to being a conventional parliamentary one from 1982, for the constitutional revision severely reduced presidential powers even though popular election remained.[15] In Greece there was also a presidential element with significant executive powers, but one weaker than in Portugal since the office-holder was elected by the Parliament and not the people. This ceased when the constitutional amendments of 1986 eliminated most of the special powers of the president and Greece also became unambiguously parliamentary.[16] The other two cases of Spain and Italy were parliamentary systems as from the beginning. King Juan Carlos, often seen as a classic instance of Huntington's 'modernizing monarch', performed a crucial 'bridging' operation during transition, but his retraction from a central political role was programmed with the party-political consensus on the parliamentary model established by the 1978 Constitution. Of course, he once again played a crucial role in 1981 in averting the coup, but that itself raises questions about when Spain moved from transition to consolidation. More specifically it reflects on informal constraints from the military as the most threatening of the *poderes de hecho*, which also exerted a kind of veto power on some government policies (notably regionalization) in the early 1980s.[17] In Italy the political parties very much controlled the process of both transition and consolidation: the monarchy had been abolished (as also happened in Greece), the armed forces had been discredited by defeat in war and association with Fascism, although the Church remained as an actor – to the advantage of one of the main parties (the DC). And together the parties created a system commonly labelled a *partitocrazia*, where they not only manage the institutions but also 'populate' the state and control most public agencies.

While acknowledging their similarities of political background and, except for Italy, their contemporaneous paths to democracy, Lijphart and others argue that 'the democratic regimes of Italy, Spain, Portugal, and Greece are neither sufficiently similar to each other nor sufficiently different from other democratic regimes to fit a distinctive model of democracy'.[18] That is, albeit parliamentary, these systems of liberal democracy nevertheless demonstrate variations of an institutional and political kind which once more relate to the scope for party-political action. The southern European democracies are examined according to two dimensions – executives-parties, and federal-unitary – of the contrast between majoritarian and consensus types of democracy. On this basis, Italy emerges as a straightforward consensus model (executive-legislative balance, multi-party system, and PR electoral system) with a high index of centralization. Portugal is similar on both counts, although there has been more executive dominance if one counts the role of the presidency up to 1982 and the tendency since for Cabinets to become more durable.[19] Greece is also distinctly unitary, but it is however clearly majoritarian given the successive dominance in government by first New Democracy and then (from 1981) PASOK. Spain moved from consensual politics during the transition period to becoming relatively majoritarian, but its structure is more federal than unitary.[20] Finally, this study predicts that these institutional and political features are likely to be maintained and even reinforced.

In other words, these variations between the southern European democracies clearly must have some bearing on the behaviour of political parties, and it is worth dwelling on this for a moment. Referring to the distinction between 'horizontal' and 'vertical' legitimation of a system,[21] Greece and Spain in this sense provide much more scope for action by individual parties when in government at the former level (one may say, therefore, for the ruling Socialist parties there in the first phases of regime consolidation). By contrast, in the other two countries, there has been much more onus on inter-party co-operation at this level. On the other hand, the Spanish case is probably the most difficult when turning to the 'vertical' level, given the extra powerful cleavage between centre and periphery. The existence of party subsystems in the regions, especially in those where regionalist parties play an important role, has provided a structural constraint on the action of the national parties. More specifically it could be said that continuing difficulties over regionalization, linked as these have been in the Basque case with terrorism, have indeed acted as a brake on regime consolidation. It would therefore appear from looking at both these levels that the ruling party in Greece has had the most scope as an agent of regime consolidation, but that presupposes much about the strategy that PASOK has adopted. A glance at its behaviour in government might suggest that this has been more concerned with party than with regime interest, although one cannot generally exclude a convergence or marriage between the two in the southern European democracies. Above all, one cannot assume that single-party behaviour is more effective than party alliances in promoting consolidation; indeed, it may be weakened where high polarization has a damaging effect on the prospects for democratic consolidation, a possible hypothesis for Greece in the 1980s.

Rather, cross-party co-operation is conceivably far more effective as a determinant of consolidation than single-party behaviour, as the emphasis on political pacts in the literature on democratic transition testifies. Whatever national variation in types of liberal democracy, it is clear that inter-party relations form a significant and perhaps crucial component in the process of consolidation. In fact, the example of Italy only shows that basic problems of inter-party relations – a powerful left–right divide, in particular with a Communist party as main opposition – served to delay the final achievement of democratic consolidation there, as Hine demonstrates in this volume (Chapter 3).

Democratic consolidation, however, requires more than the establishment and confirmation of new political structures. It also requires some 'rooting' of the system in society, where political parties are the obvious and probably crucial agents. According to Huntington, they provide the wider organizational instrument for a modernized society requiring a stable balance between participation and institutionalization: a strong party system expands participation through the system, pre-empts or diverts anomic or revolutionary political activity, and moderates participation of newly mobilized groups so as not to disrupt the system.[22] Although Huntington's own concern was with Third World countries, his argument is taken as a point of departure for assessing the southern European democracies and their success in consolidation:

> The vacuum of power and authority which exists in so many modernising countries may be filled temporarily by charismatic leadership or by military force. But it can be filled permanently only by political organisation. Either the established elites compete among themselves to organise the masses through the existing system, or dissident elites organise them to overthrow that system. In the modernising world, he who controls the future who organises its politics.[23]

Huntington's emphasis on the role of political parties in regime change recalls some of the theory on crises and sequences in political development. Again, this has a bearing, though in a much broader sense, on our theme of the prospects for parties as agents of democratic consolidation. For instance the schema of five developmental crises presented by Binder and others accommodates a wide historical sweep in approaching this question. These five developmental crises are as follows: the identity problem (i.e. of the nation-state); the legitimacy problem (acceptance of the state as the source of political decisions); the penetration problem of effective control by the state; the participation problem concerning who takes part in or has influence over political decisions; and the distribution problem (how far political decisions are used to distribute material and other benefits of society).[24] Clearly the sequence of these crises may well matter, just as an accumulation of them in a given period is also likely to create system stress.

While such a schema applies to centuries of national development, it is still useful in placing the problem of recent democratic consolidation in historical context. Opello's own application of this to the case of

Portugal shows that the resolution of these crises over time was relatively orderly, but that two of them (participation and distribution) have persisted to the present time, that is into the period of democratization.[25] This certainly helps to explain the difficulties of transition and consolidation in that country. It furthermore highlights some basic problems encountered by the parties then, such as in overcoming the lack of a tradition of political mobilization and in confronting the issue of socio-economic change following the Revolution of 1974. Referring to the other three countries in southern Europe, there is inevitably national variation in this respect. Italy may be said to have solved the identity problem largely in the nineteenth century, while penetration was solved in the Fascist period and participation following it. Difficulties have nevertheless remained over the legitimacy problem (doubts about the state's capacity) and also the distribution problem (use of state resources and the conflict here between different party interests). In Spain, the process of democratization has been less difficult compared with these two cases, although the issue of regionalization represents a form of special legitimacy problem which has clearly expressed itself through the party system there. For this reason, we include a special chapter on that problem in this volume.

So far, the discussion has identified a variety of themes relevant to regime consolidation and the role here of political parties, and it has begun to place this theme in context. But, as noted at the start of this chapter, the question of democratic consolidation does require definitional clarity, all the more when trying to assess a very contemporary development and one supposedly not yet complete.

What is democratic consolidation?

While democratic transition has occasioned several theories, broadly categorized as the functionalist and the genetic,[26] democratic consolidation has as a concept and a framework so far suffered from a poverty of theory. As Schmitter has noted, modern democratic theory has really ignored the question – being more concerned with how already existing democracies manage to function – although something relevant may be learned from literature on overcoming crises and other problems of system adaptation.[27] Compared with regime transition, consolidation is a much more nebulous concept with considerable uncertainty about its point of termination. It is in any case usually seen as a broader and deeper as well as lengthier process than transition, the latter being temporally variable ranging from a few years to possibly the first decade following authoritarian rule.

The purpose of this section therefore is to broach the question of democratic consolidation by discussing views of it and any relevant theories. In doing so, inevitable differences of interpretation will be identified in order to clarify our approach before turning to theoretical perspectives on the role of political parties in this process. As a starting-point, it is worthwhile quoting at length the most comprehensive definition of 'democratic consolidation'. According to Laurence White-head, the idea of 'consolidation'

> can only be elucidated in contrast to the notion of 'transition' that precedes it. . . . After any transition from authoritarian rule the emergent democracy will be a regime in which not all significant political actors have impeccable democratic credentials, and where democratic rules of procedure have yet to be 'internalised' by the society at large. Many established institutions must be restructured, some demoted, some virtually created anew, to make them conform to democratic rather than authoritarian modes of governance. New and inexperienced political actors enter the stage, while long-established parties and interests find themselves required to compete on a quite different basis than before. The rules of competition are up for negotiation, the outcomes are uncertain and often quite unexpected, no-one is quite sure which elements of continuity remain in place. Improbable coalitions must be formed and tested, the partners and rivals in the process having little guidance as to their specific weights. Public opinion may well be in flux, as the media fills with formerly forbidden messages, whilst the old verities are cast into oblivion. In short, the transition phase is often one of acute uncertainty and high anxiety for many social actors. Such uncertainty may be exciting and creative – spurring increased political participation and the invention of new political forms – but if it becomes too generally threatening, or if it lasts too long without any fruitful outcome, then the chances of an authoritarian relapse become very great.
>
> If the transition phase is not aborted, it may pave way for a process of democratic consolidation. The hall-mark of this process will be that the many uncertainties of the transition period are progressively diminished as the new assumptions and procedures become better known and understood, and more widely accepted. The new regime becomes *institutionalised*, its framework of open and competitive political expression becomes *internalised*, and thus in large measure the preceding uncertainties and insecurities are overcome. It is unlikely that such a process can ever be fully accomplished in less than a generation. Thus what should concern us [meanwhile] is not so much the factors assuring a *full consol-*

idation of democracy, but the conditions necessary to keep the intervening process on track.

When a democratisation process advances from end-transition to full consolidation there is a widening of the range of political actors who assume democratic conduct on the part of their adversaries; a deepening of the commitment of most actors to the mutually negotiated democratic framework (i.e. they increasingly take a 'principled' rather than 'instrumental' approach to the observance of this framework); and thus an interactive sequence akin to a round of tariff cuts, or arms reduction in international relations, whereby all participants in the democratic game withdraw some of the barriers to enhanced trust and cooperation with their rivals. By these means political actors learn to change their perceptions of themselves, their significant others, and the system as a whole. All this is likely to be accompanied by either a conscious and coordinated, or at least a tacitly agreed, campaign to 'socialise' the population at large into acceptance of democratic norms.[28]

Whitehead's excellent summary identifies many broad features of the consolidation process. It is, for instance, one that is less exclusive to the role of elites than transition, placing more attention on the relationship between the new system and society. It would appear too that the new southern European democracies are still in the earlier stages of consolidation, if we accept his argument that its full achievement takes up to a generation. This argument will be contested by some, although the Italian case – complicated as it was – did indeed take about a generation. Morlino however suggests:

It would be empirically useful to agree to a reasonable period of time at the end of which the outcome of consolidation could be examined. The European experiences of the post-war period would suggest that a decade from the end of the installation of all the principal democratic structures is, on the whole, the most appropriate. But why precisely a decade? One can attempt to answer this question and, at the same time, to justify this choice by focussing attention on the structures and norms of the regime alone. Thus, it can be maintained that consolidation is concluded, with a greater or lesser degree of success, when the passage of time no longer has an evident effect on already established practices and tested structures and norms. This seems to come about, as far as the cases under consideration are concerned, in the medium term, that is, about 10–12 years after installation.[29]

If there is any point of agreement between different versions of the temporal span of the consolidation process, it must be that a successful case shows diminishing probability of a reversal and that therefore at least the first decade of its existence is the most crucial. In this sense, Converse agrees when he says in his essay on 'Of time and partisan stability':

> What is utterly predictable . . . is that threats to the survival of a new institution will be very high in its infant stages; in the degree that it can outlast these first precarious periods, it will typically have put forth roots of sufficient strength so that challenges to its very being diminish in number and those that do occur are warded off with increasing ease.[30]

What this also makes clear is that the time for a study of political parties and democratic consolidation is now opportune, if we broadly say that the 1980s represent the first decade of consolidation following transition in the 1970s. Since Italy is said to have achieved full consolidation by or sometime during the early 1970s, this important case provides a useful historical component for comparative purposes. However, the concept of democratic consolidation still requires more contextual handling and further refinement. We do this by measuring it against other related concepts of system change and adaptation and by reference to more specific discussion of its meaning in the literature.

First, it is necessary to dwell further on the relationship with democratic transition, which preceding consolidation consequently must condition it to some degree. Consolidation may well, for instance, overlap with Rustow's 'habituation phase' as the ultimate stage of transition following the 'decision phase', which is marked by the deliberate agreement of political leaders to accept political diversity or pluralism and, to that end, to institutionalize democratic procedures as 'an act of deliberate, explicit consensus' involving in particular the constituent period. According to Rustow, the 'decision phase' is distinguished by this agreement 'being transmitted to the professional politicians and to the citizenry at large'.[31] While acknowledging that democratic consolidation is not simply a prolongation of transition, Schmitter nevertheless argues that 'the primary determinant of the type of democratic consolidation is the mode of democratic transition; this, in turn, is strongly influenced by the type of demise of authoritarian rule which is linked to the type of authoritarian regime it was'.[32] Clearly this calls for some diachronic assessment of patterns of political change leading up to and encompassing regime consolidation – with considerable scope here for national variation – but our discussion will confine itself to more direct comparison of 'transition' and 'consolidation' for the sake of differentiation between them.

In general terms, there have been two schools of regime transition theory – those known as functionalist, emphasizing environmental factors and in particular socio-economic development; and the others called genetic, stressing political factors and stressing much scope for political actors and their strategies.[33] In the former case, the time-scale is obviously longer: functionalist theories have tended to be dominated by variations on the theme that a country's chances for democratization depend crucially on its level of socio-economic development or modernization.[34] In so far as this explanation has been based on one dominant cause of transition, it has been criticized for being too deterministic. However, theories which incorporate such environmental factors and focus on interaction between them and political action are rather more convincing. This is notably true of Kirchheimer's thesis of 'confining conditions' with respect to revolutionary breakthroughs, whereby the social and economic frame of a society lays down a conditioning perimeter within which political choice has to be made and solutions sought.[35] Theories concerning political choice do not deny the importance of socio-economic factors, but they argue as does Linz that there is considerable room for political actors to make choices 'that can increase or decrease the probability of the persistence and stability of a regime'. For example, Merritt sees a key role being played by elites as instigators of change: they may be minimizers set on preserving the essential structure as it is while prepared to adapt it, or they may be potential or actual maximizers with transformative objectives, with variations between these two possibilities.[36] In the same vein, Almond has noted that 'great leaders are great coalition makers' in their capacity for building consensus; just as others have talked of 'swing men' and 'modernizing monarchs' in system change.[37] As such, these genetic theories concentrate more specifically on the transition operation, whereas the functionalist theories draw attention rather to either background factors (i.e. pre-transition) or to those relating perhaps more to the prospects for regime consolidation.

Theories on regime transition have therefore been most useful when experimenting with a range of multi-causal explanations, usually combining political and socio-economic and sometimes also cultural factors.[38] Overall, then, the tendency is to point to different modes of and paths to democratization. This also needs to be taken into account, moreover, when considering the following phase of consolidation, for clearly a particular form of transition is bound to have different consequences for consolidation from another type of transition. Indeed, some differentiation is necessary when handling the question of democratic consolidation cross-nationally, as will be noted below in further references to the literature. On the other hand, there is less likelihood for a division into different schools of interpretation when turning to consolidation, if only because it is important here to consider both political and socio-economic processes in conjunction – conceivably more so than over transition. It should also be noted that, whatever the influence of transition on consolidation, the latter is not simply an extension or prolongation of the former. Success in the first does not guarantee success in the second, for as Whitehead indicated there are qualitative differences between the two phases. Schmitter has elaborated on this as follows:

> democratic consolidation (DC) poses distinctive problems to political actors . . . to a significant degree, DC involves new actors, new rules, new processes and, perhaps, even new values and resources. This is not to say that everything changes when a polity 'shifts' into DC. Many of the persons and collectivities will be the same, but they will be facing different problems, making different calculations and behaving in different ways. . . . Moreover, the shift in problem-space may reduce the significance of actors who previously played a central role and enhance that of others who by prudence or impotence were marginal to the demise and transition.[39]

Second, in so far as democratic consolidation is a finite process, it is necessary to distinguish it also from other concepts of system change with respect to ongoing or even long-established democracies. Thus, while regime consolidation obviously has some link with the question of system stability, or rather system stabilization, none the less system stability as such is a separate problem. Conceivably systems may undergo cycles of high or low stability not automatically connected with problems of consolidation. As Dowding and Kimber have argued: 'the stability of any political object is conceptually related to the contingencies that threaten it, and its overall stability at any given time is related to the contingencies it faces at that time'.[40] Similarly Lane and Ersson agree that 'political stability is a vector of properties, each of which is more or less independent of each other and which varies over time', concluding that 'political stability is different from regime longevity or system persistence . . . the basic problem of stability is its time and space variation'.[41] The distinction of course relates to a general problem for political change is not conceptually the same as political instability, just as political stability cannot be equated with lack of change – in fact, stability may be conditional on some form of change or adaptation.[42]

Of course, much also depends on what is meant by 'change'. System change interpreted as regime change rather than (established) system adaptation is in a different category, involving something rather more basic. Even so, the distinction between instability and (regime) change should be maintained to avoid confusion between the co-existence of phenomena and a causal relationship between them. In all probability, there is an overlap between the many uncertainties of the transition phase – as explained by Whitehead – and the appearance of instability, but it does not necessarily follow that transition itself is the (main) cause of that. It is also possible that the breakdown of the previous authoritarian regime, marked by growing conflict between environmental demands for change and resistance on the part of the authorities, is rather the cause of instability, so that the move to democracy begins to relieve this problem. Similarly, the gradual disappearance of transitional uncertainties with consolidation is not as such tantamount to the achievement of stability, although obviously destabilizing occurrences may be said to delay the consolidation process.

Both preceding comparisons, with regime transition and with system stability, are at least useful as a reference point in clarifying what consolidation is not. They also help to indicate the starting and final points of the consolidation process, but we need to pursue this more specifically with further references to the literature in order to highlight the exact meaning of consolidation. Thus, it may be said that transition ends not merely once the constitution is in place but also once the system begins to function with a popularly elected government. In other words, the elites begin to work the system and to adjust accordingly. This opens the way for removing the uncertainties of transition and so the 'shift' occurs to consolidation. According to Schmitter,

> consolidation involves the process of converting patterns into structures, of endowing what are initially fortuitous interactions, episodic arrangements, ad hoc solutions, temporary pacts etc. with sufficient autonomy and value that they stand some chance of persisting; actors respond by adjusting their expectations to this likelihood and come to regard the rules and resources of these emergent structures as given, if not desirable.[43]

If the support given to the new system during transition is on the part of some political circles instrumental and even opportunistic, it may be said that consolidation sees the replacement of 'functional democrats' by 'cultural democrats' at the elite level. A commonly recognized test of progress here is a peaceful or basically uncontested transfer of power between parties in government and opposition. This is because it reflects on other attributes of democratic consolidation, such as some kind of consensus over basic policy directions and the disappearance of 'antisystem' tendencies as a viable and serious proposition. That is, the existence of the latter is likely to inhibit alternation in power and generally affect the functioning of the parliamentary institution. Clearly, too, consolidation is in train when potential challenges or threats to the new system from non-political actors (notably the military) diminish and fade.

While one dimension of the process may therefore be called 'negative consolidation', i.e. the effective removal of the prospects for system alternatives, what ultimately secures its achievement is the ongoing development of 'positive consolidation'. As already seen, this is crucial at the elite level, but our attention here is particularly directed towards the mass level. Obviously this must mean that the new system gradually acquires legitimacy. As Morlino notes about democratic consolidation, this is 'the process whereby democratic structures and norms are adapted and "frozen" and are accepted as legitimate, in part or entirely by civil society'.[44] But this is not separate from the elite level, for a decisive factor must be the interaction between both levels in that effective government performance has systemic consequences – it stores up credit for the new system. Democratic consolidation may therefore be in sight of achievement when government performance is no longer systemically important and merely reflects on the standing of the party or parties in power. This is equivalent to Easton's thesis of 'diffuse support', whereby a system takes hold despite occasional crises in performance,[45] although too many crises in the early stages of consolidation might be detrimental to it. Finally, democratic consolidation may be said to have been achieved when there is evidence that the political culture is being 're-made' in a system-supportive direction, thus removing the last of the uncertainties remaining from the transition phase.

It is difficult to state any precise time at which the consolidation process is over, although this study inclines towards Whitehead's definition of a longer-term approach. Certainly it takes distinctly longer than transition if only because consolidation is a much broader development. Its final point is bound to be rather variable nationally, but – as shown above – it is more relevant to judge this by how much the principal criteria are satisfied. This argument for differentiation may be taken further, for it is possible to speak of different levels of the consolidation process. Elaborating in effect on the two basic levels identified so far, Morlino lists the following: democratic structures and procedures which adapt and develop decisional practices; relationships between the structures, in particular over conflict management; the development of parties and the party system (organizational strengthening, identity formations, and establishing the conventions of political competition); interest structures (similar developments); relationships between intermediation structures and civil society; and relationships between intermediation structures and the regime.[46]

The conclusion is that consolidation usually proceeds at different paces at the different levels and that one may therefore speak of partial consolidation during later stages of the process. But what is also clear from Morlino's levels is that the role of parties is pertinent to virtually all of them to a greater or lesser extent. This only confirms the role of political parties as a very fundamental test of progress towards and achievement of consolidation in a liberal democracy.

Political parties and democratic consolidation: theoretical perspectives

It is clear from the foregoing discussion that any approach to the role of political parties in democratic consolidation has to be three-dimensional. Noting again that parties are crucial linkages between elite and mass levels, it is thus important to examine also separately their performance in relation to both state and society. Given too our initial hypothesis that any analysis of our subject has to focus not only on individual parties but also party systems as a whole, it follows that serious consideration has furthermore to be given to inter-party relationships. Hence, we have the outline of a general framework for this volume. But in order to develop this sufficiently, it is necessary to examine theoretical perspectives in the literature concerned directly with the role of parties and party systems and from there to identify relevant components of that framework.

We start once more with a definition, quoting again Morlino:

> Consolidation through parties is characterised, above all, by the progressive organisation and expansion of the party structures and the party system as a whole, which is then able to control and, if needs be, moderate and integrate all forms of participation. . . . Clear, long-term alignments between parties and social groups are established. Identities and the rules of internal competition among the party elites are formed. Furthermore – and this is one of the most important aspects – not only do party elites play a central part in the decision-making processes, but the parties gradually occupy the principal administrative roles and the various positions in the administration and distribution of resources at local and national level.[47]

Morlino's summary usefully highlights the importance of parties not only as agents in the institutionalization of the new regime but also as channels for developing participation, and hence for the 'rooting' of the system in society. On the actual scope for parties in the consolidation process, Morlino remarks:

> a parliamentary system can be more favourable, at the outset, to

the penetration by the groups of decision-making structures of various kinds; but this tendency can be overcome by other factors: the number of parties, the type of party system and the relationship between legislature and executive, for example, must also be taken into account.[48]

Furthermore, we have to bear in mind as always the likelihood of national variation. Here, Morlino argues – similar to our previous survey of democratic consolidation – that pre-transition developments may well have a determining influence:

> It is possible to arrive at consolidation through parties from various different traditions and situations. But, bearing in mind some European cases, it is possible to submit that the process of consolidation is more likely to follow this model if the preceding authoritarian or, indeed, totalitarian experience had profound effects on the social fabric of the country and succeeded in destroying old, traditional forms of solidarity and organisation, particularly if the system did, simultaneously, undergo considerable socio-economic transformation.[49]

This of course alludes to post-authoritarian parties as possible modernizing agents and the conditions which favour this. Paradoxically, too, it may be said that the dictatorship experience – especially if it has taken a totalitarian form – may itself facilitate subsequent 'penetration' of the system by democratic parties through the very precedent of extensive party control. The obvious European example of this would be the Federal Republic of Germany, which had undergone both thorough totalitarianism and also modernizing changes, with a consequent weakening of traditional structures both political and societal. This background opened the way, according to Loewenberg, for the 'remaking of the German party system'.[50] In the case of Italy, a somewhat weaker model of totalitarianism, some limited pluralism had persisted under the Fascist regime which did not establish full hegemony over civil society.[51] Moreover, Italy had enjoyed a democratic past with organized parties before Fascism, the latter lasting a shorter time than the dictatorships in Spain and Portugal.[52] This situation allowed parties to organize themselves in Italy before the end of the war, particularly through the Resistance, hence pre-determining their later control over the post-war system. At the same time, Italy was not a very modernized society then, so that the parties have faced difficulties in adapting to socio-economic change during the course of the post-war period. With the three new democracies, significant differences deserve mention: on the one hand, the dictatorships in Portugal and Spain lasted much longer and became more articulated than in Greece; on the other hand, modernization had commenced in Spain a decade before Franco's departure – with some influence on individual political forces there – and well ahead of that process of change in Greece and Portugal.

In view of this importance of party development and its interaction with political and social change, one may take this reasoning a stage further by referring to the role of parties in democratic transition, paralleling previous discussion of democratic consolidation. In the first instance, therefore, we can draw on or extrapolate from theories of democratic transition for approaching the role of parties in the consolidation process. In doing so, it is important to observe that parties and party systems are pertinent to both the genetic and the functionalist theories of regime change. On the first count, they provide usually the most powerful political actors and are invariably seen as strategic vehicles. On the second, parties obviously present an important linkage with and channel for the impact of socio-economic determinants on political change.

According to Rustow, the 'habituation phase' of regime transition involves a 'double process of Darwinian selectivity in favour of con-vinced democrats: one among parties in general elections and the other among politicians vying for leadership within these parties', referring to the agreement of the decision phase being transmitted to both political elites and the public.[53] He sees three elements at work here, all involving the role of parties in different ways: (1) politicians and citizens learn from the successful resolution of some issues to place their faith in new rules and apply them to new issues; (2) experience with democratic techniques and competitive recruitment confirms politicians in their democratic practices and beliefs; and (3) the population becomes fitted into the new structure by the forging of effective links of party organization 'that connect the politicians in the capital with the mass electorate throughout the country'.[54] Clearly, Rustow also identifies tasks and developments which continue into the phase of democratic consolidation. Indeed, as noted earlier, there is likely to be some overlap between Rustow's 'habituation phase' and the onset of consolidation, so that his perspectives are worth bearing in mind. Kirchheimer's thesis of 'confining conditions' in democratic transition is also somewhat long-term in its perspective and may therefore apply beyond the transition phase. According to Kirchheimer, these conditions – meaning the socio-economic frame of the country in question – limit effective political choice. At the same time, political choice itself may also (help to) modify such conditions and political outlooks may alter as a result with a consequent 'expansion of the perimeter'.[55] Certainly this suggests some scope for parties supporting the new system and identifies ways in which they may act as 'gatekeepers' in transition and afterwards. Rather similar is Pasquino's distinction between 'horizontal' (institutional) and 'vertical' (popular) legitimation in democratic transitions,[56] where parties obviously play a major role in both respects. This recalls Huntington's argument on achieving a political community in a modernized society as embracing both the 'horizontal' integration of communal groups and the 'vertical' assimilation of socio-economic classes.[57] Finally, Merritt's concern with the importance of elites in transition certainly highlights the role of party leadership, a theme accorded special attention in this volume by Pasquino's chapter. Similarly, his distinction between minimizers and maximizers alludes to the importance of party ideological motives during this formative time.[58]

It hardly requires mention that many of these functions of parties in democratic transition are carried over into the consolidation phase. Of course, any contest between minimizers and maximizers should be settled during transition, as this must be one of the salient factors of uncertainty characteristic of that phase. This is clearly seen in the Portuguese case, where early transition in 1974–6 was marked by a prolonged struggle between those with liberal-democratic and those with transformative aims. While that oversimplifies somewhat the different motives within the Armed Forces Movement – the vanguard of the 1974 Revolution – this point differentiates the parties then, especially the PS from the PCP. But, as a whole, reference above to the role of parties in transition theories does identify some problems pertinent to our discussion of consolidation, if only because they are invariably long-term and not to be confined merely to the half-decade or so of transition. At the same time, we recall Schmitter's and also Whitehead's argument that democratic consolidation is a qualitatively different process from that of democratic transition. What therefore happens to the role of parties when the 'shift' to consolidation occurs?

First, in so far as consolidation requires the progressive removal of basic uncertainties present in transition, the attitudes, strategies, and behaviour of parties must be very significant. If, as in the Portuguese case, they themselves represent or are associated with systemic alternatives, then the consolidation of liberal democracy must entail either their removal or change of strategy, or at least their neutralization or isolation. Thus, as Whitehead notes,

> if democratic consolidation is to be kept on track the revolutionary left must be either reabsorbed into democratic life or isolated and defeated; all democrats, including those on the radical left, will therefore be required to opt for defence of the regime against a continuing revolutionary challenge; but, on the other hand, persecution of the left for other than unlawful actions ... would also undermine democracy.[59]

He also pointed out that, at the same time, there is a need to be firm with hangovers from the previous regime. In other words, political parties almost certainly will be carriers of ideas identified with opposite sides of the political divide under the previous authoritarian regime. Hence, we are essentially talking here about how parties regulate political choice, and in particular how party leaderships cope with conflict management. According to Weiner and LaPalombara:

> The quality of political party leadership or, more precisely, the attitudes and skills of party leadership are an important element in how conflict is managed . . . the background and experience of party leadership in dealing with conflict is of course important. The memories of past conflicts often condition current behaviour. Individuals brought up in a political system in which coups, assassinations, political arrests, and underground movements have existed will not readily move to a political style emphasising peaceful and rational discussion.[60]

However, some willingness and effort to overcome their own past – 'burying the hatchet' historically, as it were – is clearly necessary for consolidation to proceed. This may be achieved by means of a leadership (i.e. also generational) change, or by adaptation on the part of standing party leaders and elites, but whatever method this amounts to an important aspect of the 'shift' from transition to consolidation. This recalls Di Palma's thesis about 'founding coalitions' in new democracies and a mutual 'backward' and 'forward' legitimation process. Here, ex-elites from the previous (authoritarian) regime – 'once the democratic card has proved its winning potential' – may perform a 'backward' legitimation of an incipient democracy as well as legitimizing themselves 'forward'.[61] In doing so, of course, they have no real choice but to come to terms with the legalization and ambitions of former political opponents. While the basis for such a compromise is laid during transition, democratic consolidation involves the continual testing and confirmation of that particularly if it has been the outcome of some kind of truce. This is what Rustow means by 'experience with democratic techniques and competitive recruitment', but in any case it underlines the importance of inter-party relationships in the consolidation process.

A second question concerning the role of parties in the 'shift' to consolidation refers more to their relationship with the state under the new democracy. This may take a broad or systemic form: what is to be the collective role of parties compared with other actors in the system? Taking up the point that there may be different paths to democracy,[62] it is conceivable that in transition other collective actors may be significant. However, it must be expected – given the type of liberal democracies prevalent in western Europe – that political parties will eventually come to play the central role, and that with the onset of consolidation this role is assured. This is again a pertinent example of Schmitter's argument that with consolidation new actors may emerge or, if actors remain the same, their significance may change and they invariably face different problems. As usual, interest turns first of all to the state of civil-military relations given the frequent power role of the army in previous authoritarian regimes and the requirement in standard liberal democracies that the military should be subordinated to civil rule. That is parties are obviously the principal civil actors, but their role may be challenged implicitly or explicitly by the military during transition.

For instance, the legalization of the Communist Party in Spain in 1977 – shortly before the first post-Franco parliamentary election – was commonly seen as a test-case of the military's attitude then. The uncontested decision on this, due in large part to the diplomatic mediation of the King, indicated progress in the transition, although the attempted coup four years later questioned whether transition had been accomplished and the 'shift' to consolidation had occurred. It was more likely the consequences of this event, in discrediting the reactionary military, which secured that 'shift' by removing the probability of a repeated challenge to civil rule. Significantly the alternation in power of 1982 – bringing the Socialists to power for the first time in Spanish history – occurred at this time. The period of PSOE government since then has therefore been associated with the early stages of democratic consolidation, a theme taken up by Gillespie in his chapter on Spain (Chapter 6).

Portugal, on the other hand, represents a rather different case, for here a group in the military instigated the coup which led to the 1974 Revolution and it was hardly dominated by reactionary elements. It is more true to say the military then was not cohesive, and as became clear late in 1975 it was the changed balance of power from the radical to the moderate left military (following the failed November coup) which enhanced the chances of liberal democracy. Initially therefore, the parties played more of a secondary role in the transition, at least in the turbulent events of 1974–5, although the first election in 1975 also contributed to the eventual outcome by virtue of the PS, as the most decided standard-bearer of liberal democracy, emerging as by far the strongest single party. Subsequently we see parties emerging as more central actors once the 1976 Constitution comes into force, although the military still played a parallel role at least formally through the Council of the Revolution until its abolition in the constitutional revision of 1982. All this raises the question exactly when Portugal moved from transition to consolidation. A formal answer would say with this revision, arguing therefore for a long transition. The inability of parties to manage government effectively during these years would tend to support that argument, if – as suggested earlier in this chapter – transition is achieved when the system begins to work. These difficulties of locating the Portuguese case are taken up by Gladdish in his chapter in this volume. Meanwhile, Morlino's view that 'all the difference between case and case is whether the parties have been the principal agent of consolidation or not'[63] is worth mention, while noting how much parties should in fact be the principal agents.

Third, taking the relationship with the state from a systemic to a more functional level, political parties assume both a more visible and a more regular role in consolidation through their institutionalization of the new system. By this is meant the way in which parties, acting individually and collectively, give substance to constitutional rules and thus confirm and enlarge on the formal outcome of transition. Di Palma, for instance, sees parties as having a special position in consolidation, since they formally monopolize Parliament and its accesses in representative democracies and are the key to reconciling functional interests to parliamentary politics. In his view, 'since consolidation is an ongoing process of structuration, increasingly constitutionalised political actors and their coalition strategies remain central in explaining outcomes'.[64] Parties thus perform an important legitimizing function in the crucial transfer of loyalties to the new regime by exercising decisional authority and expressing social diversity and possibly dissent.

Of course, individually their possibilities for a consolidating role usually differ at this point since some are likely to be in government and others in opposition – the departure from a transitional grand coalition (e.g. post-war Italy) or its informal version (e.g. *consenso* in post-Franco Spain) may also mark the 'shift' to consolidation. The quality of government–opposition relations may then reflect in some way on the consolidation process. This is only likely to raise serious problems if the political pact that marked transition contains an element of a truce with some basic underlying differences still unresolved. The obvious indicator of this problem is the existence of 'anti-system' parties or those suspected of harbouring 'anti-system' intentions. As Morlino has argued, 'partial consolidation' is evident when such 'anti-system' parties are significant, with pro-regime parties having a majority and carrying on the process.[65] The question of 'anti-system' parties also features in Di Palma's definition, where their existence is seen as qualifying the nature of the 'democratic compromise' and prospects for consolidation. According to him, the start of consolidation comes when constitutions succeed in imposing constrictions and regulating access to the political market.[66] Arguably, then, this has a self-reinforcing effect in terms of individual parties adapting to the new political game and making the best of it. It is only at this point one can see Rustow's 'process of Darwinian selectivity in favour of convinced democrats' beginning to really work, this being tantamount to Whitehead's view that the conditions necessary to keep the intervening process of consolidation are on track.

Ultimately two other aspects complete our discussion of the parties' relationship with the state. If system performance is to be one final test of consolidation, then parties in government have a special responsibility for its achievement which will over time have a telling effect one way or the other. This is a general rule which may be adopted cross-nationally. The other is more nationally variable, and that is the 'occupation of the state' already identified by Morlino as relevant to the theme of consolidation. But its actual relevance must be closely observed. While there has been a tendency for the expansion of party involvement with state institutions,[67] this has clearly differed between cases. According to Ware, four factors have accounted for this: the tradition of a strong state inherited from the pre-liberal-democratic era; long periods of single-party dominance under liberal democracy; the relatively early replacement of local elites by national party organizations in the organizing of elections; and, in the case of liberal democracies that collapsed in the twentieth century, the absence of legitimate rival organizations that could challenge parties when liberal democracy was restored.[68] Hence, on the one hand, the question is one of political parties strengthening their own role as the principal civil actors in new democracies through control over the state machine. On the other hand, we are talking about a theme that concerns the type or quality of liberal democracy – to what extent a system is or should be subject to partisan affiliation – and that clearly takes us above and beyond the theme of regime consolidation.

Fourth, the relationship of political parties with society furthermore identifies a variety of ways in which they act as agents of democratic consolidation. This is particularly important as it focuses attention on deeper levels at which consolidation has ultimately to be achieved. This relationship is, nevertheless, itself multifaceted. Schmitter has argued that the 'procedural minimum' for democracies is regular elections and political competition where parties play the central role. A competitive party system is therefore crucial to system legitimation in both producing effective government and in ensuring that 'losers' remain voluntarily within the system.[69] So far as consolidation is concerned, we have to assume that the high uncertainty of founding elections during transition has been removed,[70] and that the various party actors have begun to familiarize themselves with each other. As we have seen, Morlino introduces an organizational component of this relationship since this relates to the strengthening of parties' links with society. Here he sees a coincidence between the self-reinforcement of pro-system parties and democratic consolidation, in guaranteeing the decisional process and organizing and controlling mass participation.[71]

At a broader level, parties may act to promote democracy in a number of different ways, notably through interest optimilization, and as instruments of popular control and of civic orientation.[72] Apart from structuring the vote, parties also play a part in defining issues in either sectoral or cross-sectoral ways and of course they may or may not establish special or other links with interest groups. Altogether, these tasks are an element in the parties' representational and mobilizational capacity. This may well be relevant to their role in consolidation in so far as their 'penetration' of society is once more a reflection of their control in new democratic systems. Again, this can lead us on to questions about established democracies and therefore beyond the concerns of democratic consolidation. As Ware explains, there is cross-national variation in party-political 'penetration' of society and indeed also a general trend towards some weakening of this.[73]

As to a direct impact on democratic consolidation of parties qua social actors, there are various possibilities to consider. If there are certain special interests which may foster a doubtful or ambiguous attitude towards the new democracy, then it is conceivable that their links with pro-democratic parties might well help to overcome any problems and encourage their willingness to give democracy a try. For Whitehead, a key sector in the case of new democracies in southern Europe must be that of business given the problem of its reaction to the uncertainty of transition and the need for reassurances. Once consolidation is embarked upon, the game becomes rather less dramatic and more regular, as Whitehead explains:

> A vital element in the process of democratic consolidation is therefore to induce such dominant groups [business interests and the propertied classes in general] – which may have benefited considerably from previous authoritarian rule – to confine their lobbying within legitimate bounds, and to relinquish their ties with the undemocratic right. . . . More generally such implicit bargains between the democratic regime and key social sectors must be constantly renewed and renegotiated in order to keep the consolidation process on track.[74]

Clearly one way to achieve some stability here is for a link of mutual concern to be established between these interests and a political party in support of the new democratic regime. This obviously indicates a special role here for parties of the centre-right in the political spectrum.

Otherwise, so far as their relationship with society is concerned, political parties may contribute to democratic consolidation in certain broad ways. As instruments for popular control and civic orientation, they are perhaps uniquely able to influence socio-political trends. According to Weiner and LaPalombara:

> it is clear that parties are instruments for political socialisation, especially so during the early phases of political development when they are among the few institutions concerned with affecting political attitudes. In highly developed systems where there exist widely read newspapers, effective educational systems and well-established adult political attitudes, parties play a relatively minor role in inculcating feelings of being national or being a citizen. Moreover, in such systems the attitudes which parties inculcate are generally congruent with those generated by the family and by the school. In the developing areas, however, parties seek to inculcate attitudes which are often different from those which adults have learned as children.[75]

While slanted towards developing countries, this argument all the same is applicable somewhat to our southern European countries which in particular respects have been less developed than the rest of western Europe, although to varying degrees. At least the move from authoritarianism to democracy represents a significant form of political development where the above-mentioned problems have some bearing. Much therefore depends on how much civil society has developed, or been allowed to develop, before the onset of democratization. This in turn may delimit the scope for parties to emerge as socio-political actors or not. In post-war Italy, the parties developed from the beginning as very much the dominant actors here, and to some extent this has also been true of parties in Greece since 1974. In the Iberian states, that has been less the case and no doubt the longevity of their dictatorships – certainly longer-lasting than in the other two cases – helps to account for this. In Portugal, as Gladdish shows (Chapter 5), the political parties had a difficult inheritance to overcome because of the very lack of any tradition of political mobilization.

Finally, as perhaps the ultimate test of democratic consolidation, the question of the legitimizing of democracy is one where parties may perform a decisive service. While in some way linked to the matter of citizen participation, this question is subject to definitional problems because the concept is a bland one. In Przeworski's view, 'the entire problem of legitimacy is . . . incorrectly posed', for 'what matters for the stability of any regime is not the legitimacy of this particular system of domination but the presence or absence of preferable alternatives'.[76] This returns us to the role of 'anti-system' parties and their influence in society, but it does not suffice. Commenting on Przeworski, Roxborough argues:

we need to go even further: legitimacy (or active support and passive compliance) is something an actor confers on a regime, it is not an inherent quality of the regime itself; a regime is legitimate to the extent that actors give it legitimacy; hence, we need to know much more about the various different actors, their attitudes to the government and their perceptions of possible alternatives.[77]

Schmitter has taken a rather wider view of this question, including among the means of system legitimation an element of political calculation in relation to individual (one might also say sectoral) preference, and of the subjective in terms of perceptions of the effectiveness, efficiency, and fairness of political institutions.[78] On the other hand, Converse has cautioned against assumptions about the need for the (broadly-based) 're-making' of the political culture: 'the mass side of the picture is at least somewhat more perplexing, for there is a good deal of evidence that the more subtle and important of democratic values never have much more than an extremely limited absorption'.[79] Clearly at some stage, we run up against basic limitations to the role and capacity of political parties in new, not to mention established, democracies; but it is nevertheless clear from most definitions of system legitimation that there is certainly significant scope for their impact on democratic consolidation whatever facet of their relationship with society is considered.

It is evident from this discussion of political parties and democratic consolidation that we have to beware of overrating their role here and therefore of raising expectations of this too far. As noted just now and at several earlier points in this section, a firm distinction has to be drawn between the special dictates of the democratic consolidation process and the normal requirements of parties in liberal democracies. This only argues for limits to be set to the achievement of consolidation and therefore for a definite framework of analysis for pursuing the role here of political parties and party systems. The framework adopted by this volume follows; it precedes the final section which compares the results of the different chapters.

Political parties and democratic consolidation: a comparative framework

Parties and the state

1 Role of parties in the system – how much do they 'occupy' the state structure?
2 What is their relationship with the traditional agencies of power

which may have been associated with the previous regime (e.g. military, bureaucracy, monarchy, Church)?

3 The nature of the constituent process – how much have the parties been conditioned by this?

4 More broadly, how much can the individual parties be judged as system-supportive or not?

5 Going beyond that, how well have they performed (or begun to perform) as agents legitimizing the system, i.e. activated their system-supportiveness?

6 The significance of alternation in power nationally where it has occurred or not.

7 If 'anti-system' parties play a role in local government, does this actually matter?

8 What is the nature of political opposition within the system?

Inter-party relationships

1 The nature of political co-operation (alliances and coalitions) and of political competition (electoral and other) – how far is the latter well regulated?

2 The constituent process as consensual or conflictual: how far has this determined patterns of inter-party relations at the parliamentary level since democratic transition?

3 The extent of ideological space between the various parties, broadly speaking, and their potential for co-operation within the political institutions: referring to the Italian case, are there cases of 'polarized pluralism'(Sartori) or alternatively of 'centripetal pluralism'(Farneti)?

4 In looking at party strategies can they be said to aim directly or indirectly at democratic consolidation?

Parties and society

As variations on the theme of how much party systems themselves have become consolidated, the following problems arise:

1 How much have parties succeeded in the 'structuration' of state–society relations?

2 How much have they been the agents or promoters of an underlying 'social contract' supporting the new democracy?

3 More broadly, how far have they carried their system legitimation function into the public arena?

4 In performing these various functions, how have the parties related to interest groups and social movements?

5 How well-rooted are the parties in society organizationally?
6 Have they performed a role of social integration, e.g. cleavage divisions if politicized may pose some threat to new democracies, or they may delay the consolidation process.
7 Have elections become 'normal' or have they remained 'critical' as an indication of unresolved problems in the transition process?
8 What about survey evidence of public attitudes towards political parties as such (positive or negative), reflecting on acceptance of them as central actors in the 'consolidating' political system?

Political parties and the achievement of democratic consolidation

Although this framework identifies a wide range of properties of party systems in general, its particular focus therefore is on their relevance for assessing progress towards the achievement of democratic consolidation. By measuring in turn the components of consolidation, and in relating them, it becomes possible to examine the dynamics of that process. What obviously concerns us most is to establish whether, in Whitehead's words, 'the conditions necessary to keep the intervening process [towards full consolidation] on track' exist and are reinforced, given that the countries analysed in this volume are, with the exception of Italy, not yet fully consolidated democracies. At the same time, it is necessary to conclude at what stage of their consolidation the three more recent democracies have perhaps arrived; and, here, the role and performance of political parties provide a primary and a reliable indicator.

While confronting similar and largely parallel processes, this comparative framework also accommodates cross-national variation and indigenous elements in the nature of and progress towards regime consolidation. For instance, as discussed above, consolidation is regarded as both distinct from but also as clearly conditioned by transition and that in turn somewhat by the form of pre-transition developments and how the earlier regime collapsed or disintegrated. Here, the southern European democracies demonstrate diverse occasions for and trajectories of regime change, as is well known – the evolutionary course in Spain, a revolutionary point of departure in Portugal, with national defeat and Resistance mobilization leading to the restoration of parliamentary democracy in the case of Italy. It is reasonable to suppose their consolidation processes have accordingly varied somewhat in character and may be even time-variable. Certainly the length of democratic interruption has to be taken into account not least as this also reflects in some respects on the ability of parties themselves to act subsequently as agents of democratic consolidation. As Pasquino notes (Chapter 2), there are marked differences in the previous state of political organizations prior to transition, in the way in which political elites emerged at this time and also in their participation in the transition that followed. Gladdish has moreover emphasized (Chapter 5), extending this historical dimension, that the absence of patterns of political mobilization even before the authoritarian period acted as a 'confining condition' on the potential for party-political performance during the democratic transition in Portugal – combined with the kind of transition there in which the military featured prominently. This contrasts of course with the Italian case, where the political parties were the unchallenged actors in this process and where the shape of the party system was basically resolved at this time. However, as Pasquino argues, what distinguishes democratic consolidation is that it is a party-dominated process while this is not always so with democratic transition. In so far as the former has been true of all four cases – including Portugal, and to some extent Spain, where the parties were not the only main actors in transition – then a crucial condition for movement towards full consolidation exists. How, therefore, have the parties taken advantage of this to further that process?

As shown earlier, there are different levels of the consolidation process; and, indeed, our framework elaborates these. Focusing on party systems allows us to pursue these systematically, given the importance of parties as intermediary structures in liberal democracies. A first glance at some of the principal findings in this study identifies some broad differences here in the rate of consolidation between say the institutional and the socio-political levels, but also on this count between countries – not to mention individual parties within them. Thus, as Hine concludes (Chapter 3), the relationship with society has as a whole been positive for consolidation in Italy in view of the stable organizational links developed by parties (except in the south, although this did not in practice prove a serious threat to democracy), and their consistent ability to bridge strong cleavage divisions. As to their relationship with the state, the parties in that country established a firm hold over the system not least because of a weak state tradition, but their capacity for performance has been checked persistently by multi-party fragmentation and ideological distance. This has served to prolong consolidation at that level, although the well-honed practice of inter-party adjustment and accommodation has prevented these difficulties from becoming system-undermining as such.

In the case of Spain, as Gillespie shows (Chapter 6), the parties have on the other hand developed rather more as institutional than as social actors, so that consolidation has occurred sooner and more effectively at the state than at the society level. As he argues, the consolidation process is not automatically or simply cumulative; furthermore it may be hazardous or even subject to (presumably temporary) reversals in certain respects. One may usually speak of passing a succession of critical thresholds at the different levels before the consolidation process is really 'on track', as Ulrike Liebert illustrates (Chapter 7) in reference to one of the most difficult problems facing the Spanish consolidation, namely the role of the regions in the new system. This is a distinct case where the dynamics of consolidation could have turned awry, along the centre–periphery cleavage, and perhaps have self- destructed, given the direct threat of separatist terrorism in one important region on the one hand (society relationship) and the uncertain positions of some of the regionalist parties towards the evolving system on the other (relationship with the state). Nevertheless, the 'interactive sequence' (Whitehead) of consolidation proved eventually positive with a distinct trend during the 1980s away from centrifugalism to a centripetal dynamics, as she reveals. With Portugal and Greece, this broad distinction between the institutional and the socio-political levels makes them rather more like Spain than Italy, but for slightly different reasons. As Gladdish shows, the parties have invariably neglected their function as social actors owing not only to hermetic forms of elitism but also to traditional features inhibiting mobilization, as noted earlier. In Greece, however, the parties succeeded in dominating the whole system from early democratic transition as in Italy, but they have not developed nearly such stable links with society nor have they encouraged regular political participation.

At this point, it is time to turn directly to the three relationships to summarize more exactly the outcome of the consolidation process in the four countries and the role here of the political parties. This will be done in turn by use of explicit comparisons and contrasts in reference to the chapters which follow and also by drawing attention to various aspects of particular relevance to the main theme of democratic consolidation.

Parties and the state

A first and perhaps obvious variable must be the respective parties' handling of and attitude towards the constitutional settlement. While this settlement is an outcome of democratic transition, its remaining an issue of any significance or even controversy may be held as prima-facie evidence of slow consolidation and maybe of delay in embarking upon it. Here the four countries offer diverse and in some ways contrasting examples.

For instance, the political consensus pursued in Spain on the constitutional settlement (except over the regional question) meant that on these grounds the 'shift' to consolidation was straightforward. The transitional consensus was replaced by government–opposition rivalry, but this was accepted as 'normal' because of wide agreement on the rules of the game. Of course, the exception of the regional question complicated the consolidation process and can be said to have partially slowed it down. In Greece there was controversy from the beginning over the Constitution since it was not consensus-based. This may have been finally resolved by PASOK's revision of presidential powers in 1985–6 (accepted by the opposition after the 1985 election). Whether this affected consolidation seriously is not easy to say, although Susannah Verney shows (Chapter 9), using the European issue, how the lack of original consensus produced a conflictive type of consolidation process, with signs of this now diminishing. In Portugal there has been a more extensive constitutional revision and, as Gladdish emphasizes, the form of constitutional settlement is directly relevant to the problems of consolidation. This is because the radical military played a key role in its formulation, the Constitution being imbued with the ideological objectives of the 1974 Revolution. Significantly though, it was the parties that initiated and managed the later revision of the early 1980s which may be read as a sign that consolidation was at last under way.

Italy is really the least straightforward case of the four in this respect: the constitutional settlement was consensus-based, but the rupture between left and right that soon followed led to a situation where underlying differences over this settlement surfaced. As Sassoon shows in detail (Chapter 4), the question of representation and the issue of electoral reform revolved around deeper matters of constitutional interpretation and revision. They reflected a major problem of democratic consolidation, associated with the non-legitimation of the main opposition party. Italy is a telling example of the dictum that mutual trust over the rules of the political game – as both Rustow and Schmitter argue – is a *sine qua non* if not a precondition for the consolidation process.

The Italian case also advises us that the problem of 'anti-system' parties may not always be very clear cut with respect to democratic consolidation. Certainly as indicated in the comparative literature, the existence of 'anti-system' parties may hypothetically be seen as qualifying that outcome. One may further suppose – as the Italian example shows – that difficulties in accommodating such a party in a new system may retard the consolidation process. Whitehead has argued that if consolidation is to be kept 'on track' then the revolutionary left must be either reabsorbed into democratic life or isolated and defeated.[80] With Italy, we are talking about the PCI – and also originally the PSI – being isolated and later reabsorbed, although the magnitude of this problem derives from the numerical strength and political weight of the combined left. But was the PCI, as the senior party of the left, really isolated? As Sassoon shows, there were points of time when the PCI risked reverting to the position of a clear 'anti-system' party, only demonstrating how vulnerable the transition stage can be. Italy, however, reveals a few lessons which may be applicable to the other cases: it is the strategic intentions of these parties that provide an important clue to the chances for the 'shift' to consolidation (e.g. Togliatti's determination to establish the PCI as a 'loyal opposition'); and, the balance of strength within the left must affect the dynamics of the party system and hence the outcome of consolidation. In this latter respect, the other southern European countries have been different for there the (moderate left) Socialist parties have been much stronger than the (extreme left) Communist parties. This at least has facilitated alternation in power at an early stage.

Even in the more recent cases of democratization the relevance of 'anti-system' parties is, nevertheless, not so simple. It may not always be easy to categorize given parties baldly as 'anti-system'. The term itself is definitionally more complex than often recognized,[81] meaning that identification is in turn not always straightforward. For instance the PCE could be seen as having been 'defeated' (its electoral deterioration from 1982) rather than 'isolated' in Spanish politics, but in any case its significant role in *consenso* during transition and its subsequent participation in the state argue against its being called 'anti-system'. The Portuguese and Greek Communist parties (PCP and KKE) are more evidently 'anti-system', but they have remained largely isolated as well as being numerically inferior to their rival Socialist parties. If there still exist doubts on this question, then one has to look for signs that favour democratic consolidation. In the absence of the kind of useful insights provided by Sassoon on the PCI, general evidence of strategic adaptation on key issues is important. Susannah Verney examines how Greece's external links – specifically with the EC – have systemic implications and evolution here by the parties of the left (belatedly in the case of the KKE) is an indicator of democratic consolidation in progress. One may therefore also look to an international dimension to this process, although that is particularly apt in the case of Greece because of that country's background of 'foreign penetration' and its high level of left–right polarization. Italy, as another 'penetrated system', is perhaps similar in that the PCI's historic link with Moscow was an occasion for questioning its attachment to liberal democracy. As Sassoon explains, however, Togliatti regarded the Soviet model as inapplicable to Italy, although he did not make this clear in public for some while.

The question of alternative system models – surely an ultimate test of the viability of a new democracy – has otherwise not featured, except in Portugal. As Gladdish shows, the divide on this was not only between the PCP and the other parties but also between the latter and the revolutionary military, who favoured a form of socialist transformation. However, the failure of the November 1975 coup by the radical left was a decisive threshold for the new liberal democracy, and eventually the military retracted from politics. The Portuguese case also reminds us that 'anti-system' threats may lurk on the political right. Despite the 1974 Revolution, a sizeable minority of public opinion continued to regard favourably the previous authoritarian experience. But – an important point – no political force there has sought to mobilize this opinion, and so it has not in effect presented a serious challenge to the prospects for consolidation. The Alianza Popular in Spain is, however, an example of precisely a party with direct links to the previous regime (most visibly, Fraga its leader was one of Franco's ministers), but its own credibility problem has been rooted in this very fact. In Italy, the neo-Fascist MSI was founded shortly after the Second World War, but it has throughout suffered from political isolation, all the more because of the anti-Fascist consensus which has characterized post-war attitudes there. In Greece, on the other hand, New Democracy is a successful example of reconstruction on the political right.

There are thus different facets to the problem of 'anti-system' parties. Obviously this problem has consequences for the outcome of democratic consolidation and certainly the rate at which it is achieved. This is because these relate to other themes of that process. For instance, Pasquino emphasizes alternation in power as constituting 'the turning-point' in the achievement of consolidation and 'the hallmark in the achievement of a stable democratic situation'. As Hine shows, the absence of alternation is definitely linked to the presence of a party widely viewed for some time as 'anti-system' by other parties. Alternation in power must obviously be the ultimate test of confidence in the rules of the game. However, on this count, the other countries examined in this volume stand in a different category from Italy, suggesting that consolidation will be a much less lengthy process. There is a further influence from positive dynamics encouraged by alternation, for parties with some 'anti-system' tendencies may be increasingly compelled to adapt to democratic politics in line with Rustow's argument about 'Darwinian selectivity in favour of convinced democrats' during the 'habituation phase'. Pasquino throws light on this significant development, on how party leaders generally exploit opportunities for career or partisan purposes during democratic transition and use their political capital in a manner that promotes democratic consolidation. This link between party interest and the concerns of the new system must be accepted as both legitimate and positive.

However, there has been another side to this link which in some of these countries has been rather controversial. As the chapters on Greece, Spain, and notably Italy point out, the 'occupation of the state' by governing parties and their exploitation of clientelistic resources has provoked accusations of abuse of power. This has two possible points of relevance for our principal theme. Such a practice might, given the fragility of early consolidation, lead to some disillusionment with the system and not merely the party in power. But the second point might help to counter the first, for the presence of a viable opposition party – with prospects for alternation – might well act as a safety-valve for such disillusionment, that is it becomes party-channelled rather than system-oriented. Here, the dominance of the PSOE in Spain and the theme of 'Mexicanization' perhaps causes some concern – a theme which has, of course, been more prevalent in Italy. There remain, therefore, some areas for criticism, but by and large the new southern European democracies are well 'on track' towards consolidation so far as the relationship with the state is concerned.

Inter-party relationships

The focus at this level is, broadly speaking, rather more on the actual dynamics of the party systems and how developments here encourage political behaviour which promotes consolidation. One theme may be carried over from the previous discussion in reference to Whitehead's point about the reabsorption of the revolutionary left into democratic life. In contrast with the 'exclusivist' nature of previous regimes, in particular its suppression under authoritarianism or Fascism, this ideological tendency was now granted official status as a political competitor. This had implications for political competition, and also possibly for the quality of these new democracies in terms of political pluralism, but it is also historically symbolic as for instance Feather-stone notes in the case of Greece (Chapter 8).

Otherwise one may group relevant themes of inter-party relation-ships into how far party strategies are transmitted into alliance behaviour, coalitional or political; the location of parties in the ideo-logical spectrum and whether these are stable and also conducive to centripetal or centrifugal patterns; and, finally, whether political competition has had broadly positive or negative repercussions for the consolidation process.

First, the importance of political pacts has been stressed by Schmitter and others as crucial for both transition and getting 'on track' for consolidation.[82] Formal pacts have certainly marked if not dominated crucial moments of the transition stage – notably the constituent process – in post-war Italy and in Spain as well as, more uneasily, in Portugal, though not in Greece. One may surmise, however, that the 'shift' to consolidation may well be marked by an end to formal pactism as a transitional phenomenon and a release of (normal) competition between parties in government and those in opposition. Such a change must, nevertheless, be regulated by rules and also norms. It may in fact be accompanied by an element of pactism in substantial terms, that is there remains an underlying consensus on basic matters of policy, confirming implicitly if not explicitly the spirit as well as the letter of the constitutional settlement. This may, of course, be variable cross-nationally: the case of post-war Austria, where a grand coalition persisted for two decades, is explained by a background of civil strife before the war; while post-war West Germany saw precisely this change in inter-party relationships once the first government was formed. As a rule, this change must represent a sensitive moment in early consolidation, whereby its successful outcome amounts to one of those critical thresholds being passed before consolidation is set on its course.

In the case of Italy, Sassoon speaks of 'consolidation through contract', but the very delicacy of this moment is illustrated only too well by his close analysis of the line developed by Togliatti and in particular by the crisis over the issue of electoral reform surrounding the second parliamentary election in 1953. For Togliatti, this contract deriving from the consensus over the Constitution and specified in the idea of the Tripartite Coalition was crucial in the PCI's evolution as a 'loyal opposition'. There is a direct link between this line and the point, mentioned by Hine, that inter-party accommodation facilitated democratic consolidation at various critical moments, especially the 'National Solidarity' formula of the mid-1970s. From this, we may readily deduce that inter-party relationships were particularly decisive in the Italian case of democratic consolidation.

In the other countries examined in this volume, as Pasquino points out, there was a general inclination to compromise in the democratic transition which has been solidified in the 'habituation phase', i.e. it has been carried over into the consolidation process. This has been reflected in the quality of government–opposition relations and the acceptance of alternation in power. In other words, the new democracies have not as a whole been hindered by the presence of fundamentalist opposition; and, if 'anti-system' parties have existed, they have not dominated the parliamentary opposition. The only possible qualifications are not major ones. In Greece, politics has been highly polarized since the return to democracy, but its emotional tone suggests perhaps a cultural feature there rather than fundamentalism as such, this again being confirmed by alternation. In Spain, as Ulrike Liebert shows in detail, the situation in the regions has been complex. Some fundamentalist opposition has been present in certain of the regions, but at the national-parliamentary level opposition from regionalist parties has been more partial than principled.

Second, party-political locations in the ideological spectrum have caused some concern in the new democracies, though more because of uncertainty than the problem of political distance. The latter has been mainly important in post-war Italy; however, as Hine indicates, ideological distance between left and right has narrowed considerably over time, clearly in conjunction with the gradual achievement of democratic consolidation. In the other countries, uncertainty has arisen either from the changing programmatic line of individual parties (notably PASOK in Greece) or certain instabilities in the party system (as demonstrated dramatically by the total collapse of the Spanish UCD). Probably the most serious case in this respect is Portugal, where – as Gladdish stresses – party positions in the ideological spectrum have been very unpredictable, making alliances rather unstable. It could be said that, at this level, democratic consolidation there has been retarded. However, in Portugal as in Spain and Greece, the dynamics of inter-party relationships have tended to be centripetal and not centrifugal. Hence, if instability exists, it has not proved ultimately detrimental to the consolidation process.

Third, as this might suggest, political competition has had positive rather than negative repercussions. In Spain, patterns have by and large contributed to consolidation, although – again – the main problems have derived from some of the regions. Highly polarized and ideological conflict has been most common in those autonomous communities characterized by ethnic and multi-party systems. In Greece, competition while intense has been channelled within and accommodated by the system. In post-war Italy, political competition was not formally restricted but the exercise of the *conventio ad excludendum* to isolate the PCI by the parties of the right qualified the rules of competition, this being linked – in the broader sense of the 'Communist question' already discussed – to the difficulties there of democratic consolidation.

Hence this examination of inter-party relationships really shows that a general distinction may be drawn between Italy and the other three cases. This dimension was both more problematical but also – eventually – more decisive in the Italian case. In the new democracies, difficulties in democratic consolidation have focused rather on other problems with respect to the third relationship examined in this study.

Parties and society

If the first requirement here is the 'procedural minimum' of regular elections and a competitive party system (Schmitter), then the new democracies have in this sense already progressed towards democratic consolidation. In fact, they experienced an abundance of elections during the first decade after the return to democracy. As such, they have also moved beyond the stage of 'founding' elections which by definition are also 'crucial' elections in that there is high uncertainty about their outcomes with moments of great drama.[83] Democratic elections are a new experience or a revived one (depending on the duration of the previous authoritarian regime), but the strengths and in some cases the identity of political parties is difficult to predict at this point of time.

Eventually, it is assumed, partisan diversity starts to crystallize and party identification to take root. On these grounds, a general distinction has once more to be made between Italy and the other three countries, but conversely in terms of negative as against positive consequences for democratic consolidation. As noted earlier, the structuration by Italian parties of linkage mechanisms with society was achieved to a considerable degree and relatively early – indeed, within the equivalent period of time already passed by the other cases since the return to democracy. They also established a dominant hold over interest groups and social organizations, and thus they long ago asserted their control over the system at the societal level. This has generally not been replicated in the new democracies. If the argument is accepted that it is still too soon to judge them in this respect, are we therefore speaking of a lengthier process of democratic consolidation at this level? If so, how far does that matter?

An alternative explanation is that the different historical context, compared with post-war Italy, matters. The 1970s and 1980s are a period in which party identification is in relative decline in European democracies, including even Italy. The media now play a more central role as a rival linkage between politics and society, a phenomenon also evident in Spain, Greece, and Portugal. This suggests two possible effects: parties need to rely less exclusively on party organizations for influencing society; and, in line with media habits, they may seek to personalize strongly their appeals. The latter is obviously illustrated by the prominent role of charismatic personalities in several of the major parties (Gonzalez and Papandreou; and, earlier, Karamanlis and even Suarez). The former effect may well explain the determination of parties in all these countries to control the media, which at times has been a matter of controversy.

The time-frame argument may especially be important with the new democracies, suggesting that consolidation at the societal level is indeed a lengthy affair. Meanwhile, specific indicators help our assessment of this relationship, and these are discussed in the case-studies in this volume. In Greece, for instance, the under-development of civic society and the autocratic behaviour of the parties have apparently hindered consolidation at this level, although, as Featherstone notes, there are recent signs of this changing. Clearly there comes a point where cross-national variation has to be taken into account.

As to the deeper problem of instability in the relationship between parties and society – which in different ways features in the case-studies of the new democracies – it cannot be said that this represents an automatic threat to democratic consolidation there. At worst, it is a problem of consolidation being delayed. Reference is made to the distinction earlier in this chapter between system stability as a permanent and 'normal' matter and the finite process of regime consolidation. That is, instability cannot automatically be held as evidence of the latter's failure. At least the question of stability becomes pertinent when it predominates across the system in question; or, to use our framework, when it predominates at more than one level. In that event, this problem is likely to be basic system malfunction at a time when a new democracy is still vulnerable and before it has – in Easton's words – begun to acquire 'diffuse support'. Greece, Spain, and Portugal do not represent such cases.

This last point underlines that any assessment of democratic consolidation has to look also at the interaction between the different levels and not merely at these separately. For that, the reader is referred to the chapters which follow. The principal lesson of this study is therefore that progress towards democratic consolidation should not be measured with respect to certain variables alone. Any analysis has – obviously – to be systemic. Thus democratic consolidation has to be approached in a multi-dimensional or multi-level way so as not only to accommodate cross-national variation but also to evaluate the relative importance here of individual variables. In an imperfect world, it is likely that any national case of democratic consolidation will proceed at a different pace between the levels examined in this volume but also remain deficient in some respects. If those deficiencies are in fact serious ones, only then will democratic consolidation be affected considerably, as the case of Italy shows. In general, this study demonstrates that the new democracies are now well 'on track' towards democratic consolidation.

Notes

1. G. O'Donnell, P. Schmitter, and L. Whitehead (eds) *Transitions from Authoritarian Rule: Prospects for Democracy*, Baltimore, Md and London, Johns Hopkins University Press, 1986, p. 3.
2. W. Opello, *Portugal's Political Development: A Comparative Approach*, Boulder, Colo., Westview Press, 1985, p. 2.
3. R. Hague and M. Harrop, *Comparative Government and Politics*,

Basingstoke, Macmillan, 1987, pp. 141–2.
4. G. Bingham Powell, *Contemporary Democracies: Participation, Stability and Violence*, Cambridge, Mass., Harvard University Press, 1982, p. 7.
5. K. Sontheimer, 'Wie stabil sind die Demokratien Westeuropas?', *Frankfurter Allgemeine Zeitung*, 8 December 1987, p. 10.
6. Alan Ware, *Citizens, Parties and the State*, Cambridge, Polity Press, 1987, pp. 218–19.
7. See, for instance, H. Daalder and P. Mair (eds) *Western European Party Systems: Continuity and Change*, London, Sage, 1983; and S. Wolinetz (ed.) *Parties and Party Systems in Liberal Democracies*, London, Routledge, 1988.
8. Wolinetz, op. cit., p. 315.
9. Ware, op. cit., pp. 220ff and 234ff.
10. A. Bar, 'The emerging Spanish party system: is there a model?', *West European Politics*, October 1984, p. 134.
11. ibid., p. 134.
12. P. Schmitter, 'The consolidation of political democracy in Southern Europe (and Latin America)', European University Institute, conference paper, October 1985, pp. 5–6.
13. H. Penniman and E. Mujal-Leon (eds), *Spain at the Polls, 1977, 1979 and 1982*, Durham, NC, Duke University Press, 1985, p. 317.
14. O'Donnell *et al.*, op. cit., pp. 7–8.
15. A. Lijphart *et al.*, 'A Mediterranean model of democracy?', *West European Politics*, January 1988, p. 18.
16. ibid., p. 18.
17. C. Boyd and J. Boyden, 'The armed forces and the transition to democracy in Spain', in T. Lancaster and G. Prevost (eds) *Politics and Change in Spain*, New York, Praeger, 1985.
18. Lijphart *et al.*, op. cit., p. 7.
19. ibid., p. 18.
20. ibid., pp. 15–16.
21. G. Pasquino, 'L'instaurazione di regimi democratici in Grecia e Portogallo', *Il Mulino*, March–April 1975.
22. S. Huntington, *Political Order in Changing Societies*, New Haven, Conn., Yale University Press, 1968, ch. 7.
23. ibid., p. 461.
24. See L. Binder *et al.*, *Crises and Sequences in Political Development*, Princeton, NJ, Princeton University Press, 1971. This is also applied to the case of Portugal in Opello, op. cit.
25. Opello, op. cit., ch. 2.
26. These are summarized in G. Pridham, 'Comparative perspectives on the new Mediterranean democracies: a model of regime transition?', in G. Pridham (ed.) *The New Mediterranean Democracies: Regime Transition in Spain, Greece and Portugal*, London, Frank Cass, 1984, pp. 16–27.
27. Schmitter, 'The consolidation of political democracy', p. 3.
28. L. Whitehead, 'The consolidation of fragile democracies', European Consortium for Political Research (ECPR), paper 1988, pp. 6–8.
29. L. Morlino, 'Democratic consolidation: definition and models', University

of Florence, paper, March 1987, p. 15.

30. P. Converse, 'Of time and partisan stability', *Comparative Political Studies*, July 1969, p. 139.
31. D. Rustow, 'Transitions to democracy: toward a dynamic model', *Comparative Politics*, April 1970, pp. 355–61.
32. Schmitter, 'The consolidation of political democracy', p. 64.
33. See Pridham, op. cit.
34. See T. Vanhanen, 'The strategies of democratization', ECPR, paper 1988, p. 2.
35. See O. Kirchheimer, 'Confining conditions and revolutionary breakthroughs', *American Political Science Review*, December 1965, pp. 964–74.
36. R. Merritt, 'On the transformation of systems', *International Political Science Review*, 1980, no. 1, pp. 13–22.
37. Huntington, op. cit., ch. 3; G. Almond, S. Flanagan, and R. Mundt, *Crisis, Choice and Change: Historical Studies of Political Development*, Boston, Mass., Little, Brown, 1973, p. 32.
38. Vanhanen, op. cit., pp. 3ff.
39. Schmitter, 'The consolidation of political democracy', pp. 5–6.
40. K. Dowding and R. Kimber, 'The meaning and use of "political stability" ', *European Journal of Political Research*, September 1983, p. 242.
41. S. Ersson and J.-E. Lane, 'Political stability in European democracies', *European Journal of Political Research*, September 1983, pp. 257, 260–1.
42. J.-E. Lane and S. Ersson, *Politics and Society in Western Europe*, London, Sage, 1987, p. 7.
43. Schmitter, 'The consolidation of political democracy', pp. 32–3.
44. L. Morlino, 'Consolidamento democratico: definizione e modelli', *Rivista Italiana di Scienza Politica*, August 1986, pp. 203, 205.
45. See D. Easton, *A Systems Analysis of Political Life*, New York, Wiley, 1965.
46. Morlino, 'Consolidamento democratico', p. 216.
47. Morlino, 'Democratic consolidation', pp. 25–6.
48. ibid., p. 26.
49. ibid.
50. G. Loewenberg, 'The remaking of the German party system', in M. Dogan and R. Rose (eds) *European Politics: A Reader*, London, Macmillan, 1971, pp. 259–80.
51. G. Pasquino, 'The demise of the first Fascist regime and Italy's transition to democracy', in O'Donnell *et al.*, op. cit., pp. 45–7.
52. ibid., p. 69.
53. Rustow, op. cit., p. 358.
54. ibid., p. 360.
55. Kirchheimer, op. cit., pp. 965–7.
56. Pasquino, 'L'instaurazione di regimi'.
57. Huntington, op. cit., p. 397.
58. Merritt, op. cit.
59. Whitehead, 'The consolidation of fragile democracies', p. 28.
60. J. LaPalombara and M. Weiner (eds) *Political Parties and Political Development*, Princeton, NJ, Princeton University Press, 1966, p. 420.

61. G. Di Palma, 'Founding coalitions in Southern Europe: legitimacy and hegemony', *Government and Opposition*, spring 1980, p. 170.
62. E.g. A. Stepan, 'Paths toward redemocratization: theoretical and comparative considerations' in O'Donnell *et al.*, op. cit., Part III, pp. 64–84.
63. Morlino, 'Consolidamento democratico', p. 229.
64. G. Di Palma, 'Notes ai margini of the democratic consolidation project', European University Institute, conference paper, 1985, pp. 1, 6.
65. Morlino, 'Consolidamento democratico', pp. 228–9.
66. G. Di Palma, 'Party government and democratic reproducibility: the dilemma of new democracies', in F. Castles and R. Wildenmann (eds) *Visions and Realities of Party Government*, Berlin, de Gruyter, 1986, pp. 185–7.
67. Ware, op. cit., pp. 188ff.
68. ibid., p. 195.
69. Schmitter, 'The consolidation of political democracy', pp. 12–13, 28.
70. On founding elections, see ch. 6, Part IV, in O'Donnell, *et al.*, op. cit.
71. Morlino, 'Consolidamento democratico', p. 233.
72. Ware, op. cit., pp. 23–7.
73. ibid., pp. 195–6, 202.
74. Whitehead, 'The consolidation of fragile democracies', pp. 18, 22.
75. LaPalombara and Weiner, op. cit., p. 362.
76. A. Przeworski, 'Some problems in the study of the transition to democracy', in O'Donnell *et al.*, op. cit., Part III, pp. 51–2.
77. I. Roxborough, 'The dilemmas of redemocratization', *Government and Opposition*, summer 1988, p. 362.
78. Schmitter, 'The consolidation of political democracy', pp. 23–8.
79. Converse, op. cit., p. 141.
80. Whitehead, 'The consolidation of fragile democracies', p. 28.
81. G. Smith, 'Party and protest: the two faces of opposition in Western Europe', in E. Kolinsky (ed.), *Opposition in Western Europe*, London, Croom Helm, 1987, pp. 56–9.
82. O'Donnell *et al.*, op. cit., e.g. Part IV, ch. 4.
83. ibid., Part IV, pp. 61–4.

Chapter two

Party elites and democratic consolidation: cross-national comparison of southern European experience

Gianfranco Pasquino

Introduction

Analyses of the transitions from authoritarian regimes and of democratic consolidations have basically focused on the interplay of political, social, and economic organizations. In some cases, due account has been taken of the impact of external factors. In other cases, Kirchheimer's lesson on the importance of 'confining conditions' has been learned and put to use.[1] More recently, and most notably in this volume, the emphasis has been put on that very relevant political actor which is the political party (in the wake of the criticisms levelled against political parties in contemporary democracies, one has risked losing sight of their important contributions in establishing and consolidating democratic regimes). All this has been rightly done.

If party organizations are important in channelling popular support towards a new democratic regime, their rate of success (in some cases even their ability to do so) must be influenced by whether party leaders behave in such a way as to create and consolidate that democratic regime. It is not simply that politics always has a strong personality component. It is also that, in many cases, personality conflicts played a role in the demise of the pre-authoritarian regime (as, most notably, in the case of Greece); and, above all, that party leaders enjoy an unusual amount of political visibility, strategic flexibility, and tactical discretion in the phases both of transition and consolidation.

The leaders of other organizations have, in all likelihood, been discredited by their participation in the authoritarian experience – as is the case with military leaders, industrialists and, of course, members of the inner circle of authoritarian decision-makers. Officials, both in the executive and the legislative branches, are definitely too identified with authoritarianism. Church leaders, while powerful, might be more inclined to arrest unfavourable trends during transition than to get involved in what for them would be a confused and risky process. Therefore, in some cases by default, in other cases because of their control of viable organizations, party leaders emerge as very important actors in the process of democratization.

Their behaviour shapes the attitudes of party members as well as those of actual and potential supporters. Since, at least for a certain period, the politics of transition and consolidation requires agreements and pacts among a restricted group of individuals, it is party leaders who are empowered to strike these agreements (as was the case, under very different circumstances, for instance when Togliatti decided to accept the monarchy for the time being, or Soares and Cunhal acquiesced in the conditions set by the Portuguese military for participation in the first elections of April 1975). The signals party leaders produce are an indication of the limits they accept in their interaction as well as in the mobilization and activities of their followers. The need for identification with a new democracy is fulfilled by party leaders more than by any other elite. And, finally, some of them may represent a certain amount of continuity with the pre-authoritarian period, and therefore provide some reassurance of a known experience in a phase fraught with individual and collective anxiety (and expectations).

To a large extent, it had been party leaders (and their activists and followers) who played a visible role in opposing the authoritarian regime, definitely more than any other group of leaders (with the possible exception in Spain only of the trade unionists, and to a more limited extent, in Spain, in Greece, and in Portugal, of the students). If they had worked with continuity and determination, then they rightly inherited the task of bringing the transition from the authoritarian regime to a successful outcome in terms of democratic consolidation.

Of course, the outcome is dependent on a variety of conditions. But there is no doubt that the blueprints and the strategies of party leaders, especially of those who have opposed the authoritarian regime and therefore have democratic credentials to show, will have a great impact on the overall process and its conclusion. While neither the transition nor the consolidation spring full-blown from the strategies of party leaders (some of whom might just be opportunistic, others semi-convinced democrats, some just willing to play the game) as Minerva from Jupiter's head, democratic party leaders enjoy an initial advantage (because of the reaction against authoritarianism that has brought the regime to an end). It is then their task to capitalize on this advantage and to push the process to a successful democratic conclusion. It seems that, indeed, successful democratic outcomes have been associated with the presence of important and capable party leaders. There are many good reasons for this association and there are many important implications here, both for the transition and for the consolidation.

The political class in the transition

In order to understand those reasons and explore these implications, an evaluation of the nature of the previous authoritarian regimes in Italy, Portugal, Spain, and Greece is indispensable. With the partial exception of the Greek military junta (where, anyway, one leader Papadopoulos first, Ioannides next, emerged as dominant), politics was most notably characterized by the role played by the founding leader: Mussolini, Salazar, Franco. The very definition of authoritarian regimes by Juan Linz stresses the importance of a one-man leadership.[2] In societies where political and party organizations were still in a developing stage, personalities inevitably played a key role in any case. It was thus of utmost importance for the opposition to identify and to project the image of a counter-leader. Of course, this could be done more effectively where some party organizations had existed and played a role before the advent of the authoritarian regime. This was, then, more likely in Italy, because of the development of pre-Fascist parties, and in Greece, because of the democratic interlude up to 1967. It was slightly more difficult, but still possible, in Spain; rather difficult in Portugal (but then made possible first by Caetano's decompression policy and then by the ebullient transitional phase which followed).

In principle, then, one can identify different types of party elites, emerging or reappearing in the transition from authoritarian regimes. The first type is represented by the traditional political class which preceded the establishment of the authoritarian regime. Of course, the nature of this political class is somewhat determined by the state of organizational politics prevalent at the time of the authoritarian take-over. In some cases, these political elites could not be but notables, exceptionally they were leaders of political factions perhaps more than parties. It is most clearly the case of Portugal; to some extent the case of Spain as well.[3]

Another factor which influences the nature of this political class and its likelihood for playing a significant political role is simply time. Obviously again, a short-lasting authoritarian experience, such as the Greek one, cannot hope to erase the previous political class. Nor could Italian Fascism: twenty years are rather less than a political generation. On the other hand, both Salazar and Franco nourished legitimate and verifiable expectations of outliving the hated political class which preceded them. And this is exactly what happened in practice, with only few individual exceptions.

The first tentative conclusion, then, is that a combination of time and organizational features of politics determines whether the old political class will be able to survive the authoritarian regime and reassert itself. All this said, however, the first, traditional opponents remain important.

In some cases they may be able to pass on some of their legitimacy to new leaders. In the southern European cases, however, this has not been so. On the contrary, to take the dramatic case of Spain, old Communists (above all Santiago Carrillo and to a more limited extent Dolores Ibarruri) prevented the emergence of a new, endogenous party leadership with very negative consequences; old Socialists, like Rodolfo Llopis, had to be ousted in order for the renewal of the PSOE to take place. Not even in the case of Italy was the passing on of legitimacy really a factor. Where old, that is pre-Fascist, party leaders had survived, they themselves played the dominant political role.

Perhaps the first opponents played a different, though rather important role: that of showing the very possibility of opposition. In some cases, it was a 'cultural' opposition, in other cases a pedagogic opposition, in other cases still it was simply a symbolic opposition: keeping the flame alive and burning. Though often but not always revered, in subsequent phases they had to be bypassed and forgotten.

Of course, in short-lived authoritarian experiments, the first opponents may also be the ones who continue challenging the regime, survive to its demise, inherit the new situation, accompany the transition, and finally organize the democratic consolidation. It is more the case of Greece (and of some Latin American experiences) than of Italy. The Italian situation, though, is sufficiently complex to warrant more attention, later.

The first, traditional opponents, especially if they are persecuted or exiled by the authoritarian regime, maintain some or much democratic legitimacy, in any case an aura of respect and perhaps of affection. It is much more difficult for opponents born to politics under the authoritarian regime to acquire such affection and respect. As a matter of fact, the authoritarian regime will not only own, but also utilize all the instruments at its disposal to discredit the new opponents politically (the most often levelled accusation being 'communism', or bearers of chaos, or being sold out to foreign enemies) and morally (godless, corrupted, violent). Redressing these accusations will, for opponents who must dramatize their existence and provide a viable but reassuring alternative, be a very difficult operation. This is why, probably, the second-generation endogenous opponents, who enjoy some possibility of acquiring visibility and consensus, were born within the regime. They are those who joined the regime out of a moral or political stimulus, following an ideal, believing in a profound change (the supporters of Fascism-movement as contrasted with Fascism-regime, in Renzo De Felice's fruitful distinction),[4] and then became disillusioned. Their previous role provides them with some publicity in the eyes of the population at large, though more specifically with the politically conscious and active. Their previous involvement assures them, up to a point, of some impunity on the part of the regime. The limits of their challenge to the regime, and especially to its ruler (as the case of Admiral Humberto Delgado in Portugal proved) are ill-defined, as Linz would put it, but quite predictable.

Even in those few cases in which they might become successful in creating a semi-loyal opposition, the dynamics of political events does not seem to be favourable to them. It is unlikely that the regime will accept their requests. Then they are either pushed into disloyal opposition, according to the leader's evaluation (and if threatening they can be physically eliminated), or they will be co-opted again in a regime shift. Moreover, they will always appear somewhat suspect to the first-hour opponents of the regime, to those who have been confined, sent to jail, or obliged to go into exile. As a matter of fact, none of the opponents emerging within the authoritarian regime has enjoyed much success. In the Italian case, the so-called *fronda* (internal Fascist dissent) finally manifested itself in the meeting of the Grand Fascist Council which ousted Mussolini (25 July 1943). But none of its protagonists played a subsequent political role. Like revolutions, authoritarian regimes devour their oppositionist sons. Of course, former authoritarian supporters, turned into semi-loyal (or disloyal) opponents, are *not* the only opponents to emerge in an authoritarian regime.[5] On the contrary, they constitute normally a tiny fraction of the entire opposition.

Understandably the opposition is represented above all by those who have been defeated by the authoritarian leaders. Among them the most likely to survive *politically* are those who have a party affiliation, who participate in party politics, who enjoy the support of or create a party organization. Whether within the country or, more likely, in exile, party elites are therefore the most militant, most effective, most durable opponents of the authoritarian regime. Our four countries supply plenty of instances and suggest many operational differences. Definitely the most important difference is very simple: party elites and their party organizations pre-exist the authoritarian experience or are created after the establishment of the authoritarian regime.

While presented as a dichotomy, this important difference ought to be analysed by locating our four cases along a continuum. One extreme is occupied by Italy, where party politics was already in action and party elites had already acquired a recognized status when Fascism took over. To a significant extent, the three major party organizations – Socialist, Catholic, and Communist – were more than viable. They could rely on flanking organizations, had a solid social implantation, were in control of most local governments, and had developed some sense of party identification. The other extreme is occupied by Portugal. The collapse of the old Republic was in particular due to the inability of party factions to transform themselves from personalistic vehicles into party organizations. Party politics was widely discredited and party leaders did not enjoy any significant amount of respect. Portuguese civil society was too weak to sustain the creation of viable political organizations. Once defeated, the opposition to the Estado Novo had to begin a really long march through the authoritarian experience.

The other two cases can be located in between Italy and Portugal. Spain is closer to Italy in the sense that Spanish political organizations already existed which could be assimilated to political parties. But the experience with party politics and party competition had been very short-lived. Although it did not totally wipe out political traditions and political memories (whose persistence is one of the most extraordinary phenomena to be explained), it did make the creation of party opposition to the Caudillo extremely difficult. Only that modernization, that Franco tried to slow down, would offer the conditions and the resources to reorganize, albeit under severe repression, opposition political parties largely under a new leadership. Pre-military junta party leaders existed in Greece, but Greek political parties had always been an assortment of personalized factions, nourished by patronage and organized around client–patron networks. Indeed, the very label of 'party' had been eschewed (and continued to be even after 1974). Karamanlis' political vehicle was the ERE (Rally for the People); George and later Andreas Papandreou's organization was the Centre Union. Greek society was not in a position to provide many organizational resources nor to offer a solid basis for the implantation of political parties. On the positive side, however, the time bought by the military junta was not much. Old political allegiances could not be cancelled. Almost all traditional political leaders (with the exception of George Papandreou) outlived the junta. In the meantime, against all odds, Greek society and public opinion became somewhat more politicized and thus more willing to become politically organized.

It must be added that both Karamanlis and Andreas Papandreou appreciated from the beginning the need for shaping viable party organizations. The lessons of the past when the superior organization of the Centre Union had produced Karamanlis' electoral defeat, on the one hand; on the other hand, when an inability to control a diversified, indisciplined, disorganized party had prevented (George and Andreas) Papandreou's resistance to the divisive manoeuvres of the Royal establishment, had been learned. And the choice of the respective labels (New Democracy and Panhellenic Socialist Movement) indicated more than a disdain for the qualification of 'party', the intention being to cast the net very widely to encompass as many Greek voters as possible.

All in all, therefore, the prospects for the reappearance or the structuring of party politics were not unpromising in any of the countries, with the exception of Portugal. To some extent, party elites already existed in the phase of the demise or collapse of the authoritarian regime. Also, they could count on some old allegiances, on some organizational capabilities, on some social implantation. The problem, then, was how to capitalize on what already existed, in what to invest political resources, and of course which strategy to follow for the organization of democracy.

Extrication from authoritarianism

Party elites in Italy, Portugal, Greece, and Spain took part in different ways in the transition from the authoritarianism of their respective countries. In Italy, in spite of the abrupt demise of Fascism, the transition had been prepared by constant, though eventually somewhat sporadic, actions against the regime. Above all, however, the transitional phase from authoritarianism to democratic elections took almost three years and was marked by the Resistance war. In different degrees (for instance, neither the Christian Democrat De Gasperi nor the Communist Togliatti were directly involved), top party elites participated, indeed led most of these activities. For instance, the subsequent acceptance of the Communist Party in the process of building the democratic Republic was largely based on its contribution to the anti-Fascist struggle. On the other hand, Togliatti and the Communist ruling group always stressed not only their role in the Resistance but also their common experiences here with the Socialists and the Catholics (Christian Democrats).

That patrimony, though conspicuous, might have not been adequate for playing a significant political role, if Togliatti had not contributed in two other respects to reinforce it. First, there was his moderation in dealing with the issue of the transitional government (Togliatti did not ask for the immediate resignation of General Badoglio nor for the abolition of the monarchy). Second, one should mention his willingness and ability to create a mass party (this option, never entertained by the Action Party, cost it its survival in spite of its important contribution to the anti-Fascist struggle during the regime and to the Resistance). As Donald Sassoon has very aptly shown,[6] from the very beginning Togliatti convinced Communist party elites that it was time to be tactically flexible and strategically imaginative.

While the Socialists, with many contradictions and encumbered by their past, thought that the future, at least of the left, would belong to them, some sectors of the Catholics decided to build their own political future. Only Catholic organizations had enjoyed some element of freedom under Fascism. While definitely not opposed by the Church, Italian Fascism had never received that enthusiastic support which characterized the Spanish Church's attitude towards Franco at least until the mid-1960s, before developing a widespread grassroots opposition (that, again, did not characterize the Italian clergy), nor that matter-of-course allegiance offered by the Portuguese Church to Salazar. It was therefore not simply possible but even, to some extent, necessary to provide a social outlet for the activities of large sectors of Italian society. Lay Catholic organizations did exactly that. And the distance between social and political activities, at the fall of Fascism, could be easily bridged.

The issue was not so much to revive the first Catholic party, the Partito Popolare, even though its very founder, Don Luigi Sturzo, and several important members had survived Fascism. The issue was what kind of party to create to foster the interests and values of Italian Catholics and their Church. The existence of a diversified, large, well-organized, socially motivated network of Catholic organizations and associations was the initial capital to build upon. The presence of a relatively well-known political leader who had good relationships with the Vatican, as did De Gasperi, made the decision to create a political party appealing to the Catholics very likely, though not exceedingly easy. The gap between likelihood and actuality was bridged by De Gaspari's personality and commitment.

This observation raises the question of why neither in Portugal nor in Spain a Christian Democratic party emerged similar to Italian Christian Democracy. Most forecasts had indicated the creation of a Christian Democratic party in Spain as a distinct, and very likely possibility.[7] At this stage, one can only hypothesize that that possibility was consciously not entertained by some party elites, for different reasons (though in Portugal the Democratic Social Centre comes close to being a Christian Democratic party, were it not for its rightist positioning). It might also be that both in Spain and Portugal the Church had been excessively involved in the politics of the authoritarian regimes and wanted to withdraw, at least for a time. It might also be that, in the mid-1970s, the prospects for the founding of a Christian Democratic party appeared rather bleak (even the Italian DC was undergoing a major crisis). Finally, there was not enough 'social and cultural capital' to be utilized, either because the authoritarian regimes had themselves buttressed a weak church or because the Catholics were unwilling to engage, *qua* Catholics, in politics.

The task of building a political organization was not easy either for the Socialists and Communists in both Iberian countries. What already existed was more worker solidarity in trade unions (Commissiones Obreras) or peasants' organizations (for instance in the Alentejo) than party's cells or sections. Indeed, Socialist and Communist party elites were usually abroad, somewhat divorced from internal events in their respective countries. Only in 1974 did a generational revolt in the PSOE shift power back to Spain. The impressive display of years spent in prison by the members of the Portuguese Communist Party[8] cannot hide the fact that the real leader was, and remains, Alvaro Cunhal, who had been living abroad for about thirty years (an experience not dissimilar from Santiago Carrillo's).

For these party elites, therefore, the political capital had to be accumulated during the actual transition from the authoritarian regime. This accumulation could be pursued in different ways. First, the contribution of party members to the unending struggle against the dictators was highlighted also in order to boost the confidence of party members and to reward them psychologically. Second, their own personalities, though not in a blatant way, had to be idealized (Cunhal's asceticism; Ibarruri's inflexibility; Soares' uncompromising attitude; Gonzales' youthfulness: the ascent of a new generation in a new regime). Third, and most important, their behaviour under stress could be used to acquire legitimacy and consensus. The transition was not a picnic nor a gala dinner, but it definitely had some features of a popularity contest (in the negative as well as, and more so, in the positive sense): 'Se siente, se siente (Felipe or Santiago) esta presente'.

The situation was slightly easier also because it was shaped by previous personal struggles and sacrifices, for the two major Greek party leaders. The period before transition had allowed Karamanlis to enhance his stature as a towering Gaullist leader in exile (purposefully in Paris) to await the call of the motherland. It had also submitted Andreas Papandreou to an ordeal of jail, persecutions, slander, and exile. Their political capital was their past: a statesmanlike attitude and recalled capability for Karamanlis; his unflinching opposition to the military junta for Papandreou. No need to add that this was more than enough to nourish the allegiance and to maintain the identification with them of many a follower, old and young, in Greece.

In different ways, then, to which one must add the turbulent phase of military activities in Portugal, the various transitions offered time and opportunities for the most important party leaders to exhibit their qualities and their personalities. This was true for those party leaders who, like Adolfo Suarez and Manuel Fraga Iribarne, wanted in different forms and degrees, to disentangle themselves from the weight of the past and to create new political organizations. In one way or another, with more or less lasting success, party elites did exploit the time and the opportunities. But how did they invest their political resources?

When it comes to this very complex topic, an initial distinction must be clearly drawn between party elites in the government and party elites in the opposition. It may be true, of course, that the very fact of being in the government makes a difference in terms of the political resources available, presumably more. But it might also restrict the range of options. As a matter of fact, one may surmise that Suarez and to a lesser extent Karamanlis, while in charge of the government in the crucial phase of the transition, were obliged to utilize their political resources for that paramount purpose. Therefore, they could not devote enough time to the strengthening of their political organizations.[9] Again, it may be true that networks and solidarities are also the products of governmental decisions and the distribution of resources. It is one thing, however, to pursue that goal deliberately, another thing is to expect that result in the wake of appropriate governmental decisions. There is no doubt that some opposition parties, specifically the Italian and Portuguese Communists (albeit already while they shared governmental power) explicitly aimed at the creation of a wide network of social organizations. The same is true, of course, of the Italian Christian Democrats and, later, of the Spanish Socialists and, more recently of PASOK as well.

No surprise, of course, that there was a lot of image-building in the transition to democracy. Party politics was being played by party leaders. Moreover, some need for personal identification with popular leaders was felt by several sectors of the respective populations. In times of collective anxiety, as Max Weber would put it, individual leaders may provide a satisfactory answer. Again, there have been cases in which this process of image-building has been projected onto governmental institutions (in Italy, with De Gasperi; in Greece, with Karamanlis; in Spain, with Suarez). There have been cases in which the process of image-building was meant to shape and reinforce political parties (in Italy, Togliatti and the PCI; in Greece, Papandreou and PASOK; in Spain, both Gonzalez and PSOE and Carrillo and the PCE, though the latter failed; in Portugal, both Cunhal and the PCP and also Soares and the PSP, though this failed too).

Exaggerating a little, one could speak of the 'institutionalization of personal charisma'. Carrillo never really wanted to do so, distrusting his opponents-collaborators within the PCE. No wonder the process failed and the failure practically wiped out the party. Soares' appeal always remained above and beyond the organizational reach and capabilities of the Portuguese Socialist Party: the process of institutionalization might have taken place to the detriment of Soares' own strategy (and success: had he been more identified with the PSP, he might have lost the presidential elections). Cunhal has, so to speak, 'bought' the institutionalization of his charisma at the price of the immobilism of his party. Suarez decided to or could not help but, invest in the legitimation of governmental structures and processes at the cost of losing his party. Finally, Papandreou has flown on his charisma raising legitimate doubts as to the future of PASOK when the succession crisis surfaces.

If anything, one can say that recent transitions have put more emphasis on the individual role and personal image of party leaders than on political parties as such. Though this might be a product of contemporary politics and the importance of the mass media, especially television, party personalities might have assuaged the anxiety created in many by transitions from one regime to another. All in all, party leaders have shown themselves knowledgeable of the problem and willing to deal with it.[10] Their different degrees of success derive, of course, from the quantity and quality of resources available to them (organizational, positional, financial) as well as from the type of political strategy they wanted to implement. It may be just hinted at that certain leaders might not always desire to win elections. In some precise instances, the strengthening of their organization and the establishment of social networks might be considered and pursued as more important aims (this is particularly true, though it may sound ironic, for the Spanish and Portuguese Communist parties: which goes a long way to explaining their present plight).

Finally, a very important resource must be taken into account: external support. Whether accompanied by financial contributions (as apparently was the case for the DC thanks to the USA, for the PCI thanks to the Soviet Union, and more recently for the Socialist parties in Spain and Portugal thanks to a substantial commitment by the Socialist International) or not, external support is and has been relevant both for a successful transition and a successful democratic consolidation. Expressions of ideological or moral support in favour of those party elites fighting for the establishment of a democratic framework as well as explicit rejection of any return to the past have been and are important weapons in the hands of democratic party elites. As Susannah Verney has accurately portrayed,[11] and as the story of the stormy relationship between Henry Kissinger and Mario Soares, the alleged Kerenski of Portugal, shows, foreign governments do play a very important role.

Intergovernmental relationships notwithstanding, the game of transition and subsequent democratic consolidation has been fundamentally and in some cases almost exclusively played by domestic party elites. This statement might seem surprising and exaggerated. Let us then turn to some examples and the causes behind these party-elite dominated processes.

Democratic consolidation as a party dominated process

Not all the processes of transition have been party dominated; but all processes of democratic consolidation have indeed been party dominated. As we all know, thanks to Juan Linz, authoritarian regimes are characterized by limited not responsible pluralism. In all our cases, it meant that there was no *Gleichschaltung* and that some autonomous organizations and institutions survived under the authoritarian regime and played a political though minor role. While it may be difficult in some cases to evaluate their respective power and to rank them, other cases seem straightforward.

By definition, the armed forces were the dominant actor under the Greek military junta. But, more important than that is the fact that the military dictatorship became increasingly isolated 'and that the only viable alternative, the monarchy, had forfeited its chances first with its blatant and partisan interferences in the political game from 1964 to 1967, then with its ambiguous behaviour in April–May 1967, and finally with its inability openly to advocate and work for a return to a truly democratic regime. There was very limited pluralism in Greece, then, in the face of the weakness of most sectors of civil society since, after all, just a student revolt could cry that the military emperor was indeed naked. Not surprisingly, the breakdown of the armed forces opened up a transition process, where no countervailing power existed to Greek political parties and no alternative leadership could be found to 'traditional', that is well-known, definitely famous party leaders. Since all the other social, economic, cultural, and religious organizations were weak and the governmental institutions had been subordinated to the interests of the military junta, only Greek political parties remained to give shape and substance to the new regime, according to the blueprint and hopes of their most important leaders.[12]

Moving thirty years back in time, the demise of Fascism in Italy left the monarchy totally discredited, the armed forces divided, the business community with tarnished prestige and much fear, the bureaucracy weak and corrupted, and representative and governmental institutions out-dated, belonging to a past which could not be revived. The Church and its social (and later political) associations could then confront left-wing political parties in a situation of utter uncertainty for both. Party leaders behaved in a moderate way for good reasons (Rawls' veil of ignorance worked magnificently). Fortunately, but not by chance, there were no plausible alternatives to party leaders, no countervailing powers to party elites: even the Church had to enter the ground of party politics.

The socio-political and to some extent organizational configurations of the authoritarian regimes in Spain and Portugal were rather similar. However, Portugal lagged considerably behind in terms of socio-economic development and was confronted with a major international problem: colonial wars in Africa. This meant that the limited pluralism of Portugal was inevitably tilted towards the ascendancy of the armed forces (with their peculiarities). In Spain, however, the socio-economic system was slowly but irretrievably outgrowing its political crust. The balancing effort of the dictator there could only prevent the emergence of a dominant actor within the regime and, with the irony of history, pave the way to a renewed monarchy. No countervailing power or institution could block the organizational capabilities available in Spanish society, among its workers (and their Working Commissions), its students, its burgeoning professional associations. Political elites were also there of course. Their step to becoming party elites was a short one, and a relatively smooth transition made it very easy and extremely successful.[13]

Only in Portugal was the process confused and painful. Political parties had practically no roots in a far-away past. Political elites had been involved in the regime and manipulated, or put in prison or sent into exile. The overall legitimacy of party politics was definitely very low. Organizational capabilities, perhaps with the exception of the Communist party, were practically non-existent. Furthermore, the explosion caused by the collapse of the regime produced a fragmentation of groupuscules, small and fluctuating sects, and volatile associations. Once the PCP was in action, however (though still weak, as its leader recognized by looking for support within the military organization and hierarchy), all the other actual and potential competitors were obliged to follow suit within the limits of their (after all not great) capabilities. In sum, no other countervailing organization existed to the armed forces in Portugal until political parties became viable, and party leaders took over. The beginning of electoral politics immediately reduced, as some military officers had feared, the power of the armed forces and magnified the audience of party elites. The transition to democracy had then achieved a higher stage (though not yet irreversible).[14]

The performance of party elites in democratic consolidation

When it came to the issue of democratic consolidation, most party leaders were acutely aware of two major problems. The first one was how to create viable representative and governmental institutions, flexible enough to represent the opposition yet strong enough to bear its brunt. This consciousness was made on the basis of the realization of the inability of weak institutions to accommodate that conflict that led to the destruction of the previous democratic experiment. And also that some institutions are more appropriate than others for guaranteeing democratic consolidation, namely that there is nothing more damaging than a government which cannot govern (and, subordinately, than an electoral system which produces party fragmentation).

Though political elites in the four southern European countries were first and foremost really party elites, many of them had previously had direct (having been Members of Parliament themselves) or indirect (having been exposed to the workings of democratic Parliaments) experience with parliamentary government and activities. They could, therefore, appreciate the role of Parliament and the importance of parliamentary government. Only in the case of Portugal, where the military played the role of a countervailing elite to the politicians, were several different options entertained by the military themselves, by sections of the Communist party, and by a myriad of left-wing minor groups.[15] When elections for a representative assembly were first held, all those alternative options were drastically reduced, and political parties and party elites began reacquiring control over the political process (and, indeed, democratic consolidation was in the making).[16]

The second problem was how to gather political consensus. Some options had been foreclosed by the previous authoritarian experience, namely that of a plebiscitary government founded on a direct relationship between the voters and the chief executive. When the Portuguese military themselves engaged in seeking consensus for a military 'party' (by asking for a blank ballot), their performance was dismal, despite their popularity. It then became clear in Portugal that the military option, unavailable in all the other countries, was not a viable one. Even in Portugal, therefore, the game of the transition and democratic consolidation shifted into the hands of party elites.

Because of their political past and previous experience, and through a process of accelerated learning, supported and encouraged from their party friends abroad, party elites in all four countries decided to perform the three major tasks (or functions) political parties are supposedly made for (and for which there is no equally acceptable and capable replacement, Ersatz): political mobilization and participation; structuring of electoral alternatives; and selection of political and governmental personnel. By definition, democratic consolidation requires as a pre-condition free and competitive elections. Almost by definition but definitely in practice, party elites must of course participate in the electoral process. All of them decided to do so and set on course the shaping of mass democracies, that is of mobilizing and offering channels of political participation to the widest spectrum of their populations. In Italy, in 1945, this decision was an innovation both for the Communists, whose alternative model might have been the Leninist party of professional revolutionaries, and for the Catholics, whose political involvement was by no means assured. In Portugal, the process had to start practically from scratch, and proved to be difficult with ups and downs and (higher than usual?) electoral volatility. Greece and Spain, though for somewhat different reasons (in the first case, the previous democratic experiment was still very close in time; in the second, society was already available for political mobilization and participation), offered fertile ground for the implantation and activities of political parties.[17]

Party elites shrewdly exploited the various opportunities, institutional and social, political and cultural, to establish their organizations and to launch their activities. Perhaps the most important element worthy of analysis (but also badly needing some convincing empirical evidence) is the willingness and ability of party leaders to create a true political class. In some cases, for instance the three major Italian parties, a conscious attempt was made to provide a comprehensive party leadership profile, where political generations and political experiences could blend. Thus members of the pre-Fascist Giolittian parliament sat close to those born to politics opposing the Fascist regime and those who participated in the Resistance struggle. On the other hand, one is tempted to say that in parties run according to the principle of democratic centralism, that is the Portuguese and the Spanish Communist parties, the older generation, either of exiled political leaders or of imprisoned opponents of the regime, was bound to emerge as dominant – at least at the national level (and a similar reasoning should hold for the Communist Party of Greece).

For generational reasons, one would expect, on the contrary, a very large influx of a new political elite in all the other parties of Portugal and Spain, all the more so for the Spanish Socialists after the victory of the young generation at the Congress of 1974. But this was slightly less true for Conservative parties, which fished among socio-economic notables and sought to recycle some semi-opponents of the previous regime. Similar reasons, but having to do with the lack of a generational changeover because of the short period of time in which the military junta suspended party-political activities, prevented a major renewal of the political class in Greece.

However, what was not achieved or was restrained by these 'objective' (time and generation) processes, was eventually accomplished by more or less unexpected electoral outcomes. The later landslide victories of PASOK, the PSOE, and the PSD in the 1980s brought to the fore basically new party-political elites (though with some few, selected 'old' leaders still in charge), and this trend significantly enhanced the horizon of political competition. Had competition been restricted in an inter-bureaucratic manner, both the enlargement and the renewal of the political class and with it the soundness of democratic consolidation would have been jeopardized. The imperatives of electoral competition, to which parties and their leaders must be very sensitive, brought about these highly positive developments. Indeed, if the net of political development is cast wide – only political parties can do so, and only party leaders can fully appreciate its significance – more people of different generations, but especially of the young generations, will participate in politics and hence sustain the process of democratic consolidation.

In conclusion, it was because of electoral imperatives, because of a sober assessment of the inadequacy of their previous party organizations, because of an acknowledgement of the notional weakness of a democratic regime with opinion parties only, or simply because of a mixture of all these forms of motivation that party elites in the four southern European countries, at different times, made similar decisions. By so doing they have succeeded in creating, aside from the differences in institutional structures, viable mass democratic regimes.

Conclusion

In most western democracies, the conviction that 'the party's over' seems to be widespread. Moreover, all kinds of criticisms, many of them assuredly well deserved, are directed against political parties and their leaders. Often these accusations forget nevertheless the important, perhaps decisive contributions parties and party elites make to the functioning of democratic regimes, perhaps just by 'being there', that is by preventing the appearance of disagreeable alternatives: military rule, bureaucratic politics, lobby dominance, and so on.

It is *refreshing*, then, to become aware of the role played by parties and party elites in the transition from authoritarian regimes and in the consolidation of democratic ones in southern Europe, at different points in time. The differences are not very great, because the challenges were similar: how to consolidate a mass democracy in countries whose political culture was not homogeneous, whose entrenched powers retained some strength, and whose socio-economic foundations were not accepted by everybody? Party leaders provided one answer which has proved so far viable. Only party leaders could in fact link the past of their countries with the future, absorb the old generations of party politicians and mobilize a new one, blend different ideas, experiences, expectations, preferences (and suffocate desires of revenge), perform all the various functions associated with a democratic regime. And this they did.

More precisely, one can maintain that party elites succeeded in our four countries exactly where the failure of their democratic predecessors had facilitated the emergence of authoritarian regimes. That is, they succeeded in promoting and accepting conciliation and accommodation, whereas their predecessors had doomed the previous embryonic democratic experiments because of their rigidity and unwillingness to compromise. Probably because they had learned from the mistakes of the past (and some of our party leaders had been personal witnesses of those mistakes, if not outright responsible for them), probably because they had borne the brunt of the authoritarian regime, party leaders were determined not to create the conditions for a relapse.

This inclination to compromise usually appeared already in the transition phase and is characterized by the acceptance of mutual pacts, even with some sectors of the previous authoritarian regime willing to disentangle themselves from it.[18] It was then solidified by the so-called 'habituation phase'[19] (even though it must be stressed that the process of consolidation, at least in southern Europe, has been greatly helped and buttressed by international factors: the support given by some parties, specifically the Socialists and their International, to their 'brothers' in the various countries as well as the overall push for democracy coming from European governments, while previous 'habituation phases' had entailed an unbridled internal competition in early democratizing countries). Therefore this 'habituation' has had rather long, and promising, roots.

Conciliation and accommodation among party elites have also been accompanied by the possibility of alternation in power. One can, indeed, state that it was the rejection of this possibility which had previously created the conditions for an authoritarian regime. Therefore the sheer fact that party elites have accepted, as a fundamental rule of the game, the process of alternation in power (most visibly in Greece and Spain), is an excellent indicator of a successful consolidation (even though it would be incorrect to stress that lack of alternation suggests less than consolidated democratic regimes in Italy and Portugal, it certainly points to one weakness and to an unsolved problem).

One may surmise that the game played by party leaders in southern Europe has been a very shrewd one. During the transition and in the first part of the consolidation process, they consciously resorted, accepted, and put to use consociational mechanisms: to guarantee themselves against the reappearance of authoritarian temptations. In the second part of the consolidation, because a sufficient level of mutual trust had been achieved, they accepted and channelled the move towards alternation (or were caught off guard by surprising electoral developments). Then the very fact that alternation could be produced by free elections constituted the turning-point in the process of consolidation and the hallmark in the achievement of a stable democratic situation, legitimate in the eyes of party leaders and party followers (no less than of foreign observers).[20]

By this time, legitimacy has, so to speak, begun to percolate down and reach most, if not all, sectors of society. At least for a certain time to come, the implantation of party organizations and the generational turnover should prevent the emergence of the ghosts of the authoritarian past, while party leaders are still aware of the limits ('the confining conditions') to their criticism of the behaviour of other party leaders and of the very nature of the democratic regime.

Of course, democratic consolidation is one thing and the performance of the democratic regime quite another question. The matter of the quality of democracy might indeed provoke feelings of *desencanto*, but seldom has this *desencanto* resuscitated desires of returning to the authoritarian past. In any case, the commitment of almost the totality of party elites to democratic politics as well as their own behaviour and the ideas they diffuse among the population at large seem to guarantee that no breakdown of democracy is likely in the near future of southern Europe.

It may also be *instructive* for other political leaders and party elites engaged in the difficult task of ousting an authoritarian regime to be exposed to the importance of relying on party organization. Both the theory and the practice conspire in favour of the following conclusion: parties and their leaders are the decisive actors. The theory is well presented by Samuel P. Huntington:[21]

> The vacuum of power and authority which exists in so many modernising countries may be filled temporarily by charismatic leadership or by military force. But it can be filled permanently only by political organisation. Either the established elites compete among themselves to organise the masses through the existing political system or dissident elites organise them to overthrow that system. In the modernising world he controls the future who organises its politics.

The practice is convincingly shown by the overall experience of the four southern European countries here analysed. Their earlier non-authoritarian experiments were destroyed because their party politics was embryonic and deficient. Their recent democratic consolidation has been made possible by the reappearance and strength of their parties and by the lessons learned and applied by their party elites.

At this point, it is appropriate to stress that, with minor exceptions only, political parties and their southern European elites have come from a distance and that they promise to go very far. They play the role of linchpin between society and state institutions. Their epoch is not over. On the contrary, it may just be dawning for all countries and leaders who fight for a successful transition from authoritarian regimes and an equally successful consolidation of democratic regimes.

Notes

1. O. Kirchheimer, 'Confining conditions and revolutionary breakthroughs', *American Political Science Review*, 1965, vol. LIX, no. 4, pp. 964–74.
2. Specifically when Juan Linz writes that 'a leader (or occasionally a small group) exercises power within formally ill-defined limits but actually quite predictable ones' in 'An authoritarian regime: Spain', in E. Allardt and Y.

Littunen (eds) *Cleavages, Ideologies and Party Systems*, Helsinki, Academic Bookstore, 1964, p. 297.

3. Even though Mario Soares and Alvaro Cunhal in Portugal were indeed leaders of burgeoning parties, and Adolfo Suarez and Manuel Fraga Iribarne in Spain had some party background.

4. R. De Felice, *Intervista sul fascismo*, Bari, Laterza, 1975.

5. For a very accurate and imaginative analysis of the various types of oppositions under authoritarian regimes, see Juan Linz, 'Opposition to and under an authoritarian regime: the case of Spain', in R. A. Dahl (ed) *Regimes and Oppositions*, New Haven, Conn., Yale University Press, 1973, pp. 171–259.

6. In Chapter 4 in this volume.

7. For instance, the oft-quoted chapter by Juan Linz, 'The party system of Spain: past and future', in S. M. Lipset and S. Rokkan (eds) *Party Systems and Voter Alignments*, New York, Free Press, 1967, pp. 197–282.

8. See the book *Documentos politicos do Partido Comunista Portugues: IX Congresso (31 Maio, 1,2,3 Junho 1979)*, Edicoes Avante!, n.p., n.d.

9. This does not mean that a clear dilemma is posed: either statesmen or party leaders. However, it means that, in practice, some leaders might be unable, for political or organizational reasons, to allocate their time and resources satisfactorily to both tasks. ·

10. Consociational devices have, apparently, always played a significant role in the processes of transition, especially if the rupture with the past was not clean and sharp. On several of these points, see P. Schmitter 'Patti e transizioni: mezzi non-democratici a fini democratici?', *Rivista Italiana di Scienza Politica*, 1984, vol. XIV, no. 3, pp. 363–82.

11. In Chapter 9 in this volume.

12. N. Diamandouros, 'Regime change and the prospects for democracy in Greece: 1974–1983', in G. O'Donnell, P. Schmitter, and L. Whitehead (eds) *Transitions from Authoritarian Rule: Prospects for Democracy*, Baltimore, Md and London, Johns Hopkins University Press, 1986, pp. 138–64 and 200–8.

13. J. M. Maravall, *La politica de la transicion 1975–1980*, Madrid, Taurus, 1981.

14. K. Maxwell, 'Regime overthrow and the prospects for democratic transition in Portugal', in G. O'Donnell *et al.*, op. cit., pp. 109–37 and 197–200.

15. On this point, G. Pasquino, 'Le Portugal: de la dictature coporatiste a la democratie socialiste?', in L. Hamon (ed.) *Mort des dictatures?*, Paris, Economica, 1981, pp. 105–28, and the literature there cited.

16. Indeed, Soares was probably the one who had the most clearly devised strategy, as expounded in his excellent interview with Dominique Pouchin: *Portugal: quelle revolution?*, Paris, Calmann-Levy, 1976 (of course, both 'couples' – De Gasperi and Togliatti in Italy, and Karamanlis and Papandreou in Greece – had shaped their strengths in advance).

17. On some of these aspects, see H. R. Penniman and E. Mujal-Leon (eds) *Spain at the Polls, 1977, 1979, and 1982*, Durham, NC, Duke University Press, 1985, and G. Th. Mavrogordatos, *Rise of the Green Sun: The Greek Elections of 1981*, London, King's College, Centre of Contemporary Greek

Studies, occasional paper 1, 1983.
18. In addition to the article by Schmitter, quoted in note 10, see G. Di Palma, 'Founding coalitions in Southern Europe', *Government and Opposition*, 1980, vol. 15, no. 2, pp. 162–89.
19. D.A. Rustow, 'Transitions to democracy: toward a dynamic model', *Comparative Politics*, 1970, vol. II, no. 1, pp. 337–63, at p. 358.
20. On some of these points, see G. Di Palma, 'Party government and democratic reproducibility: the dilemma of new democracies', in F. G. Castles and R. Wildenmann (eds) *Visions and Realities of Party Government*, Berlin, de Gruyter, 1986, pp. 178–204.
21. S. P. Huntington, *Political Order in Changing Societies*, New Haven, Conn., Yale University Press, 1968, p. 461.

Chapter three

The consolidation of democracy in post-war Italy

David Hine

Specific features of the Italian case

The most striking feature of the consolidation of democracy in post-war Italy is the length of time the process seems to have taken. The transition phase – from Fascism to republican democracy – was fairly rapid, lasting roughly from 1943 to 1948. Consolidation, it might be argued, was completed only in the 1970s, if then. Indeed, in so far as one external manifestation of consolidation is the successful transfer of power between government and opposition, consolidation has never been completely tested, for an enduring peculiarity of Italian democracy, compared with most other European democracies, including those elsewhere in the Mediterranean, is the absence of clear-cut alternation between competing groups of parties.

However, while alternation is the ultimate test of consolidation, it is clearly not synonymous with it. It would be misleading to imply that, in the absence of a successful transition to a government of the left, Italian democracy at the start of the 1990s is no more firmly rooted than in the 1950s or 1960s. The difficulty, however, lies in devising adequate measures of the concept of consolidation. In so far as it is related to political cultures and value systems, then longitudinal comparisons of democratic consolidation should ideally be based on survey data, but there are extensive problems associated with survey data in Italy, where response rates have, until recently, tended to be disappointingly low. Even if there were a readily defined structure of elite and mass opinions which was agreed to constitute the appropriate mix of attitudes in a 'consolidated' democracy, there is for Italy no readily available source of longitudinal data which taps this structure.

At best, there are some useful, but not easily comparable, individual surveys, especially for the more recent period.[1] Much of this work, in so far as it is relevant to democratic consolidation, tends to concentrate on the issue of *perceived threats* to democracy – that is, how parties regard, trust, and interact with each other, and how they are regarded by different sections of the electorate. What emerges is a somewhat ambiguous picture. Sani's research analysed the constraints on coalition realignment almost two decades ago, and identified the persistence of extensive hostility towards both political extremes on the part of supporters of the moderate centre parties. Cross-national comparisons carried out by Sani and Sartori in the 1970s indicated that Italy had one of the broadest ideological spectra in western Europe, when defined by voters' self-locations on the left–right continuum, although differences in the cultural meaning of such a self-locating exercise make it difficult to conclude much from this about democratic consolidation.[2] Moreover, there is considerable evidence suggesting that over time there have been some important depolarizing tendencies at work. Guidorossi, for example, describes the widely quoted Doxa research, which suggests that by the later 1970s, the Italian Communist Party enjoyed a substantially more positive image among most parts of the electorate than in the 1960s. It also became clear in the 1970s that the deep-rooted antipathy between the Catholic and social-communist subcultures was in decline, with, for example, a far lower percentage of the population claiming that it was impossible to be both a good Catholic and a Socialist or Communist.[3]

Difficulties in interpreting survey evidence not originally designed to answer direct questions about democratic consolidation are compounded by the fact that mass attitudes are only one side of the story, and possibly not even the most important. Much of the recent debate about the operation of the Italian party system focuses on attitudes towards consensus and coalition-bargaining within the political elite, as we shall see later. In studying consolidation there are thus problems of definition as well as of measurement. Consolidation seems to include some notion of the *universality* of democratic values, the *institutionalization* of democratic norms and procedures, and a wide degree of mutual trust and tolerance between the main political actors. The consolidation phase is thus one in which these features are being created, but do not yet seem to be guaranteed. Rules and procedures are tentatively tested; opinion is being solidified; confidence is being built; understandings about the politically possible – not least in the realm of distributive outcomes – are being set.[4] Yet combining these features into a calculus of consolidation is little easier than defining democracy itself; most modern democracies contain at least some objectionable features, but how many they must have to be disqualified from the community of democratic states is highly debatable.

The difficulty of making inferences from indirect indicators of consolidation illustrates this. The fragility of coalitions, and the difficulty of sustaining Cabinets might be thought to be closely related to incomplete consolidation. In fact, however, while Italian politics is a by-word for coalition instability, the record in the 1980s is little better than in the past. Yet today, when there is difficulty sustaining or even forming a Cabinet, there is not the same concern that democracy may be in danger that was present until the 1970s. Democratic consolidation was long drawn out not because it took so long to learn how to build stable coalitions, but rather because the promulgation of the 1948 Constitution did not appear to resolve widespread doubts about the viability of democracy in the face of challenges from the two wings of an ideologically very wide party spectrum. If the consolidation phase has now been largely completed, as seems intuitively plausible, and as the scanty survey evidence appears to indicate, it seems to be mainly because perceptions of these challenges have changed. Here, perhaps, lies the single most important indicator of democratic consolidation – mutually endowed trust and legitimacy between the main political parties.

Admittedly the absence of mutually endowed legitimacy between political forces was not the only reason why democratic consolidation was so long drawn-out. The failure of democracy in the 1920s, the experience of Fascism and its suppression of a democratic political culture, and the survival of pre-democratic and pre-industrial habits and relationships in the southern half of the country, all combined to ensure that Italian democracy would be seen as stable only when it had been tested for a considerable period of time, and when Italian society had undergone a substantial transformation. Moreover, in the light of such a record, the impact of those developments in the later post-war years which affected many European democracies, but struck Italy with particular force (the student movement, deep-seated tensions in industrial relations, terrorism) was bound to be more threatening than elsewhere. Nevertheless, the core of the debate on Italian democracy, both partisan and academic, has been focused on the democratic credentials of supposedly extremist parties.

This chapter is not, however, aimed at resolving the perennial question of what precisely counts as an anti-system party. Attempts to resolve this issue have focused on a number of indicators: party origins and history, party aims and strategies, party statements, party behaviour (both intended and unintended) in a democratic environment, and perceptions of the party by other actors in the system. Clearly the major problem is that a party which initially looks, by some of these standards, to be an anti-system party, but which operates in a democratic environment, may, over time, and initially for very uncertain – even discreditable – reasons, come to internalize the norms and values of the environment within which it operates. If so, the process will be a gradual one, affecting different parts of the party at different times. The party is unlikely to acknowledge the change publicly, both because this could involve internal dissent, and because the party may not accept that it ever *was* 'anti-system'.[5]

Moreover, other parties are likely to refuse to recognize the change as genuine. Throwing doubt on the democratic credentials of particular parties is frequently a subjective and highly partisan activity. It has been indulged in enthusiastically not only by politicians, but also by academics, as we shall see when we return to their arguments later in the chapter. Furthermore, while the attempt to brand a party as anti-system may not be disinterested, it may nevertheless be self-fulfilling, in that the exclusion of parties from eligibility as coalition partners may make the process of sustaining governments, and preserving their popular support, more difficult.[6] It may also throw the party thus branded back on to a type of apparently intransigent opposition which it would otherwise have preferred to avoid. Such an interpretation could be placed, for example, on the events which followed the enunciation of the Truman Doctrine, and the development of the Cold War, from 1947 onwards. Faced with these events, the PCI had little option but to fall back on myths, symbols, and styles of behaviour which, so the argument would run, the leadership would have preferred to avoid.

As with many essentially contested concepts, attempts to apply the concept correctly rapidly ran into a series of contentious issues of interpretation of facts and motives, many of which involve long and complex historical sequences of events. Often, in fact, it may appear that parties are anti-system *only* in terms of their historical origins, or their unintended effects on the operation of the party system, and this may well be true of the Italian Communist Party today.

For our purposes, however, it may be sufficient to note that the problem, both as one of academic definition, and one of partisan political debate, has been more deep-rooted, and has persisted for longer, than in almost any other European democracy. This, in itself, is strong prima-facie evidence of a problem of democratic consolidation. Moreover, if today the consolidation of Italian democracy is no longer in doubt, it seems to be above all because perceptions of the parties have changed. Although the grip of party government has been eased (interest groups are more numerous and freer of party constraints, and voters are, to a degree, more mobile and instrumental in attitude – Italy is, in short, a more libertarian party democracy)[7] this has neither strengthened the existing 'extremes', nor created a space for the rise of new and dangerous anti-system movements.

Furthermore, not only has the system come through the acute test of the 1970s without the electoral polarization so feared in models of the party system based on ideological polarization, but also it has seen a marked deradicalization of the existing extremes. The Communist Party's (PCI) apparently inexorable drive towards power was halted by

1979, and the party's subsequent fortunes have dipped dramatically, but this has certainly not forced it back into the ghetto. On the contrary, the PCI is today further than ever from its Leninist past, a matter acknowledged even by the leadership of the Christian Democrat Party. As for the Socialist Party, the irreversibility of the social-democratization process which occurred under the centre-left coalitions of the 1960s has never been in serious doubt. Indeed, under Craxi, the party has often claimed to be the authentic voice of the political centre. Developments on the right have been less clear-cut, because the right still plays no role in coalition politics. But even the MSI looks less fiercesome than in the early 1970s; its leaders have even tried, however ambiguously, to achieve a measure of respectability.

Quite when these changes were complete is less clear, although there is no doubt that the 1970s represents the watershed. During that decade the parties established a substantial, if still incomplete, measure of mutual trust, and, especially at parliamentary level, the rules of the political system became far more clearly institutionalized. As a result the parties were able to overcome post-war Italian democracy's greatest challenge – the ferocious onslaught from terrorist movements of both left and right. Not only did the state, albeit belatedly, establish a firm grip on the domestic terror which created such havoc in the 1970s, but also it maintained both a basic respect for fundamental civil rights, and a high degree of inter-party solidarity.

None of this is to deny the importance of other influences on the consolidation process. Parties may lie at the core of that process – as they do in Italy – but their behaviour is strongly conditioned by economics and international politics. The discrediting and collapse of authoritarian movements elsewhere in southern Europe, for example, made Italy seem less like a fragile Mediterranean anomaly than in the days of Franco, Papadopoulos, or Caetano. The international financial integration of the 1980s, consolidating that achieved by the EEC in the 1960s and 1970s, combined with the much higher profile that this has brought Italy in the international community, to make it highly implausible that business or financial leaders would support any departure from liberal democracy. But while such changes, and the much more diffuse impact of steadily growing economic prosperity and extensive mechanisms of social redistribution, are critical to consolidation, they are no more synonymous with it than is alternation in power. If Italian democracy is today fully consolidated, it is first and foremost because the parties on the edges of the political spectrum – both left and right – are no longer seen as significant threats to the system.

Before we proceed to examine the evolution of the consolidation process, and the role of individual parties within it, we need, however, to return to the peculiarity of Italian democracy which we identified at the outset – namely, the absence of alternation. Alternation between left and right poses as yet insuperable problems, and this fact, combined with continuing problems of coalition stability, results in a rather diffuse dissatisfaction with the institutional framework, which has expressed itself, in recent years, in a continuing debate over constitutional reform. Admittedly that debate has been a leisurely one. There is little sense of an impending crisis, and what is at stake is greater decisional effectiveness in government rather than the very survival of democracy. Indeed, it is a sign of consolidation that the rules of the game *can* now be seriously debated without the fear that such debate may endanger the democratic framework. Nevertheless, while the general context of democratic institutions is hardly in doubt, the existence of this constitutional debate does partly reflect a failure on the part of the parties: a failure to provide clear-cut electoral choice, and orderly mechanisms for the transfer of power, which is, as we shall see in the latter part of this chapter, related to the way they responded to the imperatives of consolidation.

To explore these issues in a more systematic manner, we need now to examine the role of parties from the perspective of the three relationships used in other chapters in this book: the relationship between the parties and society, that between parties and the state, and inter-party relationships.

Parties and civil society

When we talk of the modern *party state,* we refer to the centrality of party in a far wider sense than simply the respective importance in the decision-making process of parties and other institutional actors such as civil servants or interest groups. A well-entrenched party state requires that parties have firm roots in society, close contacts with, or indeed the capacity to control, major social actors, and a high degree of legitimacy in the eyes of the electorate.

There is little question that on this score the transition to democracy after the Second World War stands in marked contrast to the emergence of universal (male) suffrage just before and immediately after the First World War. An important contributory factor in the failure of mass democracy in the years 1919–22 was the weakly developed party system, in which only two parties, gathering between them approx-imately half of the vote, could be said to constitute structured parties with solid organization and strong bonds with the electorate. The personalism of political relationships within the then Liberal ruling elite, and the fragmentation and instability within its parliamentary ranks, made almost impossible the formation of lasting coalitions. This, in turn, discredited democratic politics in the eyes of many voters, and undermined confidence in the capacity of central government to stand up to the apparently growing strength of the left, and the threat from Fascism.

After the Second World War, in contrast, the party system emerged with greater solidity. It is true that until after the general election of 1953 there remained a considerable degree of volatility in electoral relationships, but so there was in most European party systems in this formative post-war period.[8] In fact already by the time of the first election held under the new Republican constitution, in 1948, the shape of the party system, as it has remained almost to this day, was evident. Moreover, the parties themselves, or at least the three main ones, were based upon impressive organizational foundations. The growth of political participation which arose from the Resistance, and which turned the Communists, Socialists, and Christian Democrats into mass-based organizations enrolling between them by 1947 over 3 million members, was all the more remarkable in a country with little previous tradition of voluntary associationalism, and, even after the Second World War, with only a rather weakly developed interest-group infrastructure. Indeed an important characteristic of the post-war party state was the way in which the parties exercised a profound influence over the reconstruction of social organizations and interest groups. Many such groups were in effect captured by the parties and subordinated to the dictates of their political controllers.

Conventional wisdom on the Italian party system explains the solidity of post-war party organization and the relative stability of electoral behaviour in *subcultural* terms.[9] The two main political parties, so the argument runs, expressed natural divisions within the electorate – subcultural blocks separated by distinct ideological value-systems, the origins of which lay in the accretions of recent Italian history – the conflict between the church and the secular state, that between capital and labour, and that between Fascism and resistance. Each subculture was sustained by a wide range of associations: unions, co-operatives, professional organizations, women's groups, youth movements, etc. In recent years, of course, there has been an extensive debate about how far this subcultural model still applies, but there is little doubt that originally it was the main foundation of the post-war party system. Democratic consolidation may thus have been influenced by how effectively the two main parties handled this basic subcultural divide. Was their behaviour functional to social reconciliation and political institutionalization, or did it exacerbate major social cleavages?

Answering this question is complicated by the multidimensional nature of the subcultures themselves, and by the absence of counter-factuals telling us what would have happened to the subcultures had they not been captured by the two major parties. Subcultural politics, in fact, is not confined to the boundaries of class politics. The so-called 'socialist' subculture, largely under PCI hegemony, is politically radical, anti-clerical, and territorially concentrated. In its heartland of the Red Belt (although much less so in its second home of the Industrial Triangle), it transcends the unionized working class to include the peasantry (now much reduced in size), the independent middle strata (artisans, shopkeepers, etc.) and much of the white-collar middle class. Likewise, the Catholic subculture itself transcends class barriers, so that the Christian Democrats have always had a substantial working- class wing, allied to a trade-union confederation with an explicitly Catholic vocation.

The subcultures thus appear to have helped in transcending the cleavages of class and religion, and there is substantial evidence that both major parties have consciously sought to assemble broad inter-group alliances at the electoral level. Thus the Communist Party has always down-played the anti-clerical dimension of the Socialist subculture, from its willingness to incorporate the Lateran Pacts into the Constitution in the 1940s, to its cautious approach to demands for the liberalization of issues of personal morality in the 1970s. Similarly the Christian Democrats have frequently accepted policies of social reconciliation (welfare networks, albeit clientelistically administered; industrial subsidies; regional-aid packages; wage indexation) and have never sought to serve as the unequivocal champions of business.

The case of the Communist Party's relationship with unionized labour is more ambivalent. For nearly two decades, it resisted the notion that the unions under its influence should be integrated into a system of collective-bargaining which, even if conducted in vigorous pursuit of the immediate interests of the workers, would nevertheless be an implicit recognition of capitalist-style labour relations. Formally it abandoned the 'transmission belt' role, assigned to unions in Leninist theory, in the 1950s, and in practice it made little use of the strike weapon in an aggressively and explicitly political way. However, it retained an ideological reluctance to accept the implications of collective bargaining in a competitive labour market, particularly at plant level, and even during the Hot Autumn of labour unrest in the late 1960s, the CGIL's moves in this direction were being driven by the militancy of the Confederation's own rank-and-file members rather than by the leadership.[10]

The party's attitude has however changed considerably in the 1970s and 1980s. It is still anxious to put whatever influence it can exercise on the unions to use for its own political ends, and during the Historic Compromise it made no secret of the fact that it was exchanging a policy of wage restraint imposed on its own voters, for political influence within the parliamentary coalition. Nevertheless, the PCI now appears to accept both the basic independence of the CGIL, and the principle of union participation in a capitalist labour market. It occasionally veers towards corporatist-style tripartite agreements between labour, capital, and government, in which free collective bargaining would be much restricted. But this search for control now stems from a pessimism about the health of the Italian mixed economy, and admiration for social-democrat-style corporatism, rather than from any attempt to mobilize the labour movement towards radical or transformative goals.

On balance, therefore, we may conclude that the relationship between parties and society has been a positive one for the process of democratic consolidation. The one qualification to this pattern of a highly structured electorate, frozen into a pattern of party allegiances enduring over successive elections, is to be found in the south. There the electorate was always more volatile, and the space for anomic and spontaneous protest remained considerable, with little sustained associational experience or organizational energy. The two major parties sought in the 1950s to expand their organizations in the south, but with only limited success.[11] Christian-Democrat efforts to displace the local notables (whose loyalties to the party banner were, at best, contingent), with machine-oriented politicians who could be disciplined and controlled from the centre, resulted in the party's falling victim to the predominantly clientelistic form of political relationships characteristic of the region. The southernization of the party, in fact, was a major factor in the endemic crises of corruption that so damaged the party in the later post-war era.[12] As for the Communists, the limitations of their southern strategy were most in evidence in the mid-1970s, when the dramatic progress the PCI made in the 1975 regional and 1976 national elections evaporated in the space of three years, and demonstrated how little organizational protection the party enjoyed in the south when faced with contingent political difficulties.[13]

However, although the south clearly represents an exception to the general pattern of stable links between parties and the electorate, this was not as threatening to democracy as it might have been. Partly this was because despite frequent lawlessness, and widespread corruption, there was so little organizational energy in the south that the region could not generate an extremist protest party of its own. (This, incidently, helps explain why the south had never generated the party of territorial/peripheral defence that the Rokkanian cleavage model would predict.)[14] It was also because even if the Christian Democrats were unable to dominate southern politics by strong party organization, they were, for a long time, able to buy off protest by largesse from central government. When, in the 1970s, the appetite for patronage outstripped the centre's capacity to deliver, the DC's grip began to slip, as events from the Reggio riots onwards demonstrated, but by then the process of democratic consolidation was well advanced.[15]

Parties and the state

The second dimension of the strong party state is, of course, the hold of the parties over the institutions of the state itself. In many ways the parties established this hold by default. The discrediting of the monarchy and the army, the relative weakness of the state tradition and the state bureaucracy, and the latter's low prestige after its infiltration by Fascist habits and outlooks, all combined to create a vacuum which the parties could hardly avoid filling.

Here too, there are several features which can be seen as having contributed positively towards the consolidation process. First, parties very rapidly came to dominate the process of recruitment to political office. Generals and businessmen have not, on the whole, been parachuted into high political office after a career mostly spent elsewhere. It is true that in recent general elections parties have been in the habit of putting prestigious names on their lists of candidates, and in the last five years one or two of these have even made it into the Council of Ministers. This is the exception, however; normally the curriculum vitae of the successful national politician must be based on a party career in local government, and in local party organization, followed by election to Parliament, and finally into national office. The party is thus the filter and the legitimizer.

Moreover, parties have maintained a firm hold on the policy process, at least in the sense that they, rather than the administration, or any other public arena, are the mediators in policy disputes. This is not because the parties, like their counterparts in the Federal Republic of Germany, have possessed elaborate research and policy-making departments; on the whole they have not. However, they have faced no institutional rivals in the policy process, mainly because of the absence of a prestigious, self-consciously evangelistic, bureaucratic elite. As Cassese has shown,[16] this is a consequence of the long-term 'southernization' of the higher civil service, and its desire to trade influence over policy for career security. The core ministerial civil service has not (in contrast to France or Germany) been politicized, but this has left the parties as the arbitrators of the policy process. Even when the details of policy are effectively made by outsiders the parties maintain a strong hold over the process, in that they choose whom to consult, and whether to accept the advice: indeed they frequently decline to do so.

In addition, Italian parties are almost all structured on a system of direct internal democracy which accords a large measure of decision-making authority to party executives as opposed to parliamentary leaders. In practice, there is substantial overlap between the two, but perceived legitimacy stems, in the final instance, from party power, not parliamentary or governmental power, and leaders in government, or indeed Parliament, ignore party executives at their peril.[17] When this is combined with the workings of coalition government, it puts even more power in the hands of the parties. When major policy issues are disputed, they are subject to arbitration between party secretaries, and between parliamentary group leaders, rather than Cabinet ministers.

Strong party government may thus be presumed to have had a stabilizing effect, in so far as it was parties, rather than charismatic individuals, or bureaucrats unskilled in the art of political mediation, who controlled the policy process. Of course, this alone was not sufficient if the outputs of party government itself came to be perceived as unsatisfactory. Nor was it complete protection against the corrosive effects of indiscipline inside the parliamentary ranks of the governing parties. Such indiscipline was indeed facilitated by certain features of the operation of the Italian Parliament designed to limit party government. The drafters of the first parliamentary standing orders were sufficiently concerned about the power of party executives to include a provision (extensively used until drastically redefined in 1988) for a secret vote on the final reading of most legislation. Their intention – to weaken the power of the party whips – was similar to that behind the introduction of the preference vote in parliamentary elections.[18]

Without doubt, the secret vote did have this effect, although it is interesting to note in the present context that while it may have worked against strong party government, it did, indirectly, facilitate and encourage habits of co-operation – sometimes explicit, sometimes concealed – between government and opposition. In this sense, Parliament served as an arena which encouraged the integration of the Communist Party into the system. As has frequently been observed, there is here an important difference between the institutional access afforded to the Italian Communist Party, and the relative isolation in which the French Communist Party found itself for so many years, which may help to explain some of the key differences between the two parties. The same holds for the structure of Italian local government, especially after the introduction of regional government in 1970. Local and regional government gave the Communist Party an opportunity to test out alliances with other parties, and indeed to demonstrate its not inconsiderable administrative talents.[19]

A further important characteristic of the party state has been party occupation of the (non-civil service) administrative world, particularly the large and, until the late 1970s, constantly expanding, range of public agencies which were outside the formal ministerial structures. Partisan appointments to such bodies, which range in nature from the largest public holding companies (IRI, ENI, etc.) to the meanest local government refuse dump, have facilitated their exploitation for patronage purposes on a growing scale. Party affiliation came to be necessary not simply to be co-opted into the board of administration at the top, but gradually for permanent full-time employment lower down the agency as well. Indeed clientele politics became an important weapon in the electoral armoury of all governing parties, and the resources of the interventionist state and the welfare state fitted naturally into political relationships which only shortly before had been dominated by the local notable and his ascriptive political authority.

However, we should not conclude this part of the discussion without recognizing that the entrenchment of clientele networks was not an unqualified benefit either for the governing parties, or for democratic consolidation as a whole. As the previous section indicated, it generated difficulties for the governing parties at the point at which expenditure constraints began to undermine their ability to service their clienteles. Fortunately this became a serious factor only when consolidation was already fairly well advanced. However, it also helped undermine the reputation of the 'democratic' parties for probity and honesty, and thus seemed to preserve that credibility gap between the political class as a whole and civil society which had been a serious weakness of the pre-Fascist system, and was if anything intensified by the Fascist experience itself. Where the political class is seen to act in an unashamedly entrepreneurial fashion, rewarding its friends and penalizing its enemies, it generates little confidence that public policy-making will be informed by a search for anything like a collective long-term good. Thus what emerges clearly from cross-national survey research on political culture, despite the many well-advertised limitations of such enterprises, is the relatively low level of political trust exhibited by Italians.[20]

Inter-party relations and coalition-building

We have seen, in the previous two sections, that the development of a strong party state made important contributions to the process of democratic consolidation. Such a system locks voters into stable patterns of allegiance, reducing the pool of uncommitted voters potentially available to vote for anti-democratic flash movements, and providing the base from which the parties, and the social forces they represent, are better placed to effect compromises with one another on rules and distributive outcomes.

However, while the party system established in Italy after 1945 was a particularly strong one, it was also ideologically highly fragmented. Thus as we have already seen, although the party state was eventually part of the *solution* to the problem of consolidation, individual parties were, for some considerable period of time, the reason for the problem's persistence. After all, it is of little consequence that few voters are available to support new anti-democratic movements if some of the established parties themselves have doubtful democratic credentials. This indeed is the whole force of the 'ideological/subcultural' analysis of the Italian party system which grew up in the 1960s, and which had its two most articulate spokesmen in Giovanni Sartori and Giorgio Galli.[21] Sartori's analysis differed from that of Galli in that it was dynamic and apocalyptic, where Galli's was static and merely pessimistic. For Sartori, polarized pluralism, with anti-democratic parties at both ends of the spectrum, and a fragmented and unstable centre, implied electoral polarization and the potential collapse of the system. For Galli, deeply entrenched subcultural blocks – one Catholic, one Marxist – prevented any real change in the system, for the party expressed by one of these blocks was permanently ineligible for government, and therefore all governments had to be built around the other. But what both perspectives shared was the view that ideological distance permanently jeopardized the democratic framework.

This rather pessimistic perspective cannot, however, be the last word because in fact Italian democracy did not collapse, and indeed over time the ideological spectrum clearly narrowed considerably. Thus although the initial structure of the party system may have been unhelpful to democratic consolidation, it is possible that the behaviour of its constituent parties may, at least at critical moments, have facilitated it. This argument was developed by Paolo Farneti, whose interpretive framework, based on the notion of 'centripetal' pluralism, was designed to recognize that while the system may once have fitted Sartori's description it ceased to do so from the mid-1960s.[22] It still contained many of the properties described by Sartori, but not its crucial one: the centrifugal drive. Or more accurately if such a drive was present in the electorate, it was not reflected in the party leaderships, who regularly found ways of constructing compromises, albeit not very durable ones, to prevent the system degenerating into deadlock.

Sadly Farneti died before he could work his ideas out more fully by providing an explanation of why the centrifugal drive may under some circumstances reverse itself and become centripetal. That issue cannot be explored in detail here.[23] The significance of coalescent and accommodating behaviour on the part of party leaders who are in principle bitterly divided is nevertheless of critical importance to the process of democratic consolidation – and not just, as was Farneti's main concern, during the mid-1970s with the Historic Compromise. We can see this if we consider the strategic choices made by the parties at what are conventionally seen as the critical junctures in post-war political development: 1947/48; 1960/64; and 1973/76.[24]

1947/48

The 1947/48 crisis was, of course, different from the two subsequent ones in that the compromise essential to the preservation of the system stemmed from an outright split within one of the main parties, the PSI.[25] Nevertheless, Giuseppe Saragat's action in 1947 in agreeing to lend the support of his newly formed PSDI to a Christian-Democrat-led centrist government, thus building a bridge across a potentially dangerously wide political gap which provided parliamentary votes critical to the government's survival, merely foreshadowed subsequent and similar moves by the Socialists and Communists. Indeed the strategy pursued by the Socialist Party from 1957 onwards vindicated Saragat's judgement. Chastened by the disaster of the 1948 electoral pact with the Communists, the Socialists gradually took their distance from the PCI during the course of the 1950s. By the 1957 Venice Congress their avowed aim was an 'opening to the left' which, had they followed Lombardi and Jacometti in 1948 rather than Basso and Nenni, might have been theirs for the asking a decade earlier.[26]

1960/64

Like the PSDI secession, the Socialist Party's centre-left strategy was couched in ambitious rhetoric which concealed a decidedly defensive purpose. As sold to a sceptical membership its ostensible aim was to establish a new identity for the Socialist Party, independent of the PCI, which would attract sufficient electoral strength to serve both as an alternative to the Christian Democrats in government, and to banish the Communists to the radical fringe. To begin with, this entailed an alliance with the DC, but through reunification with the Social Democrats, and a gradual increase in electoral support for a reform-oriented non-Communist left, Nenni, the PSI leader, hoped that his party would eventually come to dominate the government.

The history of the years 1960–4 shows how this optimism rapidly gave way to a much less ambitious goal. For in 1960 the parliamentary base of the centrist coalition, always dangerously thin, fell apart. From the crisis which followed, it was clear that only two solutions were possible: an opening to the right, through which, as in 1922, the extreme right would be incorporated into the ruling coalition; or an opening to the left, by which the Socialists would replace the Liberals as the main junior partner of the Christian Democrats. The Socialists thus faced a dilemma: join the government, on terms eventually, if not in the first instance, dictated by the Christian Democrats, or risk the consequences of a clear left–right polarization of the entire political system. The crisis in fact forced the Socialist leadership to make a clear choice. It chose stability at the expense of reform, and until the end of the decade the reform programme of the centre-left was essentially set aside.

As a strategy for fundamental socio-economic reform, the centre-left was therefore a failure, but as a solution to the problem of coalition stability it was, at least during the 1960s, a qualified success. Viewed in this light the PSI's strategy can be seen as an act of national responsibility and even self-sacrifice by its leaders. They were well aware of the difficulties of creating a constituency for social reform, let alone of legislating concrete reform, as long as the Italian electorate remained frozen in its subcultural blocks; and they were equally aware of the dangers to themselves of allowing the Communists to monopolize the opposition. Yet with the PCI's democratic credentials still doubtful, there was no escaping their own indispensability to the formation of any stable coalition.

1973/76

The crisis which led to the broadly based governments of 'national solidarity' after 1976 was a long time in the making. It originated in the great upsurge of labour unrest in 1969, which in its turn made the centre-left coalition increasingly unstable. By the end of 1975 the extent to which Italy's economic strength had been undermined by the twin problems of the industrialized world in the 1970s – spiralling energy prices and a structural shift in the balance of power between management and labour – was fully apparent. Faced with such formidable obstacles, the centre-left alliance was revealed as woefully inadequate, the Socialists withdrew from it, and the electorate responded with a decisive shift to the left in favour of the PCI.

The reaction of the Communist Party to the advantages it derived from this situation was, however, just as cautious and pessimistic as the Socialist Party's behaviour in the early 1960s. Its prime concern in the Hot Autumn was to assert its control of the new forms of worker representation springing up in the work-place, and to channel the energies generated into demands that went beyond the wage packet. And when in 1976 the centre-left collapsed entirely, the party's prime concern was to restore stability – both in Parliament and in the sphere of industrial relations – through a grand coalition with the Christian Democrats and Socialists which Berlinguer had foreshadowed in his famous 'Historic Compromise' declaration three years earlier.

What followed needs little recapitulation here. The Communist Party pursued the logic of its strategy through with courageous determination, but in so doing created such strains within its own ranks, and between itself and the unions, that in 1979 it was forced to raise the price of its continued collaboration (a collaboration which, in return for only modest improvements to the dividend, the leadership probably had every intention of maintaining).[27] But the breathing space which the Historic Compromise had given Italian industry, together with the process of restructuring already well in train, encouraged the politicians of the centre-left in the belief that the emergency was over, and thus that, albeit with many initial difficulties (and under different labels) the centre-left could once more be reconstructed.

The consequences of accommodation

We thus have a sequence of crises in which successive elements of the left – first the Social Democrats, then the Socialists, and finally the Communists – agreed to make an accommodation with the parties of the centre and the moderate right, in order to support the democratic framework. The range of motives was rather different in each case, as, more evidently, was the duration of the accommodation involved. Nevertheless the common consequence of all three cases has been that at moments when parliamentary democracy has seemed close to breakdown at least one left-wing party has been willing to compromise with the parties of the centre-right, and at moments when the working class has seemed most militant, the leaders of the left have sought to establish some moderating control. In this sense, despite the unpromising structure of the party system, the behaviour of individual parties has been helpful to the process of democratic consolidation.

However, the argument is more complex than this, for we need also to examine the longer-term consequences of the broad and somewhat heterodox coalitions forced on the system by successive Cabinet crises. It is clear that one long-term consequence – both of the 1947 split in the Socialist ranks, and the centre-left coalition as it unfolded during the 1960s – was the strengthening of the Communist Party. In 1946 the Socialist Party was marginally still the largest party of the left, winning 20.7 per cent of the vote against 18.9 per cent for the PCI. By 1953 the Socialists had only 12.7 per cent, compared to 22.6 per cent for the PCI, and this set a trend in the latter's favour. The formation of the PSDI removed those very party workers and members who would have been most willing to challenge the Communist Party, and who might have helped prevent the débâcle of the electoral alliance with the PCI in the 1948 election. Admittedly it seems likely that even without a split in the Socialist ranks in 1947, the PCI would have overhauled the Socialist Party at some point, given its superior organizational resources, and the massive expansion it enjoyed in the south after 1950. But the disparity need not have been great, and had it not been, the Socialist Party might not have faced such a struggle to establish an independent and credible identity for itself in subsequent years. Nor would the draining, demoralizing, and ultimately unsuccessful attempt to reunite the two Socialist parties in the later 1960s have so damaged Socialist morale.[28]

The same may be said of the centre-left strategy. It led to a fundamental change in the PSI, for it gave the party access to the enormous patronage potential of Italian government, both nationally and locally. This in turn attracted into the party's ranks the place-seekers and opportunists who gravitate towards all governing parties in Italy. The struggle between leaders for patronage resources soon assumed serious dimensions leading to intense factional strife and a deep involvement in the seamier side of political life. The centre-left thus effectively discredited the PSI as a party of reform, undermining public perceptions of democratic socialism, and weakening its electoral base. Hence the great movement for rationalizing and redistributive reform, which grew up after 1969, found its natural focus in the Communists rather than the Socialists. For the PSI, like the Christian Democrats, therefore, the practice of patronage politics which started as a mechanism to control policy and shore up electoral support against losses to the extremes during difficult moments, ended by having the opposite effect – discrediting party politics as a whole, and driving many voters into the fold of the allegedly 'extreme' parties.

The case of the Historic Compromise is clearly different. The political accommodation practised by the Communist Party did not generate significant support for political forces even further to the left than the PCI itself. The growth of terrorism can hardly be claimed as a *mass* political movement, nor did its strategy of destabilization have the required effect. Indeed one of the chief consequences of terrorism was to evoke from the Communists what can best be described as a posture of hyper-solidarity with the democratic framework. Nor can the rise of a 'new' left, the heirs of 1968, be seen primarily as a response to the PCI's moderation. In any case, even at the peak in 1979, this group constituted only 5 per cent of the vote, the lion's share of which went to the Radical Party, which was in no sense a transformative Marxist party, and can hardly be seen as a threat to democracy.

In fact, there is a strong case to be made that of the three acts of accommodation undertaken by the parties of the left in post-war Italy, it was the last that made the greatest single contribution to the consolidation of democracy, because it enabled the Communist Party to imply by deed what it has never quite been able to make convincing in words: that it was committed to the democratic framework. Since the Historic Compromise, it has been far more difficult to sustain the view that the PCI represents a threat to democracy, and this has been of considerable importance for the general psychological climate in which politics is conducted, because it reduces perceived threats of retaliatory (or pre-emptive) action from the right, as well as those from the left.

Naturally it is not just the PCI's alliance strategy that has enhanced its legitimacy. Its response to much wider changes in Italian society has had the same effect. As we have seen the party's relationship with the range of active and well-organized pressure groups which grew up in Italy during the 1970s, while at times difficult, testified to its acceptance of the general context of party-interest group relations in a pluralist society. Moreover, in the last decade it has begun to make important changes to its own internal organization through a far-reaching process of procedural democratization.[29]

To observe these organizational, ideological, and strategic shifts is not, of course, to deny that for many years it was the party which constituted the centre of the problem of consolidation examined in this chapter. Nor is it to deny that these changes might – but for severe internal constraints in the PCI – have come earlier, thereby much reducing the time taken to consolidate Italian democracy. Moreover, there is a certain irony in the way the party has been repaid electorally for its efforts. Instead of the major pay-offs predicted if the party could finally achieve a wide measure of democratic respectability, its fortunes have steadily declined as traditional public-sector and collective solutions of all kinds have fallen out of favour in Italy as elsewhere in western Europe.

Conclusion

Since most European democracies are party-based parliamentary democracies, and since they have all generated parties as the fundamental units of representation, it would be difficult to deny that a solid, well-entrenched party system is a necessary condition of democratic consolidation. It is not, however, a sufficient condition. In the Italian case, several other factors, such as the level of economic development, particular types of institutional rules preventing 'winner-take-all' distributive outcomes, the persistence of democratic procedures over time, and an international political environment confirming the moral ascendancy of liberal political values, were also important.

The Italian parties did, however, succeed in establishing an exceptionally strong form of party state, built upon two pillars. The first was the close links between the parties and the major social actors – links which had the additional advantage of preventing a high degree of *representational* (as opposed to ideological) polarization, since both major parties assembled broad alliances of interests within their army of supporting organizations. The second, strengthening consistently over the post-war period, was the strong control established by the parties over the institutions of the state.

However, the party spectrum contained within itself several serious weaknesses of relevance to the question of democratic consolidation. Of these, the most significant were the presence of a robust and growing Communist Party on the far left, and a divided Socialist movement, which provided an inadequate counterweight to the Communists. Moreover, even the rather modest following attracted by the extreme right was sufficient to complicate the process of coalition-building to the point at which every coalition had to straddle the fragmented centre of the political spectrum, and was thus inherently unstable. The worst consequences of this situation were avoided by the accommodating behaviour of the parties of the left whenever the system appeared to be heading towards breakdown. But this had negative as well as positive effects, and probably helped to prolong the process of consolidation. It transformed the parties of the non-Communist left from parties of reform representing clear-cut alternatives to the Christian Democrats and their moderate and conservative allies, into mere adjuncts to these parties, not substantially different from them in their attitude to patronage or political probity.

Because the non-Communist left was discredited, demands for reform had to be concentrated on the Communist Party, the very party whose democratic credentials had been questioned. However, this was not, by the 1970s, as unnatural as it might have been in some other west European party systems, because the Communists already had a number of characteristics differentiating themselves from the conventional Communist model. Moreover, they were encouraged to develop these further precisely because they were presented with an opportunity of occupying the social-reform constituency. The PCI thus grew at the expense of the non-Communist left, and this further reinforced the reformist tendencies inside it. Nevertheless, even when the total left-wing vote rose to the 50 per cent level, the PCI's own pessimism about the solidity of democracy, combined with the fragmented nature of the party system (which, in a left-wing coalition, would have given substantial veto power to minor parties), prevented a government of the left. Indeed, the growth of the Communist Party in electoral terms counteracted the effect of its ideological revision. However moderate the party became, it was unlikely that the smaller parties of the centre-left, the Socialists and Social Democrats, would be willing to sink their identity in a left-wing coalition so dominated by the Communists. Even in the 1980s, therefore, Italy was condemned to be a country without a clear-cut possibility of alternation in power. The consolidation process was virtually complete and the PCI could no longer be convincingly seen as a threat to the democratic framework, but the way it was completed evidently detracted quite seriously from the quality of democracy, if no longer also from its stability.

Notes

1. See *inter alia* G. Sani, 'Mass constraints on political realignments: perceptions of anti-system parties in Italy', *British Journal of Political Science*, 1976, vol. 6, pp. 1–31; G. Almond and S. Verba, *The Civic Culture*, Boston, Mass., Little, Brown, 1965; G. Sani, 'The political culture of Italy: continuity and change'; in G. Almond and S. Verba (eds) *The Civic Culture Revisited*, Boston, Mass., Little, Brown, 1980, pp. 273–323. A useful source in Italian is G. Guidorossi, *Gli italiani e la politica*, Milan, Franco Angeli, 1984, which summarizes a mass of post-war survey research.

2. See G. Sani and G. Sartori, 'Polarization, fragmentation and competition in western democracies', in Hans Daalder and Peter Mair (eds) *Western European Party Systems: Continuity and Change*, London, Sage, 1983, 307–40.

3. See Guidorossi, op. cit., especially pp. 103–36, and pp. 241–6, which deal in some detail with this issue. See also G. Sani, 'Amici-Nemici; Parenti-Serpenti: Communists and socialists in Italy', in B.E. Brown (ed.) *Eurocommunism and Eurosocialism: The Left Confronts Modernity*, New York and London, Cyrco Press, 1979, pp. 105–42.

4. This definition draws heavily on ideas set out in a paper by L. Whitehead, 'The consolidation of fragile democracies: a discussion with illustrations', written for the Consultation on *Reinforcing Democracy in the Americas*, Atlanta, Georgia, Carter Center, 17–18 November 1986.

5. On the 'anti-system' concept see *inter alia* G. Smith, 'Party and protest: the two faces of opposition in western Europe', and G. Pridham, 'Opposition in Italy: from polarised pluralism to centripetal pluralism', both in E. Kolinsky (ed.) *Opposition in Western Europe*, London, Croom Helm, 1987, respectively pp. 49–71 and 156–94; also G. Di Palma, 'Party government and democratic reproducibility: the dilemma of new democracies', in F.G. Castles and R. Wildenmann (eds) *The Future of Party Government.*, vol. 1, *Visions and Realities of Party Government*, Berlin and New York, Walter de Gruyter, 1986.

6. See G. Sartori, *Parties and Party Systems: A Framework for Analysis*, Cambridge, Cambridge University Press, 1976, p. 133.

7. For an analysis of these changes see D. Hine, 'Parties and party government under pressure', in A. Ware (ed.) *Political Parties: Electoral Change and Structural Response*, Oxford, Basil Blackwell, 1987.

8. See M. Pedersen, 'The dynamics of European party systems: changing patterns of electoral volatility', *European Journal of Political Research*, 1979, 7, pp. 1–26.

9. See Galli and Prandi, *op. cit.*, pp. 25–71; for a recent discussion of the persistence or decline of subcultural patterns in voting behaviour, see R. Mannheimer and G. Sani, *Il mercato elettorale: identikit dell'eletore*

italiano, Bologna, Il Mulino, 1987.

10. See D. Hine, 'Communism and the Labour movement in Italy and France', in M. Kolinsky and W.E. Paterson (eds) *Social and Political Movements in Western Europe*, London, Croom Helm, 1975.

11. The classic statement of the struggle between Communists and Christian Democrats in southern Italy is S. Tarrow, *Peasant Communism in Southern Italy*, New Haven, Conn., Yale University Press, 1967.

12. See J. Chubb, 'The Christian Democratic Party: reviving or surviving?', in R. Leonardi and R. Y. Nanetti (eds) *Italian Politics: A Review*, vol. 1, London, Frances Pinter, 1986, pp. 69–86. In Italian see M. Caciagli *et al.*, *Democrazia e potere nel Mezzogiorno*, Florence, Guaraldi, 1977.

13. See J. La Palombara, 'Two steps forward, one step back: the PCI's struggle for legitimacy', in Howard R. Penniman (ed.) *Italy at the Polls: A Study of the Parliamentary Elections*, Washington, DC, American Enterprise Institute, 1981; also Marcello Fedele, 'The ambiguous alternative: the Italian Communist Party in the 1983 elections', in Howard R. Penniman (ed.) *Italy at the Polls, 1983: A Study of the National Elections*, Durham, NC, Duke University Press and American Enterprise Institute, 1987, pp. 60–77.

14. For their comments on the Italian case see S.M. Lipset and S. Rokkan, 'Cleavage structures, party systems, and voter alignments', in S.M. Lipset and S. Rokkan (eds) *Party Systems and Voter Alignments*, New York, Free Press, 1967.

15. The riots at Reggio Calabria, fomented by the extreme right, centred on the failure of the city to be nominated administrative capital of the newly created region of Calabria. The DC was itself internally divided by the issue, eventually assigning the capital to its Catanzaro faction, the new university to Cosenza, and tossing the bone of a promised new steelworks to Reggio. On the long-term problems of the Christian-Democrats in the south, see J. Chubb, *Patronage, Power, and Poverty in Southern Italy*, Cambridge, Cambridge University Press, 1982.

16. See S. Cassese, 'Esiste un Governo in Italia?', Rome, Officina Edizioni, 1980.

17. On the internal structure of Italian parties see Hine, 'Parties and party government', op. cit., pp. 78–94.

18. The preference vote enables voters not only to vote for a party's list of candidates (i.e. to choose that party as opposed to its competitors), but also to cast preferences for up to three (or in large constituencies four) candidates on the list. Proportional representation thus determines the number of candidates in any (multi-member) electoral college the party will return to Parliament. The number of preference votes received by each candidate determines *who* gets elected. .

19. On these issues see the relevant chapters in D. Blackmer and S. Tarrow (eds) *Communism in Italy and France*, Princeton, NJ, Princeton University Press, 1985, especially the concluding chapter by Tarrow.

20. Almond and Verba, *The Civic Culture*, op. cit., 1965.

21. See G. Sartori, *Parties and Party Systems: A Framework for Analysis*, Cambridge, Cambridge University Press, 1976, ch. 6; G. Galli and A.

Prandi, *Patterns of Political Participation in Italy*, New Haven, Conn., Yale University Press, 1970.

22. See P. Farneti, *The Italian Party System (1945–1980)*, London, Frances Pinter, 1985, ch. 4.

23. The likely answers lie in the historical experiences of the parties and their leaders, and in the structure of opportunities presented to them (a) by the formal rules of the system (especially those in Parliament) and (b) by the coalition-building process. The Fascist experience in particular is important here. Although its psychological impact was not as comprehensive as that of the Nazi past on post-war Germany, Fascism imbued the left with a pessimism about the solidity of Italian democracy and the behaviour under duress of the Italian middle classes which has persisted to this day. The ease with which Italy fell prey to authoritarianism, and the widespread belief that the intransigence of the labour movement was indirectly responsible, left a profound mark.

24. The following section presupposes some knowledge of the process of coalition-building in post-war Italy. Further details can be obtained, in the first instance from G. Pridham, 'Italy's party democracy', in G. Pridham (ed.) *Coalitional Behaviour in Theory and Practice*, Cambridge, Cambridge University Press, 1986, pp. 198–231.

25. Admittedly there was a split in 1964 too, but on that occasion it was a reaction to political compromise, rather than its facilitating condition.

26. On events in the Socialist Party after 1945 see R. Zariski, 'The Italian Socialist Party: a case study in factional conflict', *American Political Science Review*, June 1962, vol. LVI, no. 2, pp. 372–90.

27. But see M. Barbagli and P. Corbetta, 'After the historic compromise: a turning point for the PCI', *European Journal of Political Research*, 10, 1982. Also S. Hellman, 'The Italian Communist Party between Berlinguer and the Seventeenth Congress', in R. Leonardi and R. Nanetti (eds) *Italian Politics: A Review*, vol. I, London, Frances Pinter, 1986, pp. 47–68.

28. See D. Hine, *The Italian Socialist Party and the Centre-Left Coalition*, D. Phil. thesis, University of Oxford, 1978.

29. See Hellman, op. cit., pp. 52–61.

Chapter four

The role of the Italian Communist Party in the consolidation of parliamentary democracy in Italy

Donald Sassoon

Introduction

The establishment of the new democratic framework in post-fascist Italy was achieved largely by the political parties which had led the Resistance. They devised the new institutions and legitimized the new regime, above all by involving in it those sectors of the population which previously had been marginal or absent from political life. Christian Democracy (DC), as heir to the Partito Popolare, had to perform the task of transferring the loyalties of the rural Catholic masses – once disenfranchised by papal opposition to the new unitary Italian state – on to the new liberal-democratic framework. The Italian Communist Party (PCI), heir to the Italian Socialist tradition (or, at least, to its maximalist wing) had to do the same for the working classes.

Hence the Resistance and its component parties demonstrated that Fascism had not destroyed civil society (contrasting perhaps with Portugal, where long authoritarian rule induced political passivity). It was instrumental in mobilizing large popular sectors into politics, an important feature of Italy's transition to democracy.[1] Therefore the subsequent behaviour of these parties in channelling this activity was crucial not only to a successful transition but also to the prospects for democratic consolidation. This period is broadly equivalent to Rustow's 'habituation phase' in democratic transition, where 'both politicians and citizens learn from the successful resolution of some issues to place their faith in the new rules' and 'experience with democratic techniques and competitive recruitment will confirm the politicians in their democratic practices and beliefs'.[2] However, the Italian case is less straightforward than some other cases of the move from transition to consolidation examined in this volume. As Pasquino has noted, controversy over the post-war transition has persisted – not over its achievement and the crucial role of the parties, but over its evaluation especially concerning the defeat of the left in the 1948 election and its consequences.[3] One may therefore say that certain formative influences of transition – above

84

all, those linked with the Cold War – helped to mark the problems of democratic consolidation. Nevertheless, it goes without saying that the PCI was a decisive actor in this process. The *svolta di Salerno* (Togliatti's strategic decision in 1944 to collaborate with the other parties in government and to settle the issue of the monarchy only after the end of the war) has commonly been seen as a turning-point in the dynamics of the transition in promoting a stable institutional outcome.[4] It follows that an examination of Togliatti's views in the later 1940s and early 1950s (when Italy in effect moved from transition to consolidation) presents a significant case-study of strategic thinking at this point.

Though initially in government with all the other anti-fascist parties (1944–7), the PCI found itself in opposition with the Italian Socialist Party in 1947 when it was expelled from power by the DC prior to the first elections to the Italian Parliament (1948). Ever since that time then the PCI has remained a non-legitimized opposition party, unable to assume government. The obstacles to the acquisition of governmental power have been essentially political rather than institutional, for no formal aspect of the institutional framework prevented the formation of a government with the PCI. The democratic regime which actually emerged from the war had no intrinsic anti-communist legislative bias. The newly written Constitution and the electoral system adopted contained no clauses which in any way, either formally or informally, could be construed as penalizing the parties of the left. Moreover, the PCI had been an active participant in the construction of the new Italian Republic and its Constitution. Moreover, unlike many other left-wing parties in Europe, the PCI had not been forced to accept 'rules of the game' instituted prior to its rise to the status of a mass party. Its main competitor, the Christian Democrats (DC), was, like the PCI, a new mass party with no clear or obvious ideological or historical commitment to the liberal tradition of parliamentarism.

The aim of this chapter is to examine the theoretical and political justifications put forward by the PCI in adapting its strategy to the rules of the game of liberal democracy. The key evidence to be used here rests with the writings of the PCI leader, Palmiro Togliatti, who was in virtual control of all the party's initiatives concerning the new constitutional and institutional arrangements of post-fascist Italy. It will look first at Togliatti's views on liberal democracy, then at the issue of electoral reform turning to the PCI's role in democratic consolidation.

Interpreting liberal democracy

Togliatti established a link with liberalism on behalf of his party at an early stage, defining democracy as a 'government of the people, by the people, and for the people'.[5] This quote from Lincoln's famous speech (not attributed) represented an overt symbolic connection between the Marxist and the liberal traditions. A Leninist definition of democracy was not even attempted. Yet, for Togliatti, the Italian regime could not be 'classically' liberal-democratic (as in the French or English model): Italian democracy was the result of what he saw as a democratic revolution (the Resistance) and as such different from classical democratic revolutions.

The difference was due to the combination of three important aspects:[6] the anti-fascist nature of the Italian democratic revolution, the decisive support it enjoyed from the working class, and the fact that, because of the particular economic problems of Reconstruction which affected the country, the 'Italian revolution' could not give way to a regime based on economic liberalism. It followed that, according to Togliatti, the Italian democratic revolution, though having affinities with liberalism, could not be strictly 'liberal'. The new regime could not be the same as that existing in pre-fascist days. The new Italian Constitution should enshrine also a commitment to an economic and social renewal if Italy was to be considered a democracy.[7] 'Government of the people, by the people and for the people' must be enriched by social and economic rights. Togliatti accepted the premises of the liberal tradition but wanted to go beyond it. In a speech to the Constituent Assembly he said:

> We do not conceive of democracy in the same way as Corbino. For us a political and social regime in which the means of production and economic life are subject to the dictates and will of large capitalistic groups cannot be a democracy. We do not want it.[8]

Who, according to Togliatti, were the opponents of this conception of democracy? Clearly Corbino and the other representatives of Italian Liberalism were among them, but not the Christian Democrats since he specifically included them in the 'democratic camp' by remarking that in the conception of democracy, 'there is no significant difference between us and you, our Christian Democratic friends, if I have well understood the essence of your ideas'.[9] Thus the overall parameters which defined the new democracy were wide enough to include non-socialist forces; indeed Togliatti said later that it had not been his intention to propose an 'ideological' Constitution. By this he meant that he was not proposing a Socialist Constitution since the task before the Italian nation was 'not the construction of a socialist state'.[10] Nevertheless, there is no doubt that the Constitution would have an ideological element expressed through the inclusion of new social and economic rights; in other words, through that which supplements the otherwise classical liberal form of the Constitution itself.

This content formed the basis of a complex compromise which operated at several levels. In the first place, it made possible the reclassification of the parties of the working class as pro-system parties for the first time in Italian history. In the second place, it ensured that the working-class parties would fight their political battles with the same definition of democracy as the other parties (Togliatti frequently warned the DC and its allies that if they ever left the terrain of parliamentary democracy, then the parties of the left too would have to do the same). In other words, the only alternative to the regime of compromise being constructed would be potential or actual civil war. In the third place, it also offered the parties committed to liberalism a system of rules which included most of what is fundamental in the liberal tradition.

The new rules of the game thus allowed all the actors concerned to play it, none excluded except the 'enemies of democracy' (i.e. the Fascists who are specifically banned by the Constitution). The basis of the new Italian state therefore was not a Constitution as the expression of a majority against a minority; it is rather a Constitution which transcends this distinction and is the expression of the unity of all political parties. The dichotomy between minority and majority, which is the usual basis of parliamentarism, cannot be the basis of the Constitution.

All Constitutions, if they are to last, must be based on the near-unanimity of those who must abide by them. This is the implicit recognition of the famous Rousseauian principle:

> Indeed, if there were no earlier agreement, then how, unless the election were unanimous, could there be any obligation on the minority to accept the decision of the majority? What right have the hundred who want to have a master to vote on behalf of the ten who do not? The law of majority-voting itself rests on a covenant, and implies that there has been on at least one occasion unanimity.[11]

As we shall see later the link Togliatti established with the liberal tradition was emphasized repeatedly, but it would be a mistake to use the category of the 'liberal tradition' as if it were a static tradition which remained unrevised until the advent of Mosca, Pareto, and Schumpeter.

At the same time, there is no doubt that Togliatti demarcated himself from various aspects of the classical liberal tradition. He was clearly opposed for instance to much (though not all) of the doctrine of the separation of powers (the principle of 'checks and balances'). He also criticized the length of the legislative process, the proposed regional structure, bicameralism, the attempt to establish the categories of people who can be elected to the Senate, the attempt to establish that a vote of no-confidence must be demanded by at least 25 per cent of the members of the Assembly, and the establishment of a Constitutional Court. These proposals were all, in his view, 'deviations from the pure parliamentary democratic regime'.[12] The motivations behind them – he suspected – were all inspired by the fear that there might one day be a majority committed to a profound renewal of the economic, political, and social structure of the country. In other words, they were all established out of fear that the left would acquire control of Parliament. If transformations could not occur through Parliament, then they would occur by 'direct means'. The compromise which was being established and which Togliatti accepted gave the working classes the possibility of using the institutions in order to construct a Socialist society, but if the rules of the games were so constructed as to make this impossible, then there would be only one alternative: the return of the Communist Party to being an 'anti-system' party.[13]

To defend the central role of Parliament, thus ensuring the peaceful participation of the labour movement in national politics, Togliatti had to resort to the liberal tradition. He did not use the classical texts of liberalism or the full armoury of liberal concepts, as he would have done if his motive had been purely tactical. Instead he focused on the historical example of Giolitti's Parliament in the early twentieth century and on the concept of parliamentary control over the executive.

Giolitti is invoked not for his uninhibited use of the state machine (the Giolitti decried by Salvemini and Einaudi) but because in the first decade of the century the Italian Parliament was the central institution for the political unification of the Italian ruling class. The absence of strong party discipline and of stable majorities meant that the government was constantly involved in a bargaining process aimed at ensuring its survival. The workings of the 'trasformismo' system meant that the government regularly had to strike a number of compromises with opposition groups over virtually every piece of legislation. To ensure effective government, this form of consensus politics had to be constantly pursued in the parliamentary arena. Of course, Parliament at that time was essentially the property of the ruling groups: few of the Socialist deputies took any part in negotiations, the Catholics were excluded from political affairs by papal orders, and the suffrage was very narrow. Parliament was then a 'mirror' – not of the nation but of its ruling classes. Nevertheless when Togliatti in 1950 compared the development of the Christian Democratic regime to the Giolitti system, he unequivocally praised the latter on the grounds that in Giolitti's times Parliament was considered not only the principal arena for political debate but also an effective means whereby the nation's representatives could exercise their control over the executive.[14]

Thus the central function of Parliament was seen to be that of control. Take away control over the executive, Togliatti appeared to suggest, and you remove one of the pillars of parliamentary democracy. Here control is clearly meant in terms of day-to-day control, control over legislation and not in the sense that ultimately the government is 'controlled' because it must have a parliamentary majority: that, of course, was never in question. Parliamentary power, he said, is nothing else than control over the executive: 'Parliamentary powers are always and in each instance powers of control over the activity of governments, so much so that all constitutional theories speak of parliamentary control over the executive.'[15]

Togliatti's defence of parliamentary powers and of the principle of parliamentary control always sought the backing and supporting evidence of the (Italian) liberal tradition.[16] Yet in spite of this Togliatti was not really asserting that in Italy such a tradition had much strength and that the PCI was simply its inheritor (or one of the inheritors). The Italian liberal tradition was weak and inconsistent because the Italian bourgeoisie had been weak, inconsistent, and unable to carry out a real revolution. Taking up Gramsci's analysis of the Risorgimento, Togliatti said: 'Our country has not witnessed those social and economic transformations which, elsewhere, have been accomplished by the revolutionary forces of the bourgeoisie under the banner of the bourgeois revolution.'[17] The distinction to be made was between the Italian liberals and the liberal tradition. Italian liberals had been ineffective against Fascism and their commitment to democracy was lukewarm. Italian liberals had been unable to defend and develop 'the liberal tradition'. What was positive in this tradition could be retained by the newly emerging class: the working class and its leading party, the PCI.

To summarize so far: Togliatti redefined – in his elaboration of a specifically Italian road to Socialism – the relationship between Italian Communism and parliamentary democracy in the following way:

1 The Italian republic was to have the social rights of a democratic workers' republic with the rules of a parliamentary republic;[18]
2 Parliament must represent in proportionate terms the party political balance of forces: it must 'mirror' the constitutional pact which has sanctioned the entry of the PCI in the political system;
3 Parliament must have effective control over the executive. It must not be bypassed by any direct links between the electorate and the government.

Altogether this is what is meant by being 'representative'.

Thus the fundamental equation at the basis of the Italian road to

Socialism could be encapsulated in the formula 'liberal democracy + structural reforms' (i.e. for the transformation of economic structures). Yet it is not possible to ignore that Togliatti was at the same time seldom critical of that other road to Socialism, the Soviet road, and it was this which continued to raise doubts as to the credibility of the PCI's commitment to liberal democracy. Togliatti nevertheless viewed – to the end – the Soviet model as totally inapplicable to Italy and to western Europe, but not merely because of its disfunctions or lack of democracy. Not until 1956 (mainly in his interview to the journal *Nuovi Argomenti*) and in 1964 did he directly and openly criticize some aspects of the Soviet regime. As late as 1958 he could still write in *Rinascita* that parliamentarism was appropriate for Italy but not for the USSR. After forty years of Socialist development it was no longer possible to conceive of parliamentarism or of a pluralism of political parties in Soviet society. The Soviet Union was in any case a 'homogeneous' country with a 'democratic economy'.[19] From the 'social point of view' eastern Europe was more advanced.[20]

Is this systematic defence of the eastern European experience an instance of that 'duplicity' of which Togliatti has frequently been accused? There are many ways in which this question can be tackled. It is possible to historicize the context in which Togliatti defends 'Socialism as it really exists' by stressing the specific conjuncture in which these views are expressed: the beginning of the Cold War, the Legge Truffa, the advent of De Gaulle in France in 1958 (which Togliatti sees as paving the way for a Fascist regime in France), and so on. This, however, does not really answer the question.

The crux of the matter is that Togliatti never abandoned the view that what was being built in the USSR was a Socialist regime, with its own laws of development capable of providing their own solutions. Italy's path could not be the same, because her traditions and situation were different. It had to be based on democracy and Parliament at least so long as no one altered the rules of the games so as to force the PCI to resort to violent means. Parliament represented a guarantee to both the contending forces. To the PCI it established the possibility of advancing to Socialism without civil war, and to 'the other side' it ensured that the working-class movement would operate within parameters agreed with the representatives of the other social classes.

Representation and parliamentary centrality: the issue of electoral reform

These parameters were presented most clearly in the concept of representation Togliatti advanced in the course of the debates on the so-called Legge Truffa[21] before the 1953 national election and in his general arguments for establishing Italian democracy as Parliament-centred (as opposed to executive-centred). This is the context in which he defended the notion of proportionality in electoral systems through his use of the metaphor of 'Parliament as the mirror of the nation'. It may be seen as a significant issue at this early stage of democratic consolidation in post-war Italy.

Togliatti first wanted to establish that the mirror metaphor was part and parcel of the liberal tradition. He cited Mirabeau who said that the assembly must be like a 'geographic map' in the sense that it must be an accurate reproduction, in scale, of the various interests of the country. Togliatti also cited Sidney Sonnino, James Lorimer (the first, he claimed, to have used the metaphor of the mirror), John Stuart Mill, and Guizot.[22]

The crucial distinction which is made here is between the 'decision-making moment' and the 'representation moment'. The former must be based on the majority principle (i.e. the majority decides) but the basis of representation must have some other legitimacy, namely the principle of proportionality.[23] Parliaments take decisions on the basis of majority voting, but the majority itself cannot determine the composition of Parliament. The Legge Truffa, wrote Togliatti, was an attempt by the existing majority to impose on the minority a change in the basis of representation and so, in a sense, to determine future majorities. Moreover an electoral law should not be passed against the will of an important minority.[24] Electoral laws are intimately connected to the Constitution of the country and should not be revised unilaterally for the Rousseauian reasons mentioned above. Though the Legge Truffa was not a revision of the Constitution, Togliatti clearly intended to establish that the existing proportional system should be considered 'politically' as part of the Constitution that provided the PCI with a framework within which it could operate as a legitimate party. Hence this issue of electoral reform threatened to disrupt the process of democratic consolidation.

The seriousness of the revision brought about by the Legge Truffa was not just that it would have enabled the existing coalition to have a more solid parliamentary basis, but that it attempted unilaterally (i.e. against the parties of the left) to revise the rules of the game. The numerous quotes from Liberal thinkers used by Togliatti are, of course, meant to underline the extent to which the PCI claimed to be the authentic inheritor of the liberal tradition. They were also devised so as to enable the PCI to construct an alliance with those representatives of the liberal tradition in Italy who were objecting to the Legge Truffa. The supporters of the law had presented the measure as necessary to ensure the governability of the system. But this could not be seen as a mere technical issue since, by altering the method of representation, the distinction between the decision-making process (based on the majority principle) and the principle of representation based on the 'mirror' metaphor would disappear. A system dominated by a majority in all respects would subvert the Italian constitutional order by striking at its heart and this heart – for Togliatti – was the concept of representation.[25] It is this which enabled the PCI to function as a pro-system party even in opposition. It is therefore revealing to examine Togliatti's thinking on this point at the time.

In his speeches against the Legge Truffa, Togliatti upheld the classical thesis advanced by Burke and many others that the Member of Parliament was a representative and not a delegate. No general theory is used to demonstrate this point but, rather, an appeal to the history of the concept.[26] Medieval Parliaments, stated Togliatti,[27] had a concept of representation which coincided with the principle of delegation or of the mandate. The representatives of the medieval assemblies were the spokesmen of specific group interests usually defined in economic terms. Medieval Parliaments were elected on the basis of a preconstituted relation of forces: a fixed proportion of the seats were assigned to the representatives of specific corporate groups. Thus the task of the electoral mechanism is that of selecting personnel, not that of unveiling the real relation of forces in society. This must occur elsewhere.

The balance of political forces is the central political aspect of a pluralist society. But the medieval Parliament could not represent it adequately because it was a by-product of the balance, and not the locus in which it could appear 'as it really is', as in a Parliament which is a 'mirror' of the nation. Thus these medieval assemblies were not central institutions. Togliatti stated polemically that the Legge Truffa would introduce into the body politic the medieval principle of preconstituted relations of forces, the only significant difference being the use of political instead of economic criteria. Before the election a government, itself a coalition of parties, would prepare a common list, based on the previous electoral results with the assumption that the coalition which gained a majority previously would successfully maintain it. A fixed number of delegates would then be assigned to the majority coalition and a fixed and disproportionately inferior number of delegates would be assigned to the minority or opposition coalition.[28]

A Parliament so elected is no longer a reflection of the balance of forces: the majority would have two-thirds of the seats and the minority one-third. In this sense it could be said that the balance of forces in Parliament had been politically preconstituted. The obvious argument employed against Togliatti was that the whole system depended on one crucial assumption, namely that the majority coalition would really obtain a majority. If this did not occur (and, in fact, it did not occur in the 1953 elections and the law was repealed the following year), the mechanism of the Legge Truffa would not operate. Thus, the comparison with the medieval Parliament does not really hold. The electorate has the power to decide who is going to be the majority.

Togliatti's central objection, however, was that the Legge Truffa shifted the central focus of politics from Parliament to two mechanisms outside it: the electorate and the government. With the Legge Truffa the electorate was now able to choose between a majority and a minority, while the government became the *de facto* legislator. The first mechanism is clear. The second rests on the fact that, given the majority is preconstituted and cannot be undone by Parliament itself (unless of course the members of the coalition majority were to 'cheat' the electorate by changing sides after the elections), the government can adopt a definite programme of legislation in the knowledge it can rely on a disciplined majority in Parliament. The government defines the balance of forces, the electorate decides who is to be the majority – in other words, who is to be the government. What is being established is a direct relation between electorate and government: Parliament is therefore *de facto* eliminated because it would no longer be the place where the majority is formed:

> What is the Government? It is the expression of the majority. Where is a Government designated and a majority formed? In Parliament. . . . Only in this way a constitutional order can be said to be a parliamentary one.[29]

Thus the first important objection Togliatti moved to the Legge Truffa is that its mechanism would destroy the centrality of Parliament. It would in fact establish a system dominated by a strong executive (as in the UK). His other main objection was also linked with the principle of the centrality of Parliament: the Legge Truffa would transform representatives into delegates. This principle deals with the question of the relations between those who are elected and the electorate. It was not Togliatti's intention that Members of Parliament would not have direct contact with the electorate, or that they would have to be merely the direct agents of political parties. In trying to define the concept of representation he explained that 'We are the representative of our electors. No one can deny it: they turn towards us, they write us letters, they ask questions; we speak to them, with them we have a special link.'[30] But Members of Parliament represent not only those who elect them, but also the whole country: 'I was born in Genoa, I was elected in Rome, I represent the whole of Italy.'[31] Here Togliatti sounds like Edmund Burke addressing his Bristol electors: 'You choose a Member [of Parliament] indeed, but when you have chosen him, he is not a member of Bristol but he is a Member of Parliament.' It was in order to explain this that Togliatti began his historical excursus on the concept of representation and in particular on the metaphor of the Parliament as mirror of the country.

The metaphor of the mirror – on its own – is a naive account of the representative system: it gives no indication as to the activities of the Members of Parliament nor as to the function of Parliament apart from being a reflection. Strictly speaking it can be interpreted as entailing that, as it would be impossible for the whole people to assemble, a smaller scale version of 'the people', namely a Parliament, is convened. But the real question must be: what is it that is being represented? Is it a social characteristic of the electorate: so many rich, so many poor, so many women, so many men? This is what naive advocates of the mirror metaphor would propound as, for instance, John Adams when he argued, during the American revolutionary period, that a representative assembly 'should be an exact portrait, in miniature, of the people at large, as it should feel, reason and act'.[32]

Togliatti was not using the metaphor in this sense, first, because he also held the view that the representative represents both his/her electors and the entire nation; second, because Togliatti always assumed that representation 'works' through political parties. Political parties are the instruments which enable the masses to take part in the administration of the state. Political parties are the main instance of 'direct democracy'.[33] To make Parliament the mirror of the country means that it should provide a setting in which the party political balance of forces existing in the country is represented. It is not necessarily a question of numbers or of proportions (though Togliatti will never cease to defend proportional representation). What matters is that not just the forces be represented, but also their 'relations'. One distorts these relations when one devises a mechanism, such as the Legge Truffa, which tends to diminish artificially the power, prestige, and dignity of one of the 'forces'. In the Italian case this would occur when the exclusion of the leading political party of the working class is implemented not only at the government level but also in the parliamentary arena. This therefore amounted to a *de facto* revision of the constitutional pact, which had enshrined the relations between the three main parties. Parliament is seen as a place for the peaceful discussion of potential conflicts. It does not seek to eliminate conflicts, but rather to ensure that they do not occur outside the boundaries of legality. Of course, the Legge Truffa would not eliminate debates between minority and majority, as Togliatti seemed to imply. But it would force the minority into an opposition ghetto from which it could not hope to modify legislation.

Here we reach the core of Togliatti's objection: the Legge Truffa alters the representational nature of the system because it introduces something like a regime of plebiscites. This, for Togliatti, is not parliamentarism. The change of regime from parliamentary to 'plebiscitarian' would be a recognition that the electorate is in fact no longer voting for a Member of Parliament – or rather for a political party – but for a government. The result of such an electoral system would not be an arena where differing forces fight it out, but a government and an opposition with no mediation.

The system the Legge Truffa would produce would have many features of the British system. In Britain, the electorate is faced with a clear-cut choice between a government and an opposition and, in practice, determines the government, which can count on a relatively safe majority in the House of Commons and can proceed to implement its legislative programme. The opposition's role is to prepare for government. But the crucial difference is that the British system of weak Parliament and strong executive can be acceptable to both sides because – in reality – either side can become the government. The introduction of such a system in a country in which one of the two sides is *de facto* excluded from government means that it cannot participate effectively in the political system: it would be secluded in a Parliament without real force while being unable to achieve political power. Thus the 'mirror' metaphor described a political pact in which the proportional representation of the PCI was the *quid pro quo* for its exclusion from governmental power.

Democratic consolidation through political contract

The legitimacy of the PCI has often been doubted. Frequent demands have been made on the party to demonstrate in some way or other that it is truly committed to liberal democracy. It should be remembered that, in the situation prevailing immediately after the war in Italy and after a long period of forced illegality, the leaders of the PCI felt threatened by the climate of anti-Communism characteristic of the Cold War. They saw no reason to take for granted the commitment to democracy of the Italian establishment and assumed, quite reasonably, that the USA would intervene to protect Italian democracy only if the threat came from the left.

It followed that the PCI had to negotiate some kind of *quid pro quo* in order to obtain some guarantees from 'the other side', in exchange for its promise to become a loyal opposition: democratic consolidation works both ways. Clearly if Italian Communist activists had been convinced that the DC was no more than a front for some kind of clerico-Fascist revival (as some did think), they would have prepared for a return to clandestinity and a possible civil war, and not for the 'long march through the institutions' which has been characteristic of the PCI.

In his search for guarantees, Togliatti chose carefully those aspects of the liberal tradition which could provide a real protection for his party. He could not adopt the British model (the nearest model to the Legge Truffa system) because the direct election of a government by the electorate presupposed the political (as opposed to the formal) right of the opposition to become a government. To reinterpret the British political system through our reading of the Italian: the 'compromise' between left and right in the UK is based on the fact that the Labour Party had been able to become accepted as a legitimate party, that is as a governing party. In exchange this party 'accepted' the parliamentary system. In Italy that was not the case: the PCI could accept that it could not rule, but only as long as its electoral strength would be accurately reflected in a Parliament which had real muscle. Thus the peculiarly Italian combination of weak executive and strong Parliament is part and parcel of an informal system whereby the Italian Communist Party is in fact excluded from power.

It should thus not be surprising that Togliatti's defence of the liberal principles of parliamentary control and of the right of the minority was linked to his recognition that De Gasperi's 'counter-revolution' of 1947/8 (that is the expulsion of the left from the ruling coalition) had created a situation in which the ideology of anti-Communism would make it impossible for the Communist minority to become a majority in the foreseeable future. This meant that Togliatti did not envisage that the 'form of political rule' of the Italian road to Socialism would be a system based on a clear divide between majority and minority and alternation in power between rival coalitions. In 1947, as the DC was preparing to exclude the PCI and the PSI from the ruling coalition and to inaugurate the period of DC hegemony, Togliatti explained that the post-war 'tripartite' alliance between the DC, the PCI, and the PSI was not at all a temporary formula. There was in the country, he wrote, a clear majority in favour of a regime of 'progressive democracy' (all the main parties were then in favour of structural reforms):

> if we want the government and its policies to conform to the democratic will of the majority, the mass parties of the Left and the Christian Democratic Party must cooperate in a permanent way in a long term perspective of reconstruction. Such cooperation must not be occasional with a view to destroying each other.[34]

He then added:

> The 'tripartite' cannot and must not be, in our view, a dead formula indicating a temporary and transitional parliamentary majority. It is and must be instead a long term policy for a

government which would renew Italy, fulfilling the aspirations and the need of the great majority of the population.[35]

This position has two aspects. The main one is that the governance of Italy will not be based on the existence of a systematic opposition which aspires to become government. The connection here with the 'liberal tradition' is very tenuous. This is all the more so as Togliatti's words reveal the desire not just for a government of national unity to deal with an emergency, but for one which would be the form of government of the new Italian republic for an entire historical period. This brings us to the second aspect. What is the role of Parliament in this system? Togliatti does not specify, but it can easily be seen that it would have to be a Parliament which would reflect a balance of forces within a government majority which is already preconstituted. In fact, he even says that the necessity of tripartitism does not originate from a parliamentary requirement (presumably the lack of other possible majorities), but from popular demand: 'The need for a tripartite alliance is only indirectly (*per riflesso*) a parliamentary need.'[36] Parliament is eliminated from the circuit of people–Parliament–executive.

The words quoted are not occasional and are not aimed at a particular conjuncture. They represent a political line which Togliatti adhered to for the rest of his life (and which survived him by at least fifteen years). Its origins were in the strategy followed during the Resistance and its expression in the Constitutional pact, which enshrined the concepts not only of popular will and national unity but also that of 'social progress linked to the development of a new ruling class'.[37] The Constitutional pact took precedence in his view over any parliamentary majority, for there is a majority in the country which is more significant than a parliamentary majority. The two do not always coincide: 'Don't believe ... that an occasional parliamentary majority is sufficient to justify an abuse of power.'[38] The only parliamentary majority which was an adequate reflection of the Constitutional pact was the tripartite coalition: 'It was necessary to find a way to arrive at a deep and permanent co-operation among all the forces which had fought together for the liberation [of the country].'[39] Togliatti always kept on the table the possibility of reconstructing the lost unity – even when the divide between PCI and DC appeared to be as deep as ever. For instance a decade later in 1959, when denouncing Fanfani's 'authoritarian plans' for strengthening his leadership, he exclaimed (after Machiavelli): 'Is there a tendency, a group, a man within Christian Democracy, or elsewhere, ready to change current policies whether in foreign or internal economic affairs? Any party of the Left would be ready to offer understanding and help.'[40]

Thus the strategy of the 'Historic Compromise' – even in the much criticized interpretation of it which prevailed between 1976 and 1979 – had an unquestionably Togliattian dimension. But in Togliatti the defence of parliamentary control and of the right of the minority to be an effective opposition existed alongside a defence of Sovietism in the east (until the early 1960s) and the pursuit of 'national unity' governments in Italy. This complex line bears the scars of a national and international situation which threatened to transform one of the founding forces of the Italian republic and its Constitution into an 'outside-the-system-party'. A party which felt itself to be constantly threatened with political marginalization had at the same time to maintain a strong relationship with an international power and with its world-wide movement. Furthermore, Togliatti's PCI could not ignore that it owed its political security to its mass support and that this, in turn, partly depended on the special relationship with the 'fatherland of socialism'.

Togliatti's defence of a liberal conception of Parliament, of its 'centrality' and of the rights of the minority must be linked to the fact that the advent of the PCI to power could not occur through the normal electoral mechanism, but required the prior political legitimation of the PCI as a party of government. The mechanism which would make this possible had to be political, namely a tripartite coalition government which would underwrite the recognition of the PCI (by the DC) as a legitimate party. This would have been the Italian equivalent of the German *Grosse Koalition* which had enabled the German Social Democratic Party to become a party of government.

Unlike the PCI the DC had an alternative to tripartitism: to occupy virtually the entire political space to its right and become Italy's dominant force. In these circumstances Togliatti had to do all he could to ensure that the PCI, though unable to govern, would be at least considered as the Italian republic's 'loyal opposition'. Opposition within the system could not be adequately defended on the basis of the categories of the Communist tradition, that is Leninism and the Third International. That tradition envisaged no minority rights and no effective opposition. Only liberal concepts could 'protect' Italian Communism.

Is this an instance of that *doppiezza* (duplicity), that 'speaking with a forked tongue', of which Togliatti has been so frequently accused? To a certain extent it is, but not in the usual sense that the desired alternative to a democratic parliamentary republic was ever a Soviet one. Togliatti's alternative to 'liberal democracy' was not the Soviet model but the tripartite coalition: the only true political expression of the Constitutional pact, the only parliamentary majority which coincided with a real political majority in the country. Togliatti's famous 'duplicity' consisted in this: while defending the principle that the minority can become the majority, and while fighting against any attempt to transform the minority into an anti-system opposition, he was assuming that, sooner or later, a preconstituted government coalition of national unity would re-emerge. The role of the electorate in this would be to define the relations of forces 'within' the government, not those between government and opposition. The role of Parliament in a system without significant opposition remained unspecified and, in all probability, could not be specified a priori.

Would Parliament still be 'central'? Would it still be, to quote Disraeli, 'a mirror of the mind as well as the material interests [of the country]'?[41] I think that in Togliatti's intention Parliament would have a centrality even under his 'best scenario strategy' (the government of national unity). I can only offer here some provisional suggestions.

A country riven by great social conflicts and in need of a massive reconstruction after a devastating international conflict requires either a thorough revolution which will wipe out all traces of the previous social order and its ruling classes (the Soviet model) or an institutionalized truce between the contending parties (the Weimar model). For reasons which have been mentioned here and explained elsewhere,[42] Togliatti rejected an Italian version of the Soviet road. But what about the 'Weimar road'?

The Weimar Republic was an attempt to reconcile the differences between 'labour' and 'capital'. The economic representatives of these two social forces, organized labour (the Free Trade Unions), and organized capital (the employers) envisaged that they would succeed in circumventing Parliament and the bureaucracy (i.e. the political level) by institutionalizing their compromise on a long-term basis: the Central Working Community of German Employers and Employees (*Zentralarbeitsgemeinshaft* – ZAG) with the ambitious long-term purpose of resolving 'all economic social and legal questions touching upon industrial life'.[43] The compromise thus entered into bypassed completely the formal institutional setting and the democratic institutions. Weimar failed and for many reasons, but one of them was the fact that this compromise had no state backing and no political legitimizing.[44]

In Italy the post-war 'social pact' was however concentrated at the political level: it was a pact between political parties which had fought together, formed together a Constituent Assembly, written together a Constitution, and governed together. No social force outside them could have an independent extra-parliamentary weight. The trade unions themselves had been reconstituted by the three leading political parties. Thus the Weimar option had been foreclosed from the start: the institutions of Italian democracy, whether formal or informal, would be entirely in the hands of political parties represented in Parliament. Togliatti's strategy was to institutionalize at the political level the relations of compromise necessary to govern Italy. He was not tempted by any corporatist strategy. The parliamentary institutions would not be bypassed or weakened by the Italian road to Socialism, as had happened in Weimar, nor destroyed as in the USSR. Togliatti's defence of the powers of Parliament reached its height during the Legge Truffa debates, but the construction of Italy's parliamentary system began in the course of the Resistance and developed further during the drafting of the Constitution. Tripartitism would find its natural terrain in the parliamentary arena.

Conclusion

Italian democracy survived its crucial test when the Italian Communist Party was able to find a *modus vivendi* after its expulsion from the government, that is after the end of tripartitism. By expelling the PCI and winning the 1948 elections the DC had been tempted to marginalize the PCI by altering the rules of the game which had been jointly agreed. This, after 1948, was the most significant immediate threat to democratic consolidation by a political party. The electoral defeat of the Legge Truffa (when, in 1953, the ruling coalition obtained less than half of the votes) ensured that the parliamentary system remained sufficiently strong to ensure the participation of the PCI.

Togliatti's strategic thinking at this early stage of the process of democratic consolidation is a decisive instance of a 'political contract' at a crucial point of system stabilization, although the acceptance of it by 'the other side' was not readily apparent at first. That is itself of course one major reason why consolidation was a lengthy process in Italy, for to a significant degree the problem of the PCI's own legitimacy has paralleled this process. Nevertheless, in so far as legitimacy is something conferred on new regimes by their (principal) actors, the 'view from the PCI' discussed above corresponds to Rustow's 'habituation phase' noted at the start of this chapter. It amounts to that elimination of uncertainties which differentiates democratic consolidation from democratic transition, whereby systemic options begin to be 'closed' and the rules of the game are confirmed or, if necessary, redefined. Indeed, democratic consolidation in Italy was promoted not so much by the defeat of the left in 1947–8 as by the integration of the PCI in the new democratic system – at the level of socio-political organizations and local government as well as political institutions. That the PCI was favourable to this is only underlined by this examination of Togliatti's attitudes, contrasting somewhat with the post-1974 strategy of the Communist Party in Portugal. If the outcome in the Italian case was not always certain at the time, this illustrates the fragility of the situation which usually marks the move from transition to early consolidation.

NOTES

1. G. Pasquino, 'The demise of the first Fascist regime and Italy's transition to democracy, 1943–48', in G. O'Donnell, P. Schmitter, and L. Whitehead (eds) *Transitions from Authoritarian Rule: Prospects for Democracy*, Baltimore, Md, Johns Hopkins University Press, 1986, pp. 57–8.
2. D. Rustow, 'Transitions to democracy: toward a dynamic model', *Comparative Politics*, April 1970, p. 361.
3. Pasquino, op. cit., pp. 65–6.
4. ibid., pp. 52–4.
5. 'Discorso alla conferenza delle donne comuniste', June 1945, in Palmiro Togliatti, *Opere 1944–1955*, vol. 5, edited by L. Gruppi, Rome, Editori Riuniti, 1984, p. 147 (henceforth cited as *Opere Vol. 5*).
6. ibid., pp. 148–9.
7. *Opere Vol. 5*, p. 197.
8. Speech to the Constituent Assembly (CA), 19 February 1947, in P. Togliatti, *Discorsi Parlamentari*, Rome, Segreteria Generale Ufficio Stampa e Pubblicazioni della Camera dei Deputati, 1984, p. 44.
9. ibid.
10. Speech to the CA, 11 March 1947, in *Discorsi Parlamentari*, p. 61.
11. *The Social Contract*, Harmondsworth, Penguin edn, 1968, p. 59.
12. Speech to the CA, 11 March 1947, in *Discorsi Parlamentari*, p. 66.
13. ibid., p. 67.
14. In *Opere Vol. 5*, p. 539. On 28 May 1953 he again praised Giolitti in a commemorative speech he made in the statesman's birthplace, Cuneo; see 'Tradizione liberale e sanfedismo', in P. Togliatti, *Opere Scelte*, edited by G. Santomassimo, Rome, Riuniti, 1974, pp. 594–611.
15. In *Discorsi Parlamentari*, p. 288. As John Stuart Mill wrote: 'Instead of the function of governing, for which it is radically unfit, the proper office of a representative assembly is to watch and control the government: to throw the light of publicity on its acts: to compel a full exposition and justification of all of them which any one considers questionable; to censure them if found condemnable', in *Considerations on Representative Government*, in collection edited by H.B. Acton, J.S. Mill, *Utilitarianism, Liberty, Representative Government*, London, Dent, 1972, p. 239.
16. In *Discorsi Parlamentari*, pp. 239–50.
17. ibid., p. 300. Speech to the Chamber of Deputies (CoD), 10 June 1948.
18. Speech at the Fifth Congress of the PCI, December 1945, now in *Opere Vol. 5*, p. 210.
19. 'Le decisioni del XX Congresso e il Partito socialista italiano', *Rinascita*, October 1958, now in P. Togliatti, *Scritti sul Centrosinistra*, Florence, Istituto Gramsci and Firenze & Cooperativa Editrice Universitaria, 2 vols, 1975, p. 125 (henceforth cited as *Scritti*).

20. 'Per una sinistra europea', *Rinascita*, March 1959, now in *Scritti*, p. 238.
21. The Legge Truffa, or 'Swindle Law' as the Communists called it, was an electoral reform legislation whereby the party or coalition of parties which received more than half of the national votes would obtain a two-thirds majority in the Chamber of Deputies.
22. Cited during speech to the CoD, 8 December 1952, in *Discorsi Parlamentari*, p. 722.
23. ibid., p. 723. To back this view Togliatti quotes Guizot. The necessity for centralized decision-making is as part of the 'liberal' tradition as that of popular representation is part of the democratic one. Thomas Hobbes expressed the view that the essence of decision-making lies in its singularity: 'A Multitude of men, are made ONE Person when they are by one man, or one Person, Represented; so that it be done with the consent of every one of that Multitude in particular. For it is the UNITY of the Represeter, not the UNITY of the Represented, that maketh the Person ONE. And it is the Represeter that beareth the Person, and but one Person: and Unity, cannot otherwise be understood in Multitude', in *Leviathan*, edited by C.B. Macpherson, Harmondsworth, Penguin, 1968, ch. 16, p. 220.
24. In *Discorsi Parlamentari*, p. 740.
25. ibid., p. 719.
26. In fact, no general theory can cope with this controversy. For John Stuart Mill this could not be a matter of constitutional legislation, but of the 'ethics of representative government: . . . let the system of representation be what it may, it will be converted into one of mere delegation if the electors so choose', in op. cit., p. 315. As Hanna Pitkin has written: 'What is most striking about the mandate-independence controversy is how long it has continued without coming any nearer to a solution, despite the participation of many astute thinkers', in *The Concept of Representation*, Berkeley and Los Angeles, University of California Press, 1967, p. 148. In the modern period the concept of party representation introduces a new and fundamental variable: collective representation.
27. In *Discorsi Parlamentari*, p. 720.
28. ibid., p. 721.
29. ibid., p. 727.
30. ibid., p. 721.
31. ibid., p. 722.
32. Quoted in Pitkin, op. cit., p. 60.
33. In *Discorsi Parlamentari*, p. 1,118. Following Bernard Crick we can say the same for Britain: 'The only viable theory that would describe the actual practice of representation in Britain today is that it is "party representation": that Members are sent to Parliament by the electorate because they represent parties which, in turn, represent great collective social and economic interests', in *The Reform of Parliament*, London, Weidenfeld & Nicolson, 1970, revised 2nd edn, p. 55.
34. 'Crisi "democristiana"', *Rinascita*, January–February 1947, now in *Opere Vol. 5*, p. 241.
35. ibid.
36. ibid.

37. Speech to the CA, 11 March 1947, in *Discorsi Parlamentari*, p. 62.
38. Speech to the CA, 18 December 1947, in *Discorsi Parlamentari*, p. 265.
39. Speech to the CoD, 10 June 1948, in *Discorsi Parlamentari*, p. 303.
40. 'Invito ai socialisti', *Rinascita*, January 1959, now in *Scritti*, p.170.
41. See extract in *The Conservative Tradition,* edited by R.J. White, London, Adam & Charles Black, 1964, p. 167.
42. See my *The Strategy of the Italian Communist Party*, London, Frances Pinter, 1981.
43. See G. D. Feldman, 'German interest group alliances in war and inflation, 1914–1923' in S. Berger (ed.) *Organizing Interests in Western Europe*, Cambridge, Cambridge University Press, 1983, pp. 170–1.
44. ibid., p. 180.

Chapter five

Portugal: an open verdict

Ken Gladdish

> A purely political analysis, based exclusively on the possibilities
> opened up by a democratic system, would not be enough to
> explain how social behaviour distorts, in the Portuguese case, the
> abstract properties of democratic political theory.
>
> (Joaquim Aguiar)[1]

Introduction

The evaluation of the contribution made by political parties to
democratic consolidation presents, in the case of Portugal, a formidable
array of problems. Some of these can be regarded as generic. In the
post-1945 era, Portugal shared with a number of other European states a
battery of social and economic disadvantages in comparison with those
parts of western Europe which, over the ensuing decades, would achieve
unprecedented affluence. The experience of a prolonged period of
dictatorship was also shared with certain other states, most relevantly
with Spain. But there is a further dimension to the Portuguese
experience in that the long phase of authoritarian rule in the
mid-twentieth century had not been preceded by any process of
significant political mobilization. Neither the experience of monarchical
parliamentary government from the 1850s on, nor the efforts of the First
Republic, from 1910 to 1926, had resulted in the cultivation of a
politically organized citizenry attuned to the activities of national
parties competing in elections on the basis of universal adult suffrage.[2]
This inheritance of socio-economic backwardness and of political
passivity has acted as a strong 'confining condition' on the scope for
parties as agents of the new democracy.

Discussion of the performance and achievements of the political
parties since the overthrow of the Salazar–Caetano regime in April 1974
has therefore to be firmly predicated on that circumstance. Thus, the
parties of the new democracy have been aptly described as 'a skin over
a sharply stepped political culture'.[3] In his extended analysis of systemic

problems, from which the quotation at the head of this chapter is taken, Aguiar has characterized the contribution of the political parties under this new democracy in the following terms: 'In fact, the traditional features of Portuguese society were internalised by the parties themselves, which are now one more specific element of the clientelistic network, enclosing a circle of self-sustaining interlocked interests ... typical of a patrimonialistic society.'

Aguiar's assessment, albeit pessimistic, does raise a key question about the performance of political parties and hence their contribution to democratic consolidation in Portugal. That we are dealing here with an example of a 'difficult democracy' is evident from the extreme government overload which has marked the period since the 1974 Revolution. If for example political parties normatively preside over the allocation of resources, what happens when resources are hopelessly inadequate, or so managed as to be unable to deal with even urgent, clearly perceived needs? Parties may simply offer privileged access to limited spoils. Aguiar has furthermore identified another facet of the overall problem: 'The control of the state apparatus ... will be an impossible task when the parties have organisations so crude that they will be unable to compete with state bureaucracies, even for policy conception.' The broader question here is how well the political parties under the new democracy have confronted what has been the weightiest inheritance from previous regimes.

Such problems appear to make the Portuguese case a particularly arduous one to evaluate, for the transition to and consolidation of democracy has faced not only short-term difficulties but also long-term problems of some magnitude. However, the three relationships on which this study is based provide some framework for an interim judgement on this process. Consolidation is clearly a second-order phenomenon following upon a formative period of transition. There is already an extensive literature of analysis and interpretation concerning the early transition period in Portugal.[4] It began to emerge shortly after the military overthrow of the former regime in April 1974 and is still issuing.[5] This text is not designed as a further contribution to that exegesis. But the major lines of force of the formative phase do require to be summarized, if the dynamics of the outcome and hence the prospects for democratic consolidation are to be understood.

The essential pattern of events which comprised the transition phase is well known. A bloodless military coup on 24/25 April 1974 was followed by twenty-seven months of extempore rule filled by six successive provisional governments, each with a different complexion according to the rapidly shifting balance of political forces. The first provisional government under a civilian, Palma Carlos, lasted only two months. The next four Cabinets were all under the premiership of

Colonel Vasco Goncalves and lasted from July 1974 to September 1975. The sixth and final transitional Cabinet under Admiral Pinheiro de Azevedo held office until the first constitutional government took post on 22 July 1976.

The prominence of the military, in particular the group of officers who formed the Armed Forces Movement (MFA) and carried out the coup, was central to the entire transition phase. But it was far from being a concerted body. A recent volume on the roles of the military protagonists has grouped them in six categories, each with a different perception of what the change of regime was intended to achieve.[6] There was also a diverse array of civilian elements, each one seeking to mould the transition period towards its own preferred systemic outcome. The most active of these forces during the first eighteen months of experiment and confusion were on the radical left. They included the established, formerly clandestine Communist Party, certain members of the Armed Forces Movement, and a myriad of groupuscules at street level. Their aim was to impart to the transformation a prescriptive ideological direction. Their aspirations, at least in rhetorical terms, would be enshrined in the first two articles of the original Constitution. Also on the left was the recently constituted Socialist Party, which quickly became a protagonist of liberal democracy.

There were also forces which resisted the radical left direction on the right and in the centre, in the shape of hastily assembled political formations and of more traditional institutions – the Church, the bureaucracy, private, and corporate business – which had had varying attachments to the previous regime. Altogether, it may be said that two key dimensions of contention transected the considerable cast of social and political actors. One was the divide between the military and the politicians. The other was the conflict between the radical left and those who campaigned for a liberal state, with the bulk of the Socialist Party attempting to act as a bridge between the two. These two dimensions eventually converged somewhat uneasily in the process of constitution-making which was to set the stage for a successor regime. It is with the resultant Constitution therefore that an account of the initial phase of consolidation needs to begin.

In general, then, Portugal underwent a complex and at times turbulent transition to democracy. While the eventual choice by 1976 of a liberal democracy opened the way for regime consolidation, some features of the transition have continued to influence the achievement of the latter. It is also clear that the process of democratic consolidation has been an extended one and has not yet finished. There are certainly different levels of regime consolidation, but a crucial one with liberal democracies is the role played by competitive political parties. Indeed, as will be seen, a key point of distinction between transition and consolidation in Portugal is the emergence of parties as the central actors in the latter compared with the determining role of the military in the former.

Parties and the state

The essential features of the original Constitution, which was adopted on 25 April 1976, two years after the ending of the dictatorship, were as follows: (1) a single chamber assembly with legislative competence, directly elected by universal suffrage; (2) a presidency, also directly elected by universal suffrage, with a range of executive powers including a legislative veto, scope to dissolve the assembly and to remove the prime minister, to declare war and to ratify treaties; (3) a Council of the Revolution, composed of senior members of the armed forces, mostly appointed by the services, with powers to advise and authorize the president, notably in the interpretation of the Constitution; (4) a Council of Ministers, presided over by a prime minister appointed by the president 'after consultation with the Council of the Revolution and the parties represented in the Assembly, due regard being had to the election results' (Art. 190). The Council of Ministers not only had executive powers but also could issue decree-laws in certain circumstances. Apart from the formal structure of government, the Constitution committed the state *inter alia* to the socialization of the means of production (Art. 9c) and to the implementation of a vast list of individual and worker rights including that of full employment.

In 1982 the Constitution was amended, by the required two-thirds majority of the Assembly. The most important revisions were: (1) a closer definition of the president's powers restricting his right to dissolve the Assembly, to dismiss the prime minister, and to veto legislation; (2) the abolition of the Council of the Revolution, and its replacement by a purely consultative Council of State with no direct military membership. The original Constitution set up what amounted to a four-tier pyramid of national decision-making: the Assembly, the Council of Ministers, the Council of the Revolution, and the Presidency. The 1982 revision now reduced the number of tiers to three by eliminating the Council of the Revolution while more closely defining the presidential element. Much of the experience of operating the democratic system so far has to be viewed in the light of the complications of the constitutional structure. For instance, the 'semi-presidential' system which existed from 1976 not only divided the executive, but also affected the growth of party-political responsibility within the state structure.

Although the elaborate reasoning behind the Constitution and its revision lie beyond the scope of this chapter, some observations are crucial. The first is that both the ideological provisions of the original

Constitution (which have largely survived the 1982 revision) and the role of the Council of the Revolution (which has not) expressed the radical atmosphere out of which the new system emerged. A second point is that the off-setting of parliamentary government by the introduction of a presidency with a popular mandate and executive powers reflected both the preferences of the military in the processes of regime change and memories of the much earlier experience of failed parliamentarism under the First Republic from 1910 to 1926. These various provisions acted as an important constraint on party operations in the first phase of democracy, as Portugal moved from regime transition to early consolidation.

So the establishment of a democratic system was not a straight-forward matter of providing for responsible government within a parliamentary framework. It was from the outset hedged with 'safeguards' designed to preserve a set of ideological commitments arising from a quasi-revolutionary process, by circumscribing parliamentary sovereignty and by incorporating the Armed Forces in the constitutional order. Only the last of these was discarded in the 1982 revision. In these respects, Portugal differed from other cases examined in this volume.

The Constitution thus invested the democratic system with a plurality of somewhat conflicting aims, many of which focused upon the presidency. The duties vested in the office implied that the president would have the ultimate responsibility for ensuring that the system worked. The military had to be incorporated in its functioning, but at the same time neutralized as a political force. The ideological commitments had to be kept in mind, even though they were swiftly out-distanced by the pressing problems of a highly vulnerable economy. Finally, the president had to superintend the manoeuvres of politicians whose base in the parliamentary and ministerial tiers of the system was endowed with democratic legitimacy.

The configuration of the new constitutional structure was clearly vital to the context in which open political competition between freely formed parties proceeded. In terms of historical experience, the post-1976 political system was novel in several crucial respects. First, the holding of unconstrained and uncensored elections (all parties were prima-facie legal) grounded upon universal adult suffrage was without precedent. Under the First Republic from 1910 to 1926, none of these facilities ever became available;[7] while under the Salazar–Caetano regime both elections and the activities of the legislature were carefully stage-managed to preclude any serious challenge to authoritarian government.[8] Second, the objective was now the formation of governments clearly dependent upon parliamentary assent, notwithstanding the powers of the president and the role of the Council of the Revolution. Third, the apparatus of repression which had silenced dissent as well as determining political outcomes was now of course completely abolished.

One possible complication here, which requires comment, is that the statement of 'fundamental principles' as per Articles 1 and 2 of the Constitution might be thought an impediment to the concept of a liberal state, with no prescribed outcomes for the processes of competitive politics. These Articles ostensibly committed the Republic to 'its own transformation into a classless society' and to 'the transition to socialism by creating the conditions for democratic exercise of power by the working classes'. But the institutional provisions make it clear that whatever was in mind was not a 'guided democracy', still less a one-party state. Article 117 provides that 'political parties shall participate . . . in accordance with their democratic representativeness' and 'minorities shall have the right of democratic opposition'. So despite the overture to a certain conception of social purpose, political mobilization was it seems designed to be unrestricted.[9]

The launching of an effective system of party competition under the turbulent conditions of the transitional period from 1974 to 1976 was undoubtedly fraught with problems. Given the radical thrust of the initial stages, when the Armed Forces Movement sought to preside over the sequence of provisional governments, it was palpably easier for the left to marshal support than for the centre or the right. The most visible political formation at the outset was the Communist Party (PCP), which emerged from underground in April 1974 as the sole movement with an operational structure. Its chief rivals soon became the nascent Socialist Party and the leftist groups which mushroomed under the new conditions of free speech and free assembly.

The early phases of party activity following the abolition of dictatorship were in fact vertiginous. The arena was then controlled, or at least policed by the military, whose factions engineered a series of contrasting shifts of ideological momentum, culminating in the closure of the 'revolutionary' stage in November 1975 with the defeated coup by the radical left. By then a Constituent Assembly was in session, compiled at the first national election, in April 1975. Its largest component was the Socialist Party, which had won almost half the seats (116 out of 244), with a total vote of just under 40 per cent. Its nearest competitor was the centrist Popular Democrats (PPD), with eighty-one seats and a quarter of the poll. The Communists had come third, winning only thirty seats on one-eighth of the vote, while the leftist groupuscules had been left without representation. The remaining position of right marker in an embryonic four-party structure was held by the Social Democratic Centre (CDS), with sixteen seats on 8 per cent of the vote. This first election was nevertheless important in both encouraging the

Table 1 Parliamentary elections in Portugal, 1975–87[10]

	1975[a]		1976		1979		1980		1983		1985		1987	
	%	seats	%	seats	%	seats	%	seats	%	seats	%	seats	%	seats
PS	37.9	116	35.0	107	27.4	74	27.1	74	36.4	101	20.8	57	22.2	60
PSD	26.4	81	24.4	73	—		—		27.0	76	29.9	88	50.2	148
AD	—		—		45.2	128	47.5	134	—		—		—	
CDS	7.6	16	15.9	42	—		—		12.4	29	10.0	22	4.4	4
PCP	12.5	30	14.6	40	19.0	47	16.9	41	18.2	44	15.5	38	12.1	31
PRD	—		—		—		—		—		17.9	45	4.9	7
Other	15.6	1	10.1	1	8.4	1	8.5	1	5.0		5.9		6.2	

Key: PS: Socialist Party; PSD: Social Democratic Party; AD: Democratic Alliance (comprising PSD, CDS, and Monarchists); CDS: Social Democratic Centre; PCP: Communist Party (fought elections as APU and then CDU in 1987); PRD: Democratic Renewal Party.
Note: [a] Constituent Assembly election.

more moderate forces and strengthening the parties' role *vis-à-vis* the military as well as identifying the main party political actors for the future.

The Assembly's deliberations took place in an atmosphere of considerable conflict and uncertainty which, until the events of 24–5 November, raised the possibility of civil war.[11] The role of the military in any forthcoming system remained for the time being unresolved and the pattern of support manifested in the first election was obviously still tenuous and provisional. Even if a Constitution could be agreed, it would then have to be implemented by untried formations, charged with inaugurating a new polity while grappling with immense social and economic problems. Part of this uncertainty was eventually resolved by a pact between the military and the political parties in February 1976.[12] This set the timetable for the promulgation of the Constitution and the two elections, parliamentary and presidential, which would accompany its adoption. The framework for the passage to constitutional government was at last in place, representing an important element in the completion of regime transition. The task of democratic consolidation remained ahead and was to prove a lengthy and rather complicated process.

The first constitutional government took office in June 1976 after a national election in April, which appeared to confirm the four-party configuration of its precursor. The Socialists, again the leading party but with no overall majority, assumed power as a minority Cabinet with substantial opposition to both their right and their left. They quickly faced severe economic conditions which compelled them to seek help from the IMF and to accept a series of policy constraints. From December 1977 until December 1979 the first Parliament of the Republic was strained to its limits in its task of promoting democratic legitimacy. A surprising coalition between the Socialists and the right-wing CDS collapsed after half a year, to be followed, after the president had dismissed the Socialist leader Soares from the premiership, by three unsuccessful presidential Cabinets, including technocrats. In resisting these initiatives, the parliamentary parties were at least asserting their position *vis-à-vis* the president but in a wholly negative way, since they were unable to offer any solution to the impasse. The pattern of immobilism was finally broken by the president's dissolving the Assembly and the formation of an electoral alliance by the two right-of-centre parties – the former PPD, now re-christened Social Democrats, and the CDS.

The relative success of the Democratic Alliance (which also included a small monarchist group (PPM) and a PS splinter, the Reformadores) at the parliamentary election of December 1979, opened a new chapter in the consolidation process. With a slender overall majority in the

Assembly – 128 seats out of 250 on 45 per cent of the total vote – the Alliance was able to field the first Cabinet with prospects for an effective legislative programme. At a further election in October 1980, required under the Constitution, the AD slightly increased both its combined vote and its Assembly majority. But the prognosis for a period of effective stable government turned out to be somewhat premature. In the AD's first year of office, the Council of the Revolution exercised its veto over government measures in twenty-three cases.[13] The architect and prime inspiration of the AD, Sa Carneiro, was killed in a plane crash in December 1980 during the run-up to the presidential elections. Thereafter the principal component of the Alliance, the PSD, was plagued by leadership problems and by the end of 1982 the coalition was in disarray. It had however made two significant contributions to the prospects for consolidation. First, it had demonstrated that it was possible to construct a majority administration by the formation of an electoral and parliamentary alliance. Second, it had succeeded in enlisting the support of the PS to effect the first revision of the 1976 Constitution, thus showing that the rules of the game could be amended by consensus and due legal process.

The formula of electoral alliances had been taken up by both the Communists (from 1979) and the Socialists (from 1980), though neither were able to produce winning coalitions. After the 1983 Assembly election a further advance in coalition experience occurred when the PS, once more the leading formation, again reached across the cleavage to its right to form a majority government with the PSD. The motives behind this move were undoubtedly mixed. Soares was for instance judged to be taking advantage of the conflicts within the PSD to command the stage in his preparations for the next presidential election two years ahead. When the PSD swung to the right at its May 1985 congress,[14] the end of the uneasy partnership was signalled. In October 1985 the rank order of the two main parties was reversed. The Socialists incurred their worst ever result while the PSD achieved its best solo performance. The apparent continuity of the party system was briefly interrupted by the emergence of what was to prove a flash party – the PRD – formed around the retiring President Eanes. There were now five parties in the National Assembly, the strongest holding only a third of the seats, with no prospect of a viable coalition. A minority PSD government lasted only until the spring of 1987 when the PRD rashly manoeuvred to bring it down. President Soares promptly dissolved the Assembly and at the sixth parliamentary election in the eleven years of the Second Republic, the PSD under Cavaco Silva gained a remarkable 50.2 per cent of the vote to form the first single party majority government.[15] Thus, while persistent difficulties of government cohesion let alone performance had inhibited progress towards democratic consolidation for more than a decade, the PSD's achievement offered a serious chance for a new departure.

The relationship between the political parties and the state has a further dimension beyond their institutional performance. Responsible parliamentary government had also to deal with the possibility of countervailing power in the shape of pre-democratic forces and agencies. Here, the claims of four possible contenders for countervailing influence require to be reviewed – the armed forces, the Church, the bureaucracy, and corporate business. Much of course depends on how far they themselves have adapted to democratisation.

The armed forces – or rather, a particular group with them – were the prime agents of the switch from dictatorship to democracy. It was the Armed Forces Movement (MFA), consisting of 200–300 relatively junior officers mainly from the Army and Air Force, who organized and carried out the coup of April 1974.[16] The movement included some with left-wing affiliations and more with leftish sentiments, which contributed to the political momentum over the next eighteen months. But it would be extremely difficult to give the armed forces as a whole a clear political complexion, then or now. Gallagher, writing in 1983, reports that 'Leftist officers . . . have had a majority on the Council of the Revolution even though the military as a whole are far less radical.'[17] The most central figure in the relationship between the armed forces and the democratic system has of course been the man who ended the holiday of the left in November 1975, and then served as President of the Republic from 1976–86, General Ramalho Eanes. Committed to the Constitution, and holding, ex officio, the post of Commander-in-Chief, he symbolized the formal allegiance of the military to the democratic regime. In the presidential elections of 1980 and 1986 military candidates were canvassed by various political parties. But at no point have any high-ranking officers taken up positions outside the constitutional framework. So the armed forces have not represented any challenge to democracy, and there was no military opposition to the constitutional revision of 1982 which abolished the Council of the Revolution and thereby the military tier in the political structure. In short, although back in the turbulent days of 1974–5 some MFA circles had initially shown some hostility to civilian parties, developments since have removed any serious threat to the latter; while the constitutional revision finally allowed political parties as the central actors in the new system.

The Church has received far less attention from commentators. With one or two exceptions, the Church hierarchy was essentially acquiescent during the dictatorship.[18] Salazar, although a loyal Catholic, did not particularly advance the interests of the Church, though it received a great deal more respect under the Estado Novo than it had under the First

Republic. Since 1974 the Church has maintained a consistently low political profile, unlike in post-war Italy, and has come out strongly against only two measures of the democratic regime – the law legalizing abortion which was passed in 1984,[19] and the law passed by the parliamentary opposition in March 1987 subjecting the Catholic radio station to a reallocation of broadcasting frequencies. One political party, the CDS, has tended to align itself with the Church, though under the generalized banner of Christian Democracy. All other parties are rigorously secular, even the PSD, which predominates in the Catholic North. But the Church appears to have gracefully accepted the advent of liberal democracy, grateful no doubt that the leftist thrust of the early stages of the transition was firmly checked after 1975.

The bureaucracy is a somewhat different case, because of its pervasive and traditional influence on the state. Opello has written: 'it has been made clear (from surveys) that Portuguese political culture is a set of subjective and passive attitudinal and behavioural responses to the overwhelming power and control exercised by the administrative state'.[20] Portuguese history undoubtedly provides ample evidence of the salience of the bureaucracy, from the monarchy down to the present. The most profound experience was that under the dictatorship where the absence of any participatory institutions left the bureaucracy without rivals in its grip on the state. Gallagher writes: 'Dr Salazar allowed the state sector to expand enormously in the name of corporatist principles.'[21] The revolution of 1974 did not relax nor reduce this grip, in the sense that under democracy the national bureaucracy quickly doubled its size from 155,000 to 313,000 by 1979,[22] though this includes the results of extensive nationalization of firms, etc. There have however been considerable changes in personnel since 1974 which have removed many top officials appointed during the dictatorship. Opello writes, 'the purge carried out after the revolution of 1974 ... saw the replacement of well over one third of Portugal's Directors-General (the highest civil service rank)',[23] thus paving the way for party political patronage in the bureaucracy. There has also been a marked increase in the appointment of specialists, particularly economists, to high-level posts in ministries which has helped to alleviate the heavy hand of traditional bureaucracy. Nevertheless a sense remains in which the bureaucracy is hardly a good advertisement for Portugal's post-1974 democracy. This is certainly the view of Gallagher, who quotes the description of suffocating bureaucracy as 'fascism in freedom'.[24] The poor grasp of departmental business shown by some ministerial appointees and the absence of bureaucratic reform are hardly conducive to effective government, although the bureaucracy presents no overt threat to democracy or the role within it of political parties.

The fourth case – the higher business class – presents a mixed picture, well summarized by Makler,[25] who traces the effects of the expropriations in 1974–5. In the absence of a significant landowning class (whose remnants were further depleted by the agrarian take-overs), large business constitutes the upper echelon of the socio-economic pyramid. The state however, even under successive centre-right governments, retains control of many of the larger enterprises. The families to whom Salazar entrusted key sectors of the economy have either accepted the change of regime or remained abroad, though the first Socialist administration invited entrepreneurs to return to help the flagging industrial sector. In sum, there is probably more to fear from international corporations, should the regime lurch to the left, itself an unlikely prospect, than from the depleted native ranks of big business. Entrepreneurs undoubtedly enjoy the emphasis upon free enterprise of the present PSD government under Cavaco Silva and would certainly resist any reversion to statist economic policies.[26] But they would have little incentive, in a now modernizing EEC member country, to endorse any return to authoritarian rule.

In conclusion, while parliamentary government has a record of weakness since the 1974 Revolution, the absence of any direct challenge from traditional agencies of power has helped to entrench the choice of liberal democracy.

Inter-party relations

Virtually every prime minister and government under the Second Republic to date has been brought down by either inter- or intra-party conflict, well short of the statutory end of any parliamentary term. As a corollary, no Parliament has so far lasted more than two and a half years compared with the stipulated legislative term of four years (Art. 174). The causes of this instability can be explained on different grounds. One is the nature of parliamentary arithmetic and the degree of fragmentation or asymmetry in the party system, with fluctuations of support made more vivid by frequent and exceptional elections. A second is the very restricted scope for viable coalitions in a multi-party context where alliances have failed to hold because of rivalry and constant party manoeuvres. A third is the extent to which governmental ineffectiveness may make all Cabinets liable to a collapse of confidence in the Assembly. And fourth, there is the problem of how far the parties themselves can ensure unity, loyalty to their leadership, and discipline in parliamentary operations. All these questions are of course relevant to the contribution of parties to democratic consolidation. Given the record, they therefore raise doubts about its full achievement.

In the Portuguese case, there is much evidence under each of these headings of palpable deficiencies. If we begin with the logistics of the parliamentary components, it is evident as noted before that until the PSD breakthrough of July 1987, the shaping of vertebrate government proved an elusive and persistent task. Majority coalitions did in fact manage to survive for roughly half the period from 1976 to 1988, though each was attended by recurrent strains and sporadic defections. Importantly no coalitional pattern ever crystallized so as to point the way to a dependable formula if, as long seemed the case, no single party majorities were forthcoming.

The reasons for this are to a significant extent related to the uncertainties of party positions within the ideological spectrum. During the early transition period it was not difficult to understand why parties to the right of the PCP chose to maintain ambiguities of profile, in view of the radical atmosphere of the time. But in commenting as late as 1987, Gallagher underlined the point that 'ideological boundaries are still fluid and inexact despite the consolidation of four major parties'.[27] In fact the 1987 election suggested that only three major parties had survived at parliamentary level, but even so there remain doubts about their exact placing in programmatic terms. The pragmatism of the Socialist Party has been evident throughout the period of constitutional government, given both its policy measures while in office and its collaboration with the CDS in 1977–8 and then with the PSD in 1983–5. Neither collaboration however broadened the prospects for viable coalitions. Equally the PSD was unwilling to maintain its more obvious arrangement with the CDS after 1983. Both the leading parties, PS and PSD, in so far as their objectives can be viewed as consistent, have tended to compete as though they were not components of a multi-party system, but were within reach of dominance.[28] Even if the PSD can now point to its remarkable triumph in 1987, the PS has never been within sight of majority rule; and, of course, the PSD's achievement has yet to be confirmed as setting a new trend rather than as an exception to the rule. The difficulty since the 1987 election is to decide how far the political landscape has permanently changed. If the sixth national election does represent an abiding shift in the balance of political forces, then with the opposition divided in a ratio of 2:1 between the Socialists and the Communists, it is difficult to divine what the alternative to PSD rule could be, short of unforeseen electoral landslides.

These basic uncertainties over party ideological positions and hence profiles have made political competition complex and difficult. This is particularly true of those parties near the centre of the spectrum; while the PCP, with a clearer profile, has remained somewhat isolated in the party system. Although it participates in Parliament and is prepared to act associatively with other parties, its stance and style rule out its participation in a governing coalition. More trenchant as an explanation of generic instability has been the frequent tensions within parties, which have in turn further complicated inter-party relations.

The sheer novelty of party activity from 1974 meant that the political game had to be learnt from scratch. Free party formation was forbidden under the long-lasting dictatorship and only in the brief 'reform' phase of the Caetano period was a semi-opposition group, SEDES, allowed to operate.[29] This did provide some opportunity for debate and publicity, notably by deputies who subsequently became the founders of the PPD.[30] The CDS was also able to draw upon figures with some experience of participation in the authoritarian regime, while Communist veterans had their own background of clandestine organization. But national parties based upon mass mobilization of a fully enfranchised citizenry were unknown prior to the election for the Constituent Assembly in April 1975.

In all the major parties dominant figures have emerged but, with the exception, at least until recently, of the PCP, disputes and crises have occurred periodically, especially in the PSD, and the factor of personality has mostly over-shadowed the development of settled structures for the resolution of leadership claims. Parties have also been subject to factions and splits. Between June 1978 and April 1979 for instance, the Socialists suffered two significant breakaways – the UEDS and the Reformadores – while the PSD lost a group of MPs (ASDI) to the PS. Bruneau and MacLeod, surveying the party hierarchies, concluded (in 1986) that all were either autocracies or narrow oligarchies with little scope for effective participation in decision-making, even by middle elites let alone activists at the grass roots.[31] They present the CDS as a party of notables which has never attempted to construct a coherent organization at ground level.[32] The PSD, by contrast, does have an efficiently run national HQ in Lisbon, with computerized membership lists and impressively produced literature. But the party has been rent by factions led by *baronatos* with individual power bases, and was plagued with leadership crises throughout 1980–5. The PS, at least up to 1986, was very much the creature of its commanding personality, Mario Soares, though this did not absolve it from disputes and desertions.[33] Under its current leader, Vitor Constancio, it continues to struggle for unity, and its organization has tended to be a threadbare operation, marked by a debilitating shortage of resources. Ironically it is the two parties which make the greatest gestures towards democratic participation – the PS and PSD – which have shown the most disarray in terms of their public image. The patrician CDS has enjoyed reasonable leadership continuity under Freitas do Amaral up to 1982, and under Lucas Pires up to its electoral débâcle of July 1987. While the highly regimented PCP has generally maintained closed ranks under its veteran boss Alvaro Cunhal, though dissent has recently surfaced publicly.

Thus problems of organizational development have contributed to uncertainties over the ideological profile of the parties, a virtual conjurer's den which some analysts have dealt with in highly critical terms (Aguiar 1984). Part of the problem is that from the moment of their birth in the early transition period both the PSD and CDS had to engage in a marked shift to the left in order to conform to the revolutionary atmosphere of 1974–5. Thus the PSD, or PPD as it was initially, felt compelled to offer itself as a force for 'socialistic humanism' when its leadership was manifestly to the right of centre. The CDS adopted an even more obfuscating formula, describing itself as a party based upon 'personalistic humanism of Christian inspiration'. But it is perhaps the PS which has sought most to be all things to all voters, while pursuing a course whose only clear characteristic has been its leader's indefatigable hostility towards the PCP. It is against this baffling screen of deceptive or at best confusing signals, that an inexperienced electorate has been compelled to navigate its own way through party promises and party behaviour. While there have been subsequent shifts away from the left the formative influences of transition have continued to be felt. The consequent instability in the ideological spectrum may be said to have retarded the process of democratic consolidation.

Any attempt to evaluate the highly complex matter of how far the party system may nevertheless be acquiring fluency, articulacy, and the capacity for effective parliamentary government ultimately confronts the question of what would be an optimal pattern and performance at this stage in the development of Portuguese democracy. Until 1987 a key issue was whether stable coalition formulae would emerge in the absence of single party majorities. Another dimension was the proficiency of the national Assembly – the 'parliament without prestige' as Bruneau and MacLeod have construed it.[34] Here the electoral system, the processes of candidate selection, and the provisions for substitute attendance in Parliament have all attracted criticism. But such criticism can readily be heard in well-established democracies where system performance has become a familiar concern.

Parties and society

To the general questions relating to this dimension a variety of answers have been offered by commentators at successive stages during the brief dozen years of parliamentary rule in Portugal. Verdicts have tended to divide between qualified optimism and deep pessimism. Gallagher, for example, has consistently taken a pessimistic view of the extent to which the parties, along with other agencies, have fulfilled their tasks in relation to public needs. Others have regarded the evidence more favourably. Hammond, for instance, has argued that as early as the 1975 election for the Constituent Assembly, the brand new party system was expressing regional and class interests coherently and effectively.[35] Opello, in a lengthy discussion of the pros and cons of this matter, has given credit for the relative stability of the party system (up to 1983), but has concluded that: 'Multipartyism in Portugal seems to have as much to do with the elitism and personalism which has characterised much of modern Portuguese political history and continues today',[36] thus calling into question how far the parties have developed as forces in society. A comprehensive review of such judgements tends to yield an uncertain and confusing picture. More useful here would be a selection of the principal items which give rise to the most insistent reservations about how far the political parties have furthered the causes of democracy.

High on this list is the pattern of interest aggregation in the political arena since 1974. Since Portugal is unique within western Europe in having no intelligible background of mass mobilization prior to the present, this question inclines towards the metaphysical. Attempts to answer it require some comparative assessment, of which the most tempting is with the Spanish case.[37] Amongst the few direct examples of a bilateral treatment of the two experiences, Nancy Bermeo, in her recent study of the first elections of the transition in both countries,[38] deals with the question, 'What accounts for what emerged?' rather than, 'Did what emerge fulfil any abiding desiderata?' Even so her explanatory typology serves largely to separate the two cases, in terms of how the regimes came to be transformed, what kind of 'class structure' had developed during the authoritarian period, and what forms of semi-opposition were available in the later phase of dictatorship. Her observations on the contrasting 'class structures' which emerged in Spain and Portugal are briefly stated and confined entirely to the dynamics of the commercial and industrial bourgeoisie. This is understandable and very relevant to the behaviour of political elites, but it tells us little about the underlying stratification at mass level, nor indeed why the Socialists were eventually victorious in Spain. Attempts to probe beneath the surfaces of elite configurations have improved little on the premises of Hammond, who drew upon the early work in this field of Jorge Gaspar.[39] So the absence of sufficient research makes it difficult to deal with the aptness of the Portuguese party system *vis-à-vis* the social structure as a whole.[40]

The extent to which Portuguese parties project an image of intra-elite competition certainly seems to dwarf the aggregation of popular interests. At the most general level of analysis, what emerges is the historic social fact that only the upper bourgeoisie, a largely urban stratum, had achieved any significant degree of political influence prior to the 1970s. From the first stirrings of parliamentarism in the 1820s, the 'political class', as it came to be termed, was confined to a narrow segment of landowners, military officers, and the commercial/professional elite.[41] The installation of the First Republic in 1910 did not greatly alter this picture. In the first republican Parliament 80 per cent of the deputies held a university degree or its equivalent in a country with only one small university and extremely limited access to higher education.[42]

During the chaotic life of the First Republic, from 1910 to 1926, the 'political class' signally failed to achieve any perceptible quantum of mass mobilization. Nothing which occurred under the dictatorship made any significant impact upon the gulf between governors and subjects, so that the drive towards popular participation after 1974 confronted extremely low levels of political sophistication at the mass level. Indeed the political culture outside and even inside the cities was largely parochial and unrelated to modern ideological inputs. At the regime change in 1974 illiteracy was estimated at a third of the adult population, and despite crash programmes the official figure in 1981 was still 23 per cent.[43] Recent data suggest the level is now below 20 per cent, but it is clear that a substantial proportion of the voters since 1975 has been unable to absorb political literature directly. As late as 1986 Cravinho reckoned that 60 per cent of adults had had less than four years of formal schooling.[44] Such conditions have inevitably restricted the ability of the parties to further political modernization with the move to liberal democracy.

Given this background, the question of how far the metropolitan elite has been able to perceive and respond to mass needs remains ineluctable; and it has of course been compounded by the severe limitations of public resources during this recent period. When we come to assess policy-making, it must be remembered that social and economic difficulties have abounded under democratic rule. Inflation has undermined efforts to ensure minimum wage levels, and an expanded public sector has made heavy demands on budgets. Salaries in the public sector have however remained low and compel many public servants, including university teachers, to take additional jobs. Education is grossly under-funded as is health, welfare, and the patchy apparatus of social security. Cravinho calculates that in 1984, out of half a million unemployed, only 56,000 were receiving benefit.[45] Clearly in so far as democratic consolidation is dependent on policy performance in respect of key socio-economic indicators, these circumstances hardly appear conducive to that outcome.

In contrast to most of the evidence assembled in this chapter, the capacity of the system to cope with crises must nevertheless be rated relatively highly. This could of course be presented as an ironic reflection upon the frequency with which difficulties arise. It remains true however that both political dislocation and economic disarray have recurrently been confronted with a remarkable resilience by political elites. One has little impression when interviewing political figures that here are men, or occasionally women, who are traumatized by the intransigence of the dilemmas which face them. Instead, there is great enthusiasm for the sheer *va-et-vient* of political life, which for the unsympathetic might confirm Aguiar's view that 'the grand design (of democracy) after ten years is banalised and conditioned to the objectiveness of mere survival'.[46] This again symptomizes the extremely hermetic character of 'the political class', a study of which over the period 1976–84 revealed that the 1,600 top positions in politics and government were held by only 850 people.[47] If the masses therefore appear acquiescent, it is essentially because of their historic passivity and lack of expectation that they can affect in any way the political process.

There is however some interesting survey evidence which imparts some shape to mass attitudes towards the various forms of government under the new democracy in comparison with the dictatorship. The most accessible and impressive assessments of mass views have been carried out by Bruneau in two surveys in 1978 and 1984. Both were conducted through the agency of NORMA, the leading polling organization in Lisbon, and were reported, *inter alia*, in Graham and Wheeler (1983) and Bruneau and MacLeod (1986). In the 1978 survey 2,000 respondents were canvassed and *c*.2,400 in the 1984 survey. Of the various questions asked, what seems the most central was the following: which governments or regimes governed or govern the country best? The answers to this in percentage terms are set out in Table 2.

Table 2 Preferred governments in Portugal

	1978	1984
Salazar	7	11
Caetano	28	24
Provisional governments (1974–6)	12	5
PS (1976–7)	9	4
PS–CDS (1977–8)	—	0.5
Presidential governments (1978–9)	—	9
AD (1979–80)	—	13
AD (1980–3)	—	0.5
PS–PSD (1983–5)	—	6
Don't know/none	31	19
No response	13	7
Total	100	99

The first survey was mounted when the experience of constitutional democratic government had been extremely brief, a mere two years. At that stage 35 per cent of respondents opted for the authoritarian regime, and 44 per cent were either unable or unwilling to pronounce. This left only 21 per cent who were prepared to commend governments since the 1974 transformation, of which less than half (9 per cent) applauded the sole constitutional government of that period. By 1984 the picture had changed in respect of approval of parliamentary government. A total of 33 per cent were now prepared to opt for one or other of the constitutional governments. Of this number the largest component endorsed the brief Sa Carneiro administration of 1979–80. But the continuing affection for the dictatorship still commanded 35 per cent of the sample, and 26 per cent refused to make a judgement. If this evidence suggests not only the lack of great change in the political culture but also some mild grounds for optimism, that would seem to fit with the analysis elsewhere in this chapter that democratic consolidation in Portugal is a lengthy process and one still incomplete.

Conclusion

How far in fact does this review of the Portuguese case represent democratic consolidation? It may be said that, after more than a decade in which constitutional propriety has been observed, a new party system has become established despite its instabilities. Also, no signs of destabilization of the regime have manifested themselves, so it has to be allowed that there is some conclusive evidence of regime consolidation. What is less certain is how far this signifies the achievement of a well-functioning democracy, with wide popular support. It will therefore be instructive to see whether public attitudes will change if the present PSD government succeeds in completing a full parliamentary term and in providing the first experience so far of settled party administration. Such a development would no doubt further promote democratic consolidation, given that a persistent weakness of the new democracy has been over government performance.

It is of course not merely a matter of public attitudes which determines whether or not a polity is a genuine example of fully partici-patory democratic government and politics. For popular acquiescence may simply echo the claims of the political and managerial elites. If we refer back to Gaspar's characterization of the parties in relation to the political culture, the question becomes – has the socio-political realm evolved to a point where the parties are the mainspring of political action and directly derived from the autonomous participation of a politically aware citizenry? Or is it rather the case that the parties remain a secondary manifestation of a social structure which has not reached the stage of universal emancipation from paternalism and clientelism?

A confident verdict on this seems impossible after less than a decade and a half of political transformation from authoritarian rule in relation to a society which is still unmodernized to a large extent. Politics in Portugal still appears primarily an affair of elites whose position is defined other than by political action, office, or career. Access to posts in the higher echelons of public life still seems to be restricted to long-term members of the 'political class'. No system is immune to this feature, but what counts is its relative salience. Perhaps by the end of the century it will be possible to measure some solid progress towards a political culture in which modern characteristics prevail over traditional ingredients. But for that to be achieved, considerable social change, above all in the sphere of public education, will need to have taken place.

Acknowledgement

Support for part of the research which informs this chapter was generously provided by the Nuffield Foundation.

Notes

1. J. Aguiar, 'Hidden fluidity in an ultra-stable party system', Conference paper on Modern Portugal, University of New Hampshire, 1984. Joaquim Aguiar was political analyst to the President of the Republic, 1976–84, and author of *A Ilusao do poder: Analise do Sistema Partidario, 1976–82*, Lisbon, Publicacoes Don Quixote, 1983.
2. Although the study does not include Portugal, parts of the analysis in Nicos Mouzelis, *Politics in the Semi-Periphery, Early Parliamentarism and Late Industrialisation in the Balkans and South America*, Basingstoke, Macmillan, 1986, could be applied to the Portuguese case from *c.* 1890 to *c.* 1930.
3. Interview in April 1980 with Jorge Gaspar, co-author of *As Eleicos do 25 de Abril: Geografia e Imagen dos Partidos*, Lisbon, Livros Horizontes, 1976.
4. See Sunday Times Insight Team, *Insight on Portugal*, London, André Deutsch, 1975; J. P. Faye (ed.) *Portugal: The Revolution in the Labyrinth*, Nottingham, Spokesman Books, 1976; R. Harvey, *Portugal, Birth of a Democracy*, Basingstoke, Macmillan, 1978.
5. Recent works are H. Gil Ferreira and M. W. Marshall, *Portugal's Revolution: Ten Years On*, Cambridge, Cambridge University Press, 1986; M. Kayman, *Revolution and Counter-Revolution in Portugal*, London, Merlin Press, 1987.
6. Ferreira and Marshall, op. cit.
7. See D. Wheeler, *Republican Portugal: A Political History*, Madison, Wisconsin University Press, 1978; V. de Braganca-Cunha, *Revolutionary Portugal, 1910–36*, London, James Clarke, 1937.

8. See P. C. Schmitter, 'The impact and meaning of elections in authoritarian Portugal 1933–74', in G. Hermet *et al.* (eds), *Elections without Choice*, Basingstoke, Macmillan, 1978.

9. Discussion of this potential contradiction of motives has been curiously muted in the commentaries. T. C. Bruneau insists that the Socialist ambitions were 'not an abstract statement', but he nevertheless stresses that the system is liberal democratic: 'Continuity and change in Portuguese politics', *West European Politics*, April 1984, vol. 7, no. 2. T. Gallagher similarly contends that Article 2 was 'no mere pious generalization', but he also emphasizes that what has evolved is a 'multi-party democracy': *Parliamentary Affairs*, 1985, vol. 38, no. 2, pp. 202–3.

10. Reproduced from D. Corkill, 'Portugal's political transformation: the election of July 1987', *Parliamentary Affairs*, 1988, vol. 41, no. 2.

11. R. Robinson, *Contemporary Portugal*, London, Allen & Unwin, 1979, p. 250.

12. ibid., p. 253.

13. T. Gallagher, *Portugal: A Twentieth Century Interpretation*, Manchester, Manchester University Press, 1983, p. 240.

14. Corkill, op. cit.

15. See Corkill, op. cit.; T. Gallagher, 'Goodbye to revolution: the Portuguese election of July 1987', *West European Politics*, 1988, vol. 11, no. 1; M. Hudson, 'Portugal opts for reform', *World Today*, November 1987, vol. 43, no. 11.

16. See D. Porch, *The Portuguese Armed Forces and the Revolution*, London, Croom Helm, 1977.

17. Gallagher, *Portugal*, op. cit., p. 240.

18. Gallagher, *Portugal*, op cit., pp. 125–9. The most notable clerical opposition to Salazar was that of the Bishop of Porto, Antonio Ferreira Gomes, who spent ten years in exile from 1959 to 1969.

19. T. C. Bruneau and A. MacLeod, *Politics in Contemporary Portugal*, Boulder, Colo., Lynne Rienner, 1986, pp. 113–15.

20. W. Opello, 'The continuing impact of the old regime on Portuguese political culture', in L. Graham and D. Wheeler (eds) *In Search of Modern Portugal*, Madison, Wisconsin University Press, 1983, p. 216.

21. Gallagher, *Portugal*, op. cit., p. 248.

22. B. de Sousa Santos, 'Social crisis and the state', in K. Maxwell (ed.) *Portugal in the 1980s*, New York, Green Press, 1986, p. 178.

23. W. Opello, 'The Portuguese political elite: social origins and political attitudes', *West European Politics*, 1983, vol. 6, no. 1.

24. Gallagher, *Portugal*, op. cit., p. 249.

25. H. Makler, 'The consequences of the survival and revival of the industrial bourgeoisie', in Graham and Wheeler, op. cit.

26. This emerged strongly from interviews with industrialists in Porto, April 1987.

27. Gallagher, 'Goodbye to revolution', op. cit. Bruneau had previously made the same point in 'Continuity and change', op. cit.

28. Aguiar puts the point in the following terms: 'the party system behaved as if it were an extreme pluralism, with centrifugal strategies and non-moderate

policies – although the electorate remained fairly stable and the policies turned out to be, in practical terms, much more moderate than initially announced', 'Hidden fluidity', op. cit.

29. See N. Blume, 'SEDES: an example of opposition in a Conservative authoritarian state', *Government & Opposition*, summer 1977, vol. 12.
30. W. Opello, *Portugal's Political Development*, Boulder, Colo., and London, Westview Press, 1985, p. 100.
31. Bruneau and MacLeod, op. cit., chs 3 and 4.
32. The extremely casual organization of the CDS, even in Lisbon and Porto, is apparent to anyone visiting their party offices.
33. Opello, *Portugal's Political Development*, op. cit., pp. 97–100.
34. Bruneau and MacLeod, op. cit., ch. 8.
35. W. Opello, 'Electoral behaviour and political militancy', in L. Graham and H. Makler (eds) *Contemporary Portugal: The Revolution and its Antecedents*, Austin, University of Texas Press, 1979.
36. Opello, *Portugal's Political Development*, op. cit., p. 109.
37. For reviews of the dual literature see B. Pollack and J. Taylor, 'The transition to democracy in Spain and Portugal', *British Journal of Political Science*, 1983, vol. 13, no. 2; K. Gladdish, 'From autocracy to party government: interpreting regime changes in Spain and Portugal', *West European Politics*, July 1985, vol. 8, no. 3.
38. N. Bermeo, 'Redemocratisation and transition elections', *Comparative Politics*, 1987, vol. 19, no. 2.
39. See note 3.
40. Maria Jose Stock has however studied the party end of the equation in *Os Partidos Em Congresso 1981*, Evora, ISESE, 1985, and *Os Partidos do Poder Dez Anos Depois do 25 de Abril*, University of Evora, 1986.
41. See K. Gladdish, 'Political change in Portugal in the 20th century: succession in a transitional society', Freiburg, ECPR Planning Session on Political Succession, 1983.
42. Wheeler, op. cit., p. 73.
43. Produced by the Director-General of Adult Education, September 1981.
44. J. Cravinho, 'The Portuguese economy', in Maxwell, op. cit., p. 113.
45. ibid., p. 114. This tiny residue had presumably passed the test explained to me by the PSD vice-president, Porto, in April 1987, i.e. those who could prove they had spent a year trying to find work could claim 7,500 escudos per month (*c.* £9 per week).
46. Aguiar, 'Hidden fluidity', op. cit.
47. B. de Sousa Santos, in Maxwell, op. cit.

Chapter six

Regime consolidation in Spain: party, state, and society

Richard Gillespie

Transition and consolidation

Spain's process of democratic consolidation in the 1980s has proven at times to be one of the most hazardous of recent southern European experiences. Colonel Tejero's dramatic invasion of the Cortes in February 1981 illustrated the fragility of the new regime, which has also been challenged by the violence of the Basque separatist organization, ETA. Yet though political violence has persisted, the consolidation of the post-Franco regime has advanced during this decade, and as it has done so the character of Spain's democracy has become more evident.

Possessing several of the traits of Italy's *partitocrazia*, such as the abuse of power by governing parties, their penetration of the state, and unsupportive attitude toward independent popular organizations, Spain none the less initially differed from post-war Italy by having a less problematic 'Communist Question' to complicate the process of democratic consolidation. Unlike Italy, moreover, Spanish democracy has thus far managed to maintain single party government. Indeed, for much of the 1980s the Spanish Socialist Workers' Party (PSOE) has been an extremely dominant party, with no clear alternative emerging to challenge it. However, a decade after the first post-Franco elections the party system was still evolving and with the Socialists' popularity eventually declining, it was by no means certain that the 'predominant' character suggested by the general election results of 1982 and 1986 would be confirmed at the following election (see Table 3).

In Spain the issue of one-party predominance was central to the discussion of democratic consolidation, with many holding the liberal view that the existence of a viable alternative to the government was necessary if one were to regard the democratization process as complete. Certainly the post-Franco period has seen a succession of failed attempts to develop an effective centre-right political party. Antagonistic interests and personalities played their part in this failure, as did the political division of the economic elite when confronted with

126

Table 3 Spanish general election results

Party	1977		1979		1982		1986	
	votes[a]	seats	votes[a]	seats	votes[a]	seats	votes[a]	seats
PSOE	29.3	118	30.5	121	48.4	202	44.1	184
AP (CD, CP)	8.3	16	6.0	9	26.5	107	26.0	105
UCD	34.4	166	35.0	168	6.7	11	—	
PCE (IU)	9.4	20	10.8	23	4.1	4	4.6	7
CDS	—	—	—	—	2.8	2	9.2	19
CiU	2.8	11	2.7	8	3.7	12	5.0	18
PNV	1.6	8	1.5	7	1.8	8	1.5	6
HB and EE	0.9[b]	1[b]	1.4	4	1.4	3	1.7	7
Others	13.3	10	12.1	10	4.3	1	7.9	4
Total	100.0	350	100.0	350	100.0	350	100.0	350
Abstention	21.4		32.0		20.0		29.0	

Key: PSOE: Socialist Party; AP: Popular Alliance; CD: Democratic Coalition; CP: Popular Coalition; UCD: Union of the Democratic Centre; PCE: Communist Party; IU: United Left; CDS: Democratic and Social Centre; CiU: Catalan centre-right nationalists; PNV: Basque centre-right nationalists; HB: Basque pro-ETA nationalists; EE: Basque left party.
Sources: H.R. Penniman and E.M. Mujal-León (eds), *Spain at the Polls, 1977, 1979, and 1982; Cambio 16*, 30 June 1986.
Notes: [a] Percentage of valid votes
[b] Only EE standing

democracy, and the way in which centre-right ideological unity has been undercut by the vitality of regionalist forces. Regionalism itself provided a further obstacle to democratic consolidation. For whereas in most countries the powers of regional governments would have no bearing on the survival of a democratic regime, in Spain there is important interaction between these meso and macro levels. Regionalism here has a separatist, violent, and even a revolutionary dimension and the army, unaccustomed to democracy, sees its prime duty as being to resist this threat, military tradition dictating that it maintain the country's territorial integrity and Madrid's authority.

The character of regime consolidation has of course been much influenced by the character of the transition to democracy. Consensus at elite level was crucial to the smoothness of the post-Franco transition. Under growing pressure from below, a decisive part of the old Francoist establishment came to see that 'Francoism after Franco' was impossible. Meanwhile, there was sufficient realism in the Communist and Socialist leaderships for them to appreciate that the left in the 1970s could not alone impose a democratic regime. While both neo-Francoism and the idea of a *ruptura democrática* were frustrated, the reform process undertaken by Adolfo Suárez was swiftly fortified by an experience of consensual decision-making which involved the consultation of party leaders over the new Constitution and pressing socio-economic matters.[1] The party most credited with this process, Suárez's Union of the Democratic Centre (UCD), has been characterized as 'consociational' in that it stood for the regulation of conflict according to the quantitative and qualitative strengths of the various political and social actors.[2] Never a cohesive party, however, the UCD proved incapable of tackling the important problems confronting it following the adoption of the new Constitution in 1978. In 1981–2 it underwent the fastest disintegration of any comparable party in post-war Europe, leading what was left of it to accept dissolution in 1983.

From this early post-Franco phase, Spanish political life retained a number of features. Although trade union self-restraint should not be forgotten as a factor facilitating the success of the consensual approach,[3] the initiatives over regime development came essentially from the party leaders, and their dominance remained pronounced in the 1980s. Moreover, the pursuit of inter-party consensus became a feature of the early years of Socialist government from 1982. A further constant was the appeasement of potentially hostile *de facto* powers, such as the army, the police, and the bureaucracy; in practice this tended to undercut the promise of progressive change made by the PSOE in its electoral programme. However, the 1980s have witnessed an important development in that, although the main parties have remained united in their repudiation of *golpismo* and terrorism, they have become more competitive now that most of the basic constitutional questions have been settled. And what is more, the dominance of the 'political class', as politicians collectively are known in Spain, has begun to be challenged by both traditional and new social movements which feel disappointed, particularly by the Socialist Party in which many left-wingers had hitherto deposited their hopes.

It is not easy to be categoric about when the Spanish transition ended and consolidation began, chiefly because for a time the two processes were evidently simultaneous. Using definitions offered by Maravall and Santamaría, one can regard consolidation as beginning at least as early as 1979, when the first government was elected on the basis of the Constitution promulgated the previous year. Following Kirchheimer, these scholars define democratic consolidation in terms of

> guaranteeing the necessary conditions for the regime's regular functioning, its autonomy and reproduction. It requires the institutionalization of the regime's norms and structures, the extension of its legitimacy, and the removal of the obstacles that, in its initial phases, make its establishment difficult.[4]

The period of consolidation commences 'once the basic institutions of the new political order are organized and begin to work and to interact according to new rules of the game'; it ends after 'legal-formal institutionalization' has led on to 'political-material institutionalization'. Generally a lengthy process, consolidation is regarded by these authors as embracing four processes: the emergent regime's elimination, reduction to a minimum or incorporation of its initial ideological and institutional inconsistencies; the establishment of its autonomy *vis-à-vis* the old established powers, especially the armed forces; its mobilization of civil society into political forms of expression; and its development of a relatively stable party system, capable of guaranteeing popularly accountable government.[5]

On this basis, one certainly cannot regard the Spanish transition as ending in 1979, for by then the territorial restructuring of the state was defined only in the broadest outline. Not until 1983 was the mainland map of regional 'autonomous communities' finalized, the statutes governing the powers of the main regional governments having been negotiated individually between 1979 and 1982. The incomplete application of these statutes thereafter constituted an obstacle to democratic consolidation, especially in the Basque case where disagreement over the legitimacy of the new territorial structure and its respective powers provided Spain with a significant anti-system party in the form of the pro-ETA Herri Batasuna alliance. Yet psychologically, for many Spaniards, 1982 was the decisive year when the transition symbolically ended and consolidation advanced significantly. By achieving 'the peaceful rotation of previous opposition parties in power', Spain passed a 'critical threshold' in democratization.[6] The election of that year was virtually a plebiscite through which democratic rule was endorsed and *golpismo* condemned.[7] With the UCD and Communist parties to its right and left in crisis, the PSOE was seen by many as the only party capable in office of consolidating democracy definitively. Of course, it would be a mistake just to credit one particular party with such a complicated achievement; yet undoubtedly progress has been made since 1982 and in part this can be attributed to government initiatives and achievements.

Parties and the state

With the important exception of the regional question, Spain's post-Franco constitutional settlement has been surrounded by considerable political consensus. In contrast to Portugal, constitutional reform has not been an issue for the major Spanish parties. Acceptance of the monarchy has been enhanced by repeated demonstrations of King Juan Carlos's support for the Constitution, most crucially on the night of 23 February 1981. And there has been less friction than in Greece over issues likely to upset Church–state relations. Certainly there was Catholic Church opposition to legislation on divorce (1981), abortion (1983), and education (1984), but subsequently there was no great movement of Catholic conservatives demanding a return to the *status quo ante*. Today the Church is too divided politically to constitute a serious challenge to a democratic regime, as it was in the 1930s, while on the left traditional anti-clericalism has been undermined both by partial liberalization within the Church and by the entry into the PSOE of a growing proportion of religious believers (up from 39 per cent of the membership in 1980 to just over 50 per cent by 1986).[8]

The constitutional settlement is questioned only by the micro-nationalist political forces of the Spanish periphery. Of concern to some observers has therefore been the rise in the Basque and Catalan nationalist votes. However, by far the most popular regional forces have been the more moderate parties, such as the Basque Nationalist Party (PNV) and Catalan Convergence and Union (CiU). Under the first administration headed by Felipe González (1982–6), there were some improvements in relations between Madrid and the regional governments headed by these parties, and Catalan nationalism anyway has weaker separatist tendencies than Basque nationalism. In the Basque case, PNV relations with central government improved following the downfall of Carlos Garaikoetxea as *Lehendakari* (regional president) in December 1984, and his replacement by José Antonio Ardanza. When this power struggle eventually split the PNV in September 1986, a period of instability ensued during which it proved difficult to form a viable regional government. At this time various Basque parties made distinctly ambiguous declarations regarding the existing level of regional autonomy, and although a regional coalition was finally formed by the PNV and PSOE in February 1987, it would appear that Madrid's decision to drop the more draconian clauses of the 1985 Anti-Terrorist Act was a precondition.

Despite the second González government's transfer of most of the remaining powers to which the region is legally entitled, with the aim of removing one nationalist grievance, the Basque Country is likely to remain the Achilles' heel of the post-Franco regime. For here the anti-system Herri Batasuna, which increased its vote in the regional election of late 1986, has some capacity to destabilize political life by suspending its traditional policy of not occupying the seats it wins in Vitoria or Madrid. Its first parliamentary intervention came during the Basque governmental crisis of early 1987 when it threatened to contribute its regional deputies to any blocking manoeuvre that was necessary to prevent the PSOE from acquiring the post of *Lehendakari*. On the other hand, ETA suffered some serious military setbacks during this period, mainly as a result of co-operation between the Spanish and French authorities.

While the constitutional settlement thus commands widespread support among the major Spanish parties, certain anti-democratic tendencies persist in the military and in public administration. In the case of the former, much progress has been achieved since 1982 in relation to democratic consolidation and there has been no major coup attempt since February 1981. The public outcry against the military rebels served to deprive *golpismo* of its lingering legitimacy, as did the decisive intervention of the King on that occasion. The televised images of Colonel Tejero's violent intrusion into the Cortes presented the public with a salutary shock that left many Spaniards more supportive of the new regime. For some 'democracy' had been associated with economic hardship and political violence, but a glimpse of a real anti-democratic alternative sufficed for most Spaniards to confirm their commitment to the new regime. This experience, and the retirement of the last batch of officers who participated in the 'Crusade' of the 1930s, are examples of consolidation developing independently of party initiatives. However, the latter were also crucial. The first Socialist government did much to reconcile the military with the new regime: by simply demonstrating that they could govern (unlike the weak preceding UCD administration), by taking firm disciplinary action against outspoken *golpistas*, by greatly increasing military expenditure in order to modernize the armed forces, by bringing military pay into line with that of civilian counterparts, by enacting military reforms that subordinated the men in uniform to civilian ministers, and through its limited successes in its dealings with regional governments and the fight against ETA.[9] Meanwhile, the PSOE's volte-face over membership of NATO was calculated, among other things, to democratize military thinking through international contact. None the less the domestication of the military was a slow process, in no way helped by the high levels of self-recruitment and inter-marriage among military families, which maintained the officer corps as a caste apart.[10] González awaited re-election in 1986 before moving to rehabilitate democratic officers who had been purged from the army in the mid-1970s, and a revision of military training programmes was not contemplated until towards the end of his second administration.

While some progress is evident in the case of the military, the civil service has proved resilient to change. Here some encroachment on the traditional powers of the old *cuerpos* was implied by Socialist legislation (the *Reforma de la Función Pública*) that increased the government's role in making appointments. However, successful bureaucratic opposition to change has meant that even the Socialist regulations stipulating that civil servants should work full office hours have not been effective. Civil service reform is the key to the success of a number of other reforms (e.g. of the health service), yet it was delayed by the Socialists for fear of disruption during their early years in office. Resorting instead to co-optation and patronage, the Socialists filled about 25,000 administrative posts between 1984 and 1987, having in 1982 estimated that only 4,000 political appointments would be made.[11] Associated with this trend were demonstrations of the *patrimonialismo* that the PSOE had accused the UCD of in the past. The use of state resources for party purposes has been most obvious in the case of television, but there was also apparent discrimination when it came to the allocation of public meeting places during the NATO referendum campaign in 1986.[12]

Although colonization and partisan penetration of the state were sanctioned by the political culture of the Franco era, they were rather alien to what had been promised by the Socialists while they were in opposition. The continuities in the style of Spanish politics led to much liberal criticism of the PSOE, while some disillusioned left-wingers even spoke about there being a 'Mexicanization' of political life, a charge that had also been made under the preceding UCD administrations. What were being criticized were abuses of power and certain institutional devices that were unconducive to fair party competition. Both the electoral law and the system of state financial subsidies for parties favoured the major political parties, while placing obstacles in the path of the minor parties' development. The PSOE was able to take full advantage of these arrangements, both because of its effective quasi-Leninist internal discipline, which made it appear united at election time, and because its massive voting appeal gave it absolute control over the two Houses of Parliament.

Opposition parties, often crippled by their own internal problems, have also found it difficult to oppose the government constructively as a result of the way in which Parliament is organized. The quality of debate is adversely affected by strict internal party procedures and by parliamentary regulations that ensure that the official spokesmen of the parliamentary groups dominate the agenda. Government dominance was further reinforced in 1985 by a Constitutional Tribunal ruling that the opposition's use of 'prior appeals' against bills, to prevent them becoming law, was unconstitutional. Exacerbating this situation has been the government's contemptuous attitude toward opposition bills. These have been ignored, regardless of their intrinsic merits. As with the UCD before them, a 'winner takes all' attitude has prevailed among the Socialist leaders, and the prestige of the Cortes has suffered as a result. A sign of this tendency was González's absence from it for a full seven months prior to the 'state of the nation debate' in February 1987. The less prestigious of the two chambers is the Senate, where the autonomous communities currently have only token representation, though there is some support for a 'federalization' of the existing government structures.

None the less the behaviour of opposition parties towards the state invariably affects the process of democratic consolidation, as well as political stability more generally. Although detractors have occasionally questioned their commitment to the constitutional system, in practice both the Popular Alliance (AP) and the Communist Party (PCE) have done much to legitimize it. True, there have been some instances of AP apologetics on behalf of military subversives, as befitted a party seeking votes on the right, and Fraga's recommendation of abstention from voting in the NATO referendum in 1986 was potentially destabilizing; but overriding these postures has been the very presence of this 'natural party of authoritarianism'[13] within the system, which contributed to regime legitimacy in the eyes of many former Francoists.

The contribution of the Communists to the establishment of democracy is widely recognized, and during the consolidation phase their commitment has remained firm. However, it should be noted that the PCE's internal crisis of the early 1980s, which led to its fragmentation into three parts, had adverse consequences for the climate of industrial relations. The electoral slump of the official PCE in 1982 left the Workers' Commissions (CCOO) as the crucial remaining avenue for Communist influence; over the next few years militant industrial action and street mobilizations would be seen as the most effective means of undermining the prestige of Socialist governments, though of course the motives behind such activity were not solely political.

Thus to conclude this section, one can say that at the national level the 1980s has seen a reinforcement of the authority of elected civilian governments dominated by party elites. The most striking difference with the situation pertaining a decade earlier has been in the field of civilian–military relations. On the other hand, the further ascendancy of party elites has brought with it a different kind of questioning of the democratic credentials of the Spanish regime. Provisional characterizations such as 'Spain: conditional democracy'[14] have been invalidated, but both the institutional arrangements and an increased governmental resort to patronage for partisan purposes certainly make it difficult for oppositions to replace governments in Spain. However, the problem here is not simply a product of the characteristics of the Spanish regime. It also reflects the extraordinary electoral popularity of one political party and the internal incoherencies of its main rivals. And of course a radical change in electoral fortunes has already permitted one alternation of the parties in power in 1982.

Inter-party relations

Consensus politics have as a whole contributed to democratic consolidation in the 1980s, though perhaps to a lesser extent than to which the Moncloa Pact eased the transition to democracy in the later 1970s. In the aftermath of the 1981 coup attempt the UCD and PSOE closed ranks, reaching a series of agreements on how best to undermine support for *golpismo*. The main outcome of these was the LOAPA, a law designed to suspend the extension of regional autonomy. There was also a PSOE offer to join a coalition, but this was declined by the UCD. Since the UCD was well on the way to disintegration, this collaboration did not last long, but it did help to stabilize the political situation at a crucial moment. Meanwhile, there had for several years been co-operation between the PSOE and PCE of a pragmatic kind, confined to the municipal level. The Socialist leaders had no desire for a return to the politics of the *Frente Popular*, and their agreement with the Communists to achieve left-wing control of the major cities came after the local elections of 1979 and not before. This marriage of convenience would soon be affected by the PCE crisis, but in places it worked well, producing energetic local administrations with a record of municipal improvement.

Focusing more generally on the 1980s and above all on national politics, the most interesting inter-party relationship has been that between the governing PSOE and the opposition AP. The 1982 general election result left these as the principal forces at the national level, with over six-sevenths of the seats in the lower house between them. The party system became more polarized, if one compares the greater ideological distance between the PSOE and AP with that previously separating the UCD and PSOE. Yet at the same time the virtual disappearance of the UCD and the extremist forces from the party system reduced tensions that formerly had resulted from strong bilateral competition on both sides of the spectrum. Centripetal competition tended to be encouraged, even though AP often proved unresponsive to the logic of the system.[15]

On a few major issues, such as education and abortion, Fraga's party resorted to intransigent opposition – including street mobilizations, obstruction in the Cortes (for example over 4,000 amendments were tabled in response to the Socialists' education bill), and 'prior appeals' to the Constitutional Tribunal to delay the conversion of bills into legislation. Over the NATO referendum of 1986, it adopted tactics that other European conservative forces regarded as dangerous. Some feared that the call for a boycott could give victory to the anti-NATO camp: Spain might withdraw from the Alliance because an electorally inadequate party of the right saw in this tactic its only means of undermining the Socialist government.

One must set against these instances an important degree of PSOE–AP bipartisanship. The Socialists' liberal economic policies drew eulogies from the world of capital, where their industrial restructuring policies were commended in particular; it was even acknowledged that the PSOE was implementing unpopular job-cutting measures that AP could never have got away with.[16] The incumbent Socialists also drifted rightwards on key issues of foreign policy, further reducing the distance between government and opposition stances.[17] On key 'nationalist' issues, such as Gibraltar, there were successful efforts by the Socialists to develop a bipartisan approach, though of course there were other areas, such as Central America, over which there was obvious disagreement.

Having everything to gain from an 'unpresentable' right-wing party being its main electoral rival, the Socialists deliberately promoted AP, and especially Fraga, as the principal forces of Spanish conservatism. In December 1982 the Socialists decided to regard Fraga as if he were a British-style 'Leader of the Opposition'. The AP leader was given an official car, two secretaries, and an office, paid for out of the parliamentary budget. Early in 1984 Fraga decided to name a Shadow Cabinet, even though his standing in opinion polls never showed him to be gaining ground on the PSOE. Considerable consensus between Fraga and González was apparent during the 'state of the nation' debate in October 1985, when the opposition leader said there were 'many acceptable things' in the work of the government. It even seemed to some observers that AP was offering the Socialists help over winning the NATO referendum. This spectacle led leaders of the smaller parties to allege that a 'PSOE–AP' pact existed to avoid conflictive issues. And indeed there is some evidence of the two leaders having agreed upon a secret 'non-aggression pact' designed to keep Spain in NATO, and having reached consensus over similar 'matters of state' at meetings in October and November of that year.[18] Certainly by the following March Fraga was adopting a less accommodating public attitude over the referendum, but he was waging a low-key campaign around it.

The experiment in bipartisanship lost momentum following right-wing setbacks in the referendum and ensuing general election. After the June 1986 poll, AP's electoral partners in the Popular Coalition (CP) – the Christian Democratic PDP and right-wing Liberal Party – abandoned the conservative alliance to form their own parliamentary subgroups. This together with the fallout from AP factionalism signified for Fraga the loss of one-third of the 105 deputies who had been elected on the CP ticket. AP's financial situation became critical, leaving it not only more dependent on the bankers but also readier to reaffirm its loyalty to the political system, since the other means of economic salvation lay in government action to remove party debts. Fraga resigned as AP leader in December 1986, his attempt to construct a successful broad centre-right alliance having failed. This put an end to AP's standing as the official opposition party. Its parliamentary weight had declined, its new leader Antonio Hernández Mancha was not even a deputy, and the position of leader of the opposition had never really become institutionalized. The minor parties expressed pleasure at the ending of what they saw as the 'two-party fiction', designed to squeeze them out of the decision-making arena. However, they were soon to find that the main effect of AP's decline was a reinforcement of the dominance of the governing Socialists.

This brief survey of inter-party relations in the 1980s indicates some positive trends for democratic consolidation. There have been moves towards defining more clearly the relationship between government and opposition, though these have stopped short of institutionalization. Clearly there have been some periods when AP saw its future best served by becoming a responsible opposition and a credible, officially recognized alternative to the existing government. The parties that have felt excluded from consultation have been ones that, with the important exception of some regional nationalist forces, are unlikely to impede democratic consolidation, for they are not only small but also centre parties, and hence ideologically opposed to destabilizing the new political system.

These smaller parties seem likely to continue to play some role in the Spanish party system. The conservative dream of establishing a *gran derecha* is unlikely to materialize, given AP's own post-1986 decline and the obstacles to unity presented by *personalismo* and *protagonismo* in the various parties of the centre-right. Suárez, whose Social and Democratic Centre (CDS) became a party to be reckoned with in 1986, is still hated by Spanish conservatives and distrusted by the bankers, the Church, and the army; the old guard who were bypassed by Juan Carlos in 1976 still regard Suárez as something of an upstart, and the conservative right still feel that he betrayed them by legalizing the PCE the following year. Moreover, the ideological basis for a broad centre-right coalition is weakened by the strength of the regional parties: these may not be much less conservative than the Spanish right, but they are naturally incompatible with its inbred centralism. An attempt to launch a new, more progressive, conservative party, the Democratic Reformist Party (PRD) under the leadership of Miquel Roca, ended in complete failure at the 1986 general election, primarily because the conservative constituency in Spain remains largely centralist and antagonistic to the Catalanist base of the PRD.

Therefore, while consensus politics in the 1980s have facilitated democratic consolidation, this pattern has been fragile because of continuing instabilities in the party system itself. This problem will be explored more fully in the next section.

Parties and society

Leaving aside the regional dimension (which is examined elsewhere in this volume), there are two other important areas where Spain's democracy may be regarded as not yet completely consolidated, and both are to be found at the interface between parties and society. One is the structure of the party system, clues to whose identity have been provided by the results of four general elections between 1977 and 1986. And the other concerns the social 'rooting' of the parties: the extent to which Spanish society basically identifies with the main political parties and the regime that they represent.

Elections in Spain are still 'critical', not because their outcome is crucial to the preservation of the new regime as such, but rather because the results show the evolving party system to be still defying classification. Between 1979 and 1986, general elections suggested in turn the emergence of various different types of party system. That of 1982 for instance offered such varied images of the emerging party system that no consensus was possible among analysts: some emphasized the evidence of 'predominance' in the system, exercised by the PSOE, while others believed that a two-party or 'two-plus' party system was in the offing.[19] The tendencies in the development of the party system were in no way unilinear. However, on the basis of the election results themselves, and using Sartori's typology of party systems,[20] it is clear that the idea of an emergent two-party system is negated both by the large discrepancy between the electoral performances of the two leading parties and by their inadequate combined share of the total vote. From the 1982 election the two major forces emerged with 75 per cent of the votes, with the PSOE enjoying a lead of 22 percentage points over its nearest rival, the AP–PDP alliance. No confirmation of the 'two-party' thesis was provided in 1986 when, although the PSOE lead dropped slightly to 18 points, the two leading forces' joint dominance declined to 70 per cent of the votes. Minority representation grew, with twelve parties rather than ten winning seats in the Cortes. The success of the Social and Democratic Centre (CDS) – up from 2.8 to 9.2 per cent – allowed its leader Suárez and the new Communist-dominated United Left (IU) to proclaim the end of *bipartidismo imperfecto*, a development which they saw confirmed when the frustrated AP and its associated Popular Coalition entered into crisis after the election.

Mathematically the elections of 1982–6 suggested the emergence of a 'predominant' party system, for on both occasions the PSOE enjoyed a huge lead over its nearest rival and ended up with an absolute majority of the seats in both Houses of Parliament. However, still applying Sartori, a minimum of three consecutive general elections producing this kind of result is necessary before one can classify a party system as 'predominant', and after 1986 this eventuality seemed less likely. The Socialists' standing in surveys of voting intentions fell quite markedly and their decline was also registered in the results of the triple (municipal, regional, and European) election held in mid-1987. By mid-1988 the nature of the party system was still extremely unclear, for the PSOE's losses did not immediately translate into gains for their rivals; instead the camp of the undecided voters grew to more than 40 per cent of the total.

It should be noted that, although the party system has evidently not yet stabilized, there has been considerable consistency in electoral behaviour. The great turn in the evolution of the party system seen in 1982 owed more to party crises than to voter volatility.[21] Partly for this reason, democratic consolidation may still be achieved even without the stabilization of the party system to which Maravall and Santamaría attach importance. What is more crucial is that tendencies towards 'predominance' in the party system do not inhibit its development. For although some predominant systems may be reasonably democratic in practice, it is in their nature to create special obstacles to democratic consolidation. Some observers would go further than this to insist that the emergence of a coherent centre-right alternative to the PSOE is a *sine qua non* for democratic consolidation in Spain.[22]

It is still possible that the Spanish party system might stabilize on a basis suggested more by the election results of the 1970s than those of the early or mid-1980s.[23] But as Mario Caciagli has argued, even provisional classification is inadvisable: Spain's parties have a high potential for instability, having evolved more as institutional than as socio-political forces.[24] Antonio Bar has offered a total of seven reasons for the lack of party system consolidation: the newness of several of the parties, their lack of organizational consolidation and ideological differentiation, their lack of internal democracy, the popular mistrust of parties, the difficulties encountered in establishing stable inter-party alliances, the retention of autonomy by *de facto* powers, and the presence of an influential regional subsystem.[25] To these may be added two further causes of instability: (1) the political disunity of the economic elites, which has contributed to fragmentation of the opposition by their rather diffuse and tentative financial support for the forces of the right, with at times traditional, conservative parties and at others more modern, progressive parties being sponsored; and (2) the Socialists' attempt while in office to shed what remains of their old working-class image and acquire national, supra-class appeal.

Although one cannot therefore be categoric about the structure of the party system, it seems likely on the basis of the existing evidence that competition for the centre ground will continue to determine the evolution of the system.[26] This itself should prove beneficial to democratic consolidation, unless it were to involve the parties somehow becoming out of touch with an electorate that was growing more radical, alienated, or issue-conscious.

Here one must look beyond individual election results and examine the significance of the parties' weak 'rooting' in society. Survey evidence during the early period of Socialist government certainly pointed to democratic consolidation at a broad attitudinal level: democracy seemed more stable, was regarded in more positive terms, and by the end of 1984 only one-tenth of Spaniards expressed a preference for an alternative regime. The military establishment was deemed to have lost political influence and 70 per cent of Spaniards felt that a military coup was now less likely to occur.[27] In November 1985 the King in fact declared that Spain's democracy was at last 'consolidated'.[28] Yet some reason for doubt is provided by survey evidence of a progressive decline in the government's standing amidst increased social unrest both early in 1987 and in spring of the following year. Since this did not strengthen the standing of the opposition parties, there existed the hypothetical possibility that the unrest might acquire an anti-system dimension.

Clearly one cannot draw a firm conclusion from what may eventually prove to be passing phenomena. More serious meanwhile is the persistent low level of involvement in political parties and the reasons behind it. Although in the mid-1980s one in twenty-five adults claimed a current party affiliation and 10 per cent said they had belonged to parties in the past, the real party membership figures were rather lower.[29] A Centro de Investigaciones Sociológicas survey in March 1984 revealed a total of 440,000 Spaniards to be party members (i.e. just over 1 per cent). Some 75 per cent of the respondents said they never attended political meetings and 87 per cent said they never took part in political activity, even as sympathizers. Only 3 per cent regularly engaged in political activity and relatively few of them were women. Levels of political participation had been stationary over the previous four years.[30] A later survey found that the Spanish level of interest in politics (28 per cent) was 13 points below the EC average, and that only 4 per cent were politically involved.[31]

Even after two successful elections, through which it became a major dispenser of state patronage, the PSOE's membership was no higher than 215,000 in 1988 (the pre-government figure having remained at around 100,000). The involvement of women was disappointing – even though the proportion rose from 9 to 16 per cent between 1980 and 1988 – and anxiety was also felt about a membership weakness among the young.[32] A disappointing, unadventurous university reform and an unemployment rate of 43 per cent for the under-25s, who rarely qualified for social security, help explain various manifestations of youth disaffection. High unemployment of around 3 million by 1987 also sheds light on the very low levels of trade union membership: in total about 16.5 per cent of the work-force by the late 1980s.[33]

Of course, the rooting of democracy – including the implantation of participatory norms of political behaviour – tends to be a slow process anyway and in the Spanish case one should not forget the longevity of Franco's authoritarian regime with its suppression of these norms. Even if democratization had not coincided with economic recession, one should not have expected the relatively high levels of political interest and involvement of the transition period in 1977–8 to be maintained. For one thing, associations at that time were insufficiently prepared and organized to integrate those who wanted to join. It may even be the case that weak 'rooting', in the participatory sense, is an inevitable and perhaps lasting feature of democratization in a time of rapid modernization, when the communications media are already quite advanced so that party elites are therefore able to communicate with their electorates directly, with little mediation necessary on the part of the rank-and-file. If true, the party elites bear some responsibility for this state of affairs.

Without doubt, the parties have nevertheless attempted to build up mass memberships. Special mention should be made of the 1988

Socialist and Communist party congress decisions to encourage female participation by establishing quotas for the presence of women on deliberative party bodies. However, the left's approach to the 'new social movements' has tended to be one of developing supportive associations there rather than welcoming the emergence of independent non-party associations.

Even party-building has been hampered by the party leaders' near obsession with internal unity and 'coherence', especially since witnessing the advantage that these traits gave the PSOE in 1982. During the following years dissenting party members were either silenced or excluded. This was even largely true of the PSOE, a party previously regarded by many as a model of internal democracy. Scenes of virtual unanimity in policy votes and executive elections at Socialist Party congresses contributed to the party's public image of coherence, but they also made some Spaniards rather sceptical about democracy. The early years of Socialist government saw a decline in local branch activity to such an extent that one influential newspaper editor described the PSOE as simply 'a fabulous electoral machine and a political job centre'.[34]

Public cynicism concerning the parties was nurtured in particular by the way in which the two main parties adopted NATO referendum positions that were at odds with the real views of most of their members.[35] Indeed, the NATO volte-face was the key turning-point in the PSOE's loss of moral authority in Spanish political life. Contributing to this also was the party's increasing indulgence in clientelism, its arrogantly dismissive attitude towards criticism from other political forces, and several cases of corruption. But undoubtedly the major factor in losing the PSOE support on the left was the way in which it overrode very widespread anti-NATO feeling to secure its referendum victory, 'in the interests of Spain', by threats about the dire political and economic consequences of leaving, rather than by engaging in a debate about the country's defence needs. The referendum result was immediately conducive to stability, yet in the longer term the manner in which it was achieved may not be conducive to democratic consolidation, for it reinforced old feelings about the *clase política* being an elite apart, not representing the Spanish people.

Also of relevance here is the way in which the PSOE in the 1980s has adopted far more of an institutional approach to political activity. During the 1970s when socialism and democracy were the party keynotes, the PSOE's strategic discourse emphasized the need to reinforce parliamentary activity with social mobilization. The shift to a 'demobilizing' emphasis was a consequence of the party's move to the right, its assumption of office, and fears about provoking a further military intervention in politics. The PCE's evolution has been similar, at least to the extent of preferring controlled mobilizations to the 'assemblyism' that was associated with the Workers' Commissions in the mid-1970s. Thus the left parties, which one might expect to be most committed to promoting democratic participation, have tended to discourage participation of a spontaneous and uncontrolled nature.

Institutionalized participation, on the other hand, has been encouraged, and for a while it involved labour and employers' associations in broad agreements designed to shape social and economic policies. Even though these pacts, such as the Economic and Social Agreement (AES) signed in 1984, limited wage rises, they promised compensation to the unions in the form of job creation schemes, improved social security coverage, and so on. While such social contracts were in force, they contributed to democratic consolidation by regulating industrial relations and limiting the level of strikes and the social unrest that usually accompanies them (given the weakness of the unions). From the mid-1980s fresh agreements of this type proved more difficult to achieve, largely because of a deterioration in the relations between the Socialist government and the unions. With the González government committed to liberal economic policies and especially determined to make the Spanish economy more competitive so as to meet the challenges of EC membership from 1986, the labour movement found the government increasingly unsympathetic to its demands. Failing to fulfil its electoral promises in regard to job creation, the government presided over a rise in unemployment from 2.2 to 3 million between 1982 and 1987, while social security coverage for the victims in fact fell, to reach only 27 per cent of the unemployed. Although on paper the Socialists had strengthened the juridical position of the unions, and in this way had made a further contribution to democratic consolidation, the social cost of their industrial restructuring and economic policies proved too high to enable the government to maintain good relations with the more conciliatory union, the Socialist General Workers' Union (UGT). In addition to serving its own members' interests, the UGT's behaviour was influenced by the existence of a more militant rival in the form of the Workers' Commissions. Though it defeated the Commissions in the work-place elections of 1982 and 1986, a revival of the Communist-led union in some of the larger enterprises in 1986 encouraged the UGT to assert its independence of the government and of the PSOE, and indeed to campaign together with the CCOO from 1988 for a more socially oriented economic strategy.

While surveys have consistently shown unemployment to be considered Spain's major problem, voters have not tended to blame governments automatically for this phenomenon; there is broad recognition that job losses in certain traditional sectors of the economy are unavoidable. Yet the persistence of high unemployment may in the long run affect attitudes to the new regime, especially given that its predecessor provided more job security for workers and benefited from the economic boom of the 1960s. 'Under Franco we lived better' has been the sentiment of only a small nostalgic right-wing majority, but there is an economic basis for a broader alienation, especially among the young.

This is by no means the only policy area where government may appear unsympathetic to the ordinary Spaniard and in relation to which critical attitudes about the new regime have been expressed. The ministry least disturbed by the 'change' promised in 1982 has been the Interior Ministry, headed initially by José Barrionuevo. The democratic credentials, and hence the legitimacy, of the present regime have been called into question on several occasions as a result of incidents linked to this ministry. Cases of prisoners being tortured, dying, or in one case 'disappearing' have not been adequately investigated, and in March 1987 it was revealed that nineteen policemen accused of torture had not even been suspended by the ministry.[36] Ministry personnel have even been accused of involvement in the mysterious GAL death squad which in the mid-1980s killed a number of ETA suspects living in France.

Alienation from a regime is difficult to measure and of course apathy to some degree may be regarded as functional in a representative democracy. Apart from the survey evidence, electoral abstention levels and to a lesser degree strike data may be relevant in the long term. Abstention fell by 12 points between 1979 and 1982, but from 20 per cent in 1982 it rose to 29 per cent in 1986 (and 40 per cent in the NATO referendum). There is no long-term trend to be derived yet from this. Meanwhile annual data indicating the number of days not worked as a result of strikes do correlate industrial conflict with the absence of social agreements being in force in 1984 and 1987.[37] Alienation from the political system cannot be deduced from such data, but it would at least seem that general stability is enhanced when such agreements are in force.

Assessment

To what extent then has Spanish democracy been consolidated? Spain certainly passed a critical threshold of party alternation in office in 1982 and since that time the threat posed by an unintegrated army has declined, in part owing to certain initiatives by the party in office. However, it would be a mistake to regard democratic consolidation, in all its facets, as simply cumulative: progress may be interrupted or overturned by crises, or even fade through inertia. Undoubtedly there has been progress in relation to devolution, the military weakening of ETA (with French help), and the subordination of the military to civilian authority. Little progress has been made in relation to the parties and democracy more generally becoming rooted in society, despite – but also because of – the parties' central role in the post-Franco democratization process. And certainly the party system has not yet become stable, though as argued instability here need not in itself be an impediment to the process of consolidation.

The Socialists in office thus deserve some credit in respect of democratic consolidation, particularly for increasing governmental authority *vis-à-vis* the military. More open to criticism is the way in which they have downplayed the role of Parliament and failed to reform public administration. Moreover, as a party they have been over-preoccupied with unity and have discouraged criticism and open debate, both within and outside their ranks. The resort to clientelistic approaches to party development has disappointed many democrats. Yet change may come through an electoral weakening of the PSOE's tentative 'predominance' in the party system; Parliament, at least, might then acquire more vitality. At the same time, the social unrest of 1987–8 has led the Socialists to reflect upon existing political practices and to seek ways of tackling the growing problem of youth alienation.

Equally one must recognize that, even in a political system that offers many advantages to the governing party over its rivals, opposition parties have contributed to the process of democratic consolidation by avoiding the persistent use of confrontational and disruptive tactics. Against examples of such negative behaviour, one must weigh the examples of bipartisanship and a general readiness to adhere to certain 'rules of the game'. Thus the parties have made an important collective contribution to the continuing process of democratic consolidation. However, their political prominence should not be allowed to eclipse the contributions made by Spaniards more generally, both by means of major socio-economic groups such as the UGT and employers' CEOE, or directly through voting in elections and manifesting public opinion by peaceable demonstrations, petitioning, and other activities. All in all, while it would be premature to declare the process of democratic consolidation complete, there can be no doubt that in several respects the process has advanced significantly since the coup attempt of February 1981.

Notes

1. On the transition to democracy see especially D. Gilmour, *The Transformation of Spain*, London, Quartet, 1985, and P. Preston, *The Triumph of Democracy in Spain*, London, Methuen, 1986. For further bibliography see A. de Blas Guerrero, 'La transición democrática en España como objeto de estudio: Una nota bibliográfica', *Sistema*, 1985, no. 68–9,

pp. 141–8, and J.A. Gómez Yáñez, 'Bibliografía básica sobre la transición democrática en España', ibid., pp. 149–73.

2. C. Huneeus, *La Unión de Centro Democrático y la transición a la democracia en España*, Madrid, Centro de Investigaciones Sociológicas-Siglo XXI de Madrid, 1985, pp. 14–26.

3. A case for this is made in M. Guindal and R. Serrano, *La otra transición. Nicolás Redondo: El sindicalismo socialista*, Madrid, Unión Editorial, 1986. See also J.W. Foweraker, 'The role of labor organizations in the transition to democracy in Spain', in R.P. Clark and R.H. Haltzel (eds) *Spain in the 1980s*, Cambridge, Mass., Ballinger, 1987.

4. O. Kirchheimer, 'Confining conditions and revolutionary breakthroughs', *American Political Science Review*, 1965, vol. 59, pp. 964–74; J.M. Maravall and J. Santamaría, 'Political change in Spain and the prospects for democracy', in G. O'Donnell, P.C. Schmitter, and L. Whitehead (eds) *Transitions from Authoritarian Rule*, Baltimore, Md, Johns Hopkins University Press, 1986, part 1, p. 89.

5. Maravall and Santamaría, op. cit., p. 73.

6. P.C. Schmitter, 'An introduction to Southern European transitions from authoritarian rule: Italy, Greece, Portugal, Spain and Turkey', in O'Donnell *et al.,* op. cit., p. 9.

7. R. López Pintor, 'The October 1982 general election and the evolution of the Spanish party system', in H.R. Penniman and E.M. Mujal-León (eds) *Spain at the Polls, 1977, 1979, and 1982*, Durham, NC, Duke University Press, 1985, p. 296.

8. 'Encuesta', *El Socialista*, September 1986, no. 12, p. 8.

9. J. Hooper, *The Spaniards*, revd edn, Harmondsworth, Penguin, 1987, ch. 14; *Anuario El País 1986*, 1986, pp. 86–9.

10. J. Steele, 'By the Left, slow march', *Guardian*, 26 March 1987.

11. *El País*, 2 September 1982; 5 July 1987.

12. E. López-Escobar and A. Faus-Belau, 'Broadcasting in Spain: a history of heavy-handed state control', *West European Politics*, 1985, vol. 8, no. 2; R. Gillespie, 'Spain's referendum on NATO', *West European Politics*, 1986, vol. 9, no. 4. According to a *Guardian* review of Spain, 6 March 1987, some 65 per cent of Spaniards have television as their sole source of news.

13. B. Pollack and J. Grugel, 'Opposition in contemporary Spain: tradition against modernity', in Eva Kolinsky (ed.) *Opposition in Western Europe*, London, Croom Helm, 1987, p. 258.

14. See for example C. Abel and N. Torrents (eds) *Spain: Conditional Democracy*, London, Croom Helm, 1984.

15. Maravall and Santamaría, op. cit., pp. 100–8.

16. *El País*, 9 November 1986.

17. Gillespie, 'Spanish socialism in the 1980s', in T. Gallagher and Alan Williams (eds) *Southern European Socialism*, Manchester, Manchester University Press, 1989.

18. *El País*, 16/17 October 1985; 1 November 1985; 5 November 1985.

19. Pollack and Grugel, op. cit., p. 248; Maravall and Santamaría, op. cit., p. 103; E.M. Mujal-León and R. López Pintor, 'Conclusion', in Penniman and Mujal-León, op. cit., p. 314; R. Gunther, G. Sani, and G. Shabad, *Spain after*

Franco: The Making of a Competitive Party System, Berkeley, Calif., University of California Press, 1986, p. 104; Sani and Shabad, '¿Adversarios o competidores?: La polarización del electorado', in J.J. Linz and J.R. Montero (eds) *Crisis y cambio: Electores y partidos en la España de los años ochenta*, Madrid, Centro de Estudios Constitucionales, 1986, ch. 13.

20. G. Sartori, *Parties and Party Systems: A Framework for Analysis*, Cambridge, Cambridge University Press, 1976, especially chs 5 and 6.
21. S.H. Barnes, P. McDonough, and A. López Piña, 'Volatile parties and stable voters in Spain', *Government and Opposition*, 1986, vol. 21, no. 1.
22. P. del Castillo and G. Sani, 'Las elecciones de 1986: Continuidad sin consolidación', in Linz and Montero, op. cit., p. 642; F. Jaúregui, *La derecha después de Fraga*, Madrid, Ediciones El País, 1987, p. 9.
23. A. Bar, 'The emerging Spanish party system: is there a model?', *West European Politics*, 1984, vol. 7, no. 4.
24. M. Caciagli, 'Spain: parties and the party system in the transition', *West European Politics*, 1984, vol. 7, no. 2.
25. Bar, op. cit., pp. 131–4.
26. Maravall and Santamaría, op. cit., pp. 106–7. A Centro de Investigaciones Sociológicas survey found in 1986 that 62 per cent of the electorate saw themselves as being in the centre or on the centre-left or centre-right, with three to four times as many on the centre-left as on the centre-right (*Guardian* review, 6 March 1987).
27. Maravall and Santamaría, op. cit., pp. 101–2.
28. *El País*, 23 November 1985.
29. Maravall and Santamaría, op. cit., p. 105.
30. *El País*, 27 March 1984.
31. *El País*, 9 January 1985.
32. *El Socialista*, 15 October 1987, no. 438/9, p. 1; ibid., 31 December 1987, no. 444, p. 14.
33. *El País*, 29 May 1989.
34. J.L. Cebrián, 'Los vicios de la democracia española', *El País*, 21 February 1987.
35. Gillespie, 'Spain's referendum', pp. 240–4.
36. *El País*, 18 March 1987.
37. 'Guía completa de manifestaciones, huelgas y protestas', *Cambio 16*, 16 March 1987, no. 798.

Chapter seven

From polarization to pluralism: regional-nationalist parties in the process of democratic consolidation in post-Franco Spain

Ulrike Liebert

Introduction

If the consolidation of democracy consists mainly in a process of 'freezing-adaptation of modes of peaceful conflict-resolution',[1] we may tend to expect major problems produced by the proliferation of parties at the subnational level: fragmentation of political forces, increased conflictiveness, eventually polarization between them within the regional ambit, which could translate into a major fragmentation and even segmentation of the national party system. Such a party system, divided by centre–periphery cleavages, might also lead to instability and a lack of legitimacy of a new democracy.[2]

However, if democratic consolidation, rather, is primarily understood as a process of structuration of a variety of 'partial regimes' – 'networks of power among interdependent or hierarchically ordered institutions' – which promote 'satisfactory participation', 'account-ability to citizen preferences', and 'responsiveness of authorities to individuals and groups',[3] we will rather welcome a more complex, territorial, and political pluralism 'in order to reinforce commitment to the regional realities and to the democratic system'.[4]

Hence there may be conditions under which subnational parties may not only articulate the differentiated demands of regionally based electorates, but also channel their participatory claims, safeguard the accountability and responsiveness of government towards them, and mobilize regional support for the regime. In certain cases centre–periphery conflict may become polarized, lead to regionally based anti-regime opposition, and threaten the legitimacy of a new democratic regime, putting its very survival into question.

Spain, more than any other country in western Europe, and especially in southern Europe, has known these threats since the massive irruption of regional parties in the 1977, and particularly since the 1979 elections. The Spanish party system resembles other systems with respect to the role of class and religious divisions. But it differs considerably from most other European societies . . . in the extent to which centre–periphery cleavages are the source of political conflict – at the national level, between the culturally and linguistically distinct minorities and the Castilian majority, and even within the peripheral regions themselves.[5]

A national leader of the government party UCD characterized these threats of exacerbated centre–periphery conflict in 1981:

The fact that the Basque and Catalan party systems are different, and that we run the danger of an additional Galician party system, as well as of further Andalusian, of Canarian parties, opens the question if we are not in front of a radical crisis of the party system which could imply a crisis of the democratic system.[6]

The crisis of the party and the democratic system materialized with the collapse of the governing party UCD and the resignation of Prime Minister Suarez, and with the failed attempt at government formation by Calvo Sotelo and the military coup, all of which occurred in the first two months of 1981.

How far was this evident crisis of ungovernability indeed enhanced by regional-nationalist parties from the 'historical nationalities', Catalonia, and the Basque Country, or even from some of the 'new' regions, for instance Andalusia? And to what extent was the crisis and realignment of the party system in 1981–2 – itself a crucial development in democratic consolidation – due to the rise and decline of regional-nationalist parties which lacked a consolidated structure? Did regional-nationalist parties in fact engage in irresponsible mobilization of the regional populations, thus putting the stability of the democratic order in danger, as they were frequently accused of doing? Or, can we rather argue, on the contrary, that some of the regional-nationalist forces played a pertinent role not only in the process of structuration of the 'State of the Autonomies', but also with respect to the containment and regulation of centre–periphery conflict, or with respect to reinforcing citizen commitment to the new democratic institutions? These are some of the questions which come to mind if we try to analyse the process of democratic consolidation in Spain from a regional perspective. After more than ten years of democracy, and in spite of the doubts which the consolidation and the type of the Spanish party system still occasion, we may try to draw a balance.

This task, however, is complex. In part, we may draw on the available electoral data[7] and on classifications of territorially differentiated electoral behaviour which have been advanced recently.[8] How far are we allowed, however, to limit our consideration to the different, subnational electoral and party systems of the Basque Country, Navarra,

Catalonia, and Galicia? Do we not also have to include 'new' regions – like Aragon, the Canary Islands, the Balearic Islands, Valencia – in which relatively strong regionalist minorities emerged as oppositions, coalition partners, or even governing parties and were reinforced by the 1987 regional elections? Of course, the historical and cultural origins and differences between the 'old' and the 'new' regional-nationalist parties are important and can be explained. However, the main focus of the present study is on their role in the process of democratic consolidation.

The scope of the present contribution will necessarily be limited, due to the fact that there have been only four general and two or three series of regional elections, and also because there are gaps in the systematic comparative data available. But we will provide at least a framework of comparison, and develop some hypotheses. We will start with an account of the strategies of regional-nationalist parties with respect to the design, institutionalization, and functioning of the new state institutions. Then we will try to classify the different types of subnational party systems which have emerged in the seventeen 'Comunidades Autonomas' so far, and analyse their implications for conflict regulation. Finally, we will try to evaluate how far these parties have been able to penetrate regional societies, and have managed to consolidate themselves.

Regional parties and the state

After having been designed by the constituent legislature, the new state institutions in Spain at the central and regional level have experienced a conflictive period of implementation before entering the stage of 'normal functioning'. Regionalist and nationalist parties have to different degrees intervened, in some stage or the other, at the central, or only at the regional level. A pre-eminent role, of course, has been played in all stages and on both levels by the Basque and Catalan nationalists, which have been present in the Cortes since the first general elections in 1977. The strengthening of and the increase in the number of regional-nationalist forces in the 1979 elections, and – after their decline in 1982, in the aftermath of the military coup – their new successes in the 1986 general elections and in the two regional elections, are further indicators of the incidence of other regional-nationalist parties in the institutionalization of the new state institutions.[9]

In this highly conflictive and rather explosive process we may distinguish between a number of particularly crucial challenges: (1) parliamentary constitution-building (1977–8); (2) the constitutional referendum (December 1978); (3) the institutionalization of pre-regional governments (1977–8); (4) the containment of terrorist separatism; (5) the achievement of regional government by Catalonia, the Basque Country, Galicia, and Andalusia (1978–80); (6) the problem of governability (May 1980–February 1981); (7) regional-nationalist parties in opposition after 1982; (8) regional-nationalist parties in regional government.

The parties which successfully obtained seats in some of the four general and the two or three series of regional elections held up to now were in total twenty-two from twelve out of the seventeen autonomous communities. In particular, we can identify seven which were represented in the Cortes for only one or two legislative terms; four held representation during all legislatures. A third group of eleven regionalist or nationalist parties achieved representation only at the regional level after 1983 (see Tables 4 and 5).

At this point I intend to recapitulate the major strategies of some of these parties with respect to the aforementioned crucial 'challenges' which have brought about the new institutional structure of the Spanish state. These developments also mark the stage when the new Spanish democracy moved from transition to consolidation.

Parliamentary constitution-building (1977–8)

There were four principal regional-nationalist parliamentary groups which played an active role in the constituent legislature: 'Minoria Catalana' (MC), and the 'Grupo Nacionalista Vasco', both of which were flanked by one representative of the more radical-nationalist brand of Basque and Catalan nationalism, 'Euskadiko Ezkerra' (EE), and 'Esquerra de Catalunya'. The MC displayed an unambiguous, pro-constitutional position, while the Basque nationalists of the 'Partido Nacionalista Vasco' (PNV) maintained a somewhat more ambiguous position, and the two radical nationalist parties opposed the constitutional compromise, especially with respect to paragraph VIII of the Constitution on the 'territorial organization of the state'.

The party with the longest historical tradition, the Basque PNV (which was founded as early as 1892 and had formed the provisional Basque government at the end of the Second Republic), was with its eight seats in the Congress and one representative in the subcommittee which drafted the constitutional text, subject to severe pressures from its own base. In order not to be considered as 'espanolista', the PNV had to maintain throughout the constitutional debate an ambiguous position towards the Constitution by arguing that the legitimation of Basque autonomy could not come from the new Constitution, but only from the Basque 'historical rights', from its history and its ancient sovereignty.[10] In the final voting on the Constitution in October 1978, six of its eight deputies abstained, the other two were absent.

Table 4 Regional parties and coalitions in the various legislatures in Spain, 1977–88

	Represented in Congress legislatures	Represented in regional legislatures
(a) parties with permanent representation in the Cortes (Congress)		
Convergencia i Unio (CiU)	C, I, II, III	I, II, III
Partido Nacionalista Vasco (PNV)	C, I, II, III	I, II, III
Euskadiko Ezkerra (EE)	C, I, II, III	I, II, III
Herri Batasuna (HB)	I, II, III	II, III
(b) parties with limited representation in Congress		
Esquerra Republicana de Catal. (ERC)	C, I, II	II, III
Partido Aragones Regionalista (PAR)	I, III	I, II
Coalicion Galega (CG)	·	II
Partido Social. de Andalucia (PSA–PA)	I	I, II
Union del Pueblo Canario (UPC)	I	I
Agrupacion Independ. Canaria (AIC)	III	II
Union Valenciana (UV)	III	II
(c) parties with only representation in autonomic legislatures		
Union del Pueblo Navarro (UPN)	–	I, II
Partido Nac. Vasco/Navarra (PNV)	–	I
Euska Alkartasuna (EA)	–	II
Euskadiko Esquerra/Navarra (EE)	–	II
Herri Batasuna/Navarra (HB)	–	I, II
Partito Socialista de Mallorca (PSM)	–	I, II
Unio Mallorquina (UM)	–	I, II
Bloque Nacionalista Galego (BNG)	–	I, II
Esquerda Galega (EG)	–	I, II
Partido Regionalista de Cantabria (PRC)	–	I, II
Extremadura Unida (EU)	–	I, II
Partido Regionalista/Rioja (PRP)	–	I, II
Partido Socialista de Andalucia/ Catalunya (PSA)	–	I
Asamblea Majorera/Canarias (AM)	–	II
AC–INC	–	II

Source: Own elaboration of data provided by CIS, and *Anuario El Pais 1988*, pp. 130ff.

Table 5: Regional-nationalist parties in autonomic government in Spain

| Comunidad Autonoma | Government-formula in legislature | | |
	I	II	III
Catalunya	CiU-Minority	CiU-Majority	CiU-Majority
Basque Country	PNV-Majority	PNV-Majority	PNV-PSOE
Galicia		CG-PSOE	
Aragon		PAR-Minority	
Canarias		AIC-CDS-AP	
Baleares		UM-AP	

Source: *Anuario El Pais 1988*, pp. 140–1.

The only deputy of 'Euskadiko Ezkerra', a coalition of the radical nationalist and leftist EIA (Party of the Basque Revolution) with the Spanish leftist 'Movimiento Comunista de Euskadi', opposed the constitutional compromise and voted against it, maintaining an anti-system opposition similar to that of the Basque underground organization ETA. Both branches of the armed organization – 'militar' and 'politico-militar' – 'complemented' the legal activities of the Basque nationalist forces in Parliament with 'the most violent terrorist campaign ever realized from the beginning of its activity (in 1968) on'.[11] This intensification of terrorist activity reached its height in the year of the constitutional debates, 1978, when 107 people were killed. ETA's declared motive was 'to support through military means the negotiations with the government which should lead to the recognition of Euskadi's national sovereignty' (ibid.).

'Minoria Catalana', on the contrary, from the beginning showed a favourable attitude towards the constitutional agreement. MC comprised three Catalan electoral alliances – the centre-left 'Pacte Democratic per Catalunya' (PDC) – consisting of four groups, among them as nucleus the nationalist, Social Democratic 'Convergencia Democratica de Catalunya' (CDC), founded in 1974 by Jordi Pujol, with eleven deputies; the more rightist, Christian Democratic 'Coalicion Electoral Unio del Centre i la Democracia Cristiana de Catalunya' (UC-DCC) (a product of a pact between the historical UDC and 'Centre Catala') with two seats.[12] MC lost four of its initial thirteen members during the constitutional debates. In the final vote two of its remaining members abstained. The left-wing, nationalist 'Esquerra de Catalunya' (EC), which held one mandate, was the only one to vote against the Constitution.[13]

The constitutional referendum (December 1978)

In the campaign for the constitutional referendum, the PNV maintained its ambiguous stance and called for abstention. EE called explicitly for 'no to the constitution'. The 1978 newly constituted coalition of 'Herri Batasuna' – which included among more moderate socialist formations extremist separatist groups as 'HASI' and 'LAIA' – campaigned as well against the Constitution, defending either the 'no' position or abstention. The results of the referendum in the Basque Country only demonstrated the weak incorporation of the Basque community into the new Spanish political democracy: not even one-third of the Basques voted in favour of the new Constitution, more than 11 per cent were against it, and nearly 50 per cent of the electorate abstained. Subsequently the argument that 'Euskadi did not approve the Constitution' became of greatest political importance for negotiations over the regions.

In Catalonia, where the major nationalist forces campaigned in favour of the Constitution, the rate of abstentionism was only 23 per cent, hence much below the national average of 32 per cent.[14] Here only Esquerra Republicana de Catalunya had campaigned for abstention. In Galicia, where the 'Bloque Nacional Galego' had called for abstention, the rate of abstentionism was indeed the highest of all regions (46 per cent in Galicia-Asturias). To a large extent, this was due, however, to traditionalism and apolitical attitudes of the Galician population (ibid.).

The institutionalization of pre-regional governments (1977–8)

The institutionalization of pre-regional governments from 1977 onwards by governmental decree, provoked very different reactions on the part of regional-nationalist parties.

In the Catalan case, the symbolically important return of the 'historical' Catalan President Tarradellas from exile and his investiture as the head of the 'pre-autonomic Generalitat' as early as in 1977 reinforced the co-operation and integration of the parliamentary nationalist forces, even if they called into question the claim of Tarradellas that the 'spokesman' of Catalonia should be always its president.[15] For instance, the leader of CDC, Pujol, was one of the alternative proponents of 'efficient relations with the Spanish government' by means of political pacts.[16]

In the Basque case, on the other hand, the parliamentary nationalist parties found themselves excluded from this highly symbolic institution, given that UCD helped the Socialists to occupy the presidency of the pre-regional executive, which was created four months after the Catalan one. Marginalized from pre-regional Basque government, the Basque nationalists exploited public opinion and blamed the PSOE for being principally responsible for the insufficiencies of the regionalization process, the nature of which had little to do with the aspirations of a great part of the Basque population.[17] We can assume that the exclusion of the nationalist forces from pre-regional government may have constituted one source for the subsequent radicalization of the strong anti-centralist feeling in the Basque Country. Another outcome of this could have been even the reinforcement of separatist demands leading up to support for violent struggle.

Also in Andalusia, the regionalist mobilization pursued by 'Partido Socialista de Andalucia' benefited from the doubtful 'Andalusist' image of the first president of the pre-regional 'Junta de Andalucia', the Socialist Fernandez Viagas, who was in office from January 1978 to mid-1979.[18] As an effect of the electoral successes of PSA in 1979, the Socialists had to replace him by Rafael Escuredo who represented a current with a more regionalist–nationalist orientation within the Andalusian PSOE.

The containment of terrorist separatism

By 1977/8, the beginnings of terrorist separatism could be found in territories other than just the Basque Country, and regional-nationalist parties had to take positions with regard to their operations in public.

In Catalonia, from about 1968 until after 1979, a large number of groups emerged and dissolved

> without reaching their objective: to organize the sectors who totally rejected that Catalonia belongs to the Spanish state and who claim the independence of the 'Paisos Catalans' (Catalan countries). The more reformist separatist 'Nacionalistes d'Esquerra', for instance, gained 60,000 votes in the first and 40,000 votes in the second regional elections, without obtaining any seats. Catalan separatist armed groups – Terra Lluire; Independentistes dels Paisos Catalans (IPC), PSAN, and other minoritarian groups – since their emergence in 1979 were persecuted closely by the police forces and soon lost their logistical capacity and propagandistic impact. Radical separatism was incapable of implanting itself in the society or occupying institutional positions during transition.[19]

Neither did terrorist separatism succeed in the *Canary Islands*. Here the 'Movimiento por la Autodeterminacion y la Independencia del Archipielago Canario' (MPAIAC), which since its creation in 1963 in Algeria, had advocated armed struggle and committed a number of violent actions, split after the second general elections in 1979 into an internal and a foreign branch. The former renounced political violence. The impact of the latter was also greatly reduced, after it increasingly lost its international support.[20] This process was accelerated after the first elect-oral success of moderate Canarian nationalism in the 1979 elections.

In the *Basque Country*, the parliamentary nationalist parties had a more ambiguous position towards terrorist separatism, among other things influenced by public opinion there. The number of people killed by ETA reached its climax with more than 100 victims in 1978, and decreased somewhat in 1979 (nearly 80 victims). In the same year 40 per cent of the PNV voters held positive attitudes towards terrorists and considered them as 'patriots' or 'idealists'. Among the voters of EE, as many as 85 per cent shared the same view – the same proportion as in the case of HB voters. Even 46 per cent of the PSOE voters supported this attitude. By continuing to kill people after the failed military coup of 1981 ETA began to isolate itself from a widening sector of the Basque population. This is shown by the results of a second mass survey conducted in 1982: those who considered the terrorists as 'crazy' or 'criminals' had increased significantly from only 13 per cent in 1979 to 58 per cent in 1982. However, the share of those who described terrorists as 'patriots' or 'idealists' had, on the whole, remained nearly stable.[21] The most drastic change in attitudes occurred among the electorates of the PSOE, PNV, and EE.

The voters of PSOE, only 15 per cent of which had perceived terrorists as 'crazy' or 'criminal' in 1979, in 1982 rejected terrorism by a large majority (80 per cent); from the EE voters, 31 per cent had come to reject terrorists as 'crazy' or 'criminal' in 1982, compared to 0 per cent in 1979. Meanwhile, EE had clearly renounced any form of support for armed struggle, and thanks to its pressure, a conspicuous number of ETA's activists gave up their arms.[22]

Among PNV-supporters opponents of terrorism increased from 18 to 57 per cent; only within the HB electorate, the proportion of those who rejected terrorists as 'criminals' or 'crazy', was extremely low (6 per cent), while the share of those who believed them 'idealists' or 'patriots' had increased. At the same time, the leaders of Herri Batasuna pursued recognition of ETA as the nationalist movement's spokesman.[23]

Regional statutes and referenda in the 'historical nationalities' and Andalusia (1978–80)

The establishment of institutions in the various regions was influenced to very different degrees by regional-nationalist parties: in Galicia it was

dominated by the government party against the impotent protest of
leftist 'Nationalism'; in Catalonia it saw a consensus between nationalist and other parliamentary forces; in the Basque Country it took place
under the leadership of PNV and the pressure of radical nationalism and
led to highly controversial results; and in the Andalusian case, it was
guided by the left, under the pressure of Andalusian nationalism, and
occasioned a profound crisis of the Spanish government and helped the
beginning of a realignment of the Spanish party system.

In Galicia, UCD held an absolute majority and hence could follow its
own conception of a limited autonomy. The statutes were ratified
against the PSOE minority. The extreme leftist nationalist party
coalition BNPG, which had presented itself in the 1977 elections
without success, defended a maximalist, radical separatist position
towards the Constitution and the Galician statutes from its extra-
parliamentary position. Nevertheless, it remained completely impotent.
The call of BNPG for abstention in the regional referendum in
December 1980 may have reinforced, but by no means produced the
extremely low level of participation – only 28 per cent of the population
went to the polls.[24]

The consensus on the Catalan statutes embraced all parliamentary
forces, among which the Catalan Socialists PSC (PSC-PSOE) was
predominant, followed by UCD and – equally strong – CiU, and finally
the Communist PSUC. The ERC deputy, although rejecting the statutes,
in 1979 joined the campaign for the regional referendum. The process
was rich in polemics – for instance, with respect to 'Tarradellism',[25] but
did not give rise to a principled opposition.

In the Basque Country, EE, the second nationalist force, which
before had been one of the principled anti-constitutional forces, now
changed its attitude with respect to the autonomy statutes. Between the
approval of the new Spanish Constitution and the second general
elections in March 1979, EE moved towards a more moderate
nationalist, pro-institutional position, and accepted the opportunities for
regionalization, which had been opened by the Constitution. Hence the
assembly of Basque deputies, in which PNV and EE held a relative
majority *vis-à-vis* PSOE and UCD, approved the project of Basque
autonomy statutes only three weeks after the constitutional referendum.
Due to the effective threat produced by the results of the constitutional
referendum in the region, PNV was in the position to make all parties,
even the Spanish ones, accept its claims for far-reaching regional
powers, including the 'Conciertos Economicos' and its conception of a
potentially confederal model of the Spanish state.[26] The Basque regional
powers in these areas, which were also finally approved by the Cortes as
'organic laws', are hence significantly stronger than the Catalan or
Galician ones, thus raising the question of the 'harmonization' of the

rather different levels of autonomy. However, Herri Batasuna remained constant in its anti-institutional position and called for abstention in the referendum on the Basque regional statutes in October 1979. The Basque results, however – more than 40 per cent of abstentions, and 5 per cent of contrary votes – paradoxically resembled the Catalan ones, without any force having called here for non-participation or 'no'.[27]

Perhaps the most complicated route to regional government was the Andalusian one. The PSA, the first major regionalist–nationalist party in an area where no movement of this type had previously existed, was founded only in 1974 and did not obtain any notable success in the 1977 elections. Its leftist-regionalist programme, based on the claim for political autonomy similar in type and scope to the Basque and Catalan one, in order to develop the densely populated, but backward regional economy,[28] nevertheless attracted in the 1979 elections over 11 per cent of the regional votes, and made the dominant PSOE lose some points. This new regional constellation, as well as the five PSA deputies receiving group status in the Congress – *vis-à-vis* the UCD minority government, which was always in need of legislative support – created an unforeseeable dynamics. In a few months, under pressure from the PSA, a leftist-regionalist block was formed in Andalusia which pursued the rapid way to Andalusian government against the firm intentions of the UCD government. After having been obliged to cede to the Basque regional demands shortly before, the government decided to use all its means to block the Andalusian proposal which could have created a model for further regions. The government's call for abstention or 'no' in the regional referendum brought it into conflict not only with 'Andalucistas' and the parties of the left, but also with parts of its own Andalusian section. The desertion of some prominent Andalusian and ex-government members, and finally the defeat of UCD in the referendum, caused a deep crisis of the UCD.

The PSA, on the other hand, exercised together with the other regionalist and nationalist forces in Andalusia an important role with respect to the design of the regional structure of Spain. After the second regional referendum in October 1981, Andalusia was the fourth region after Catalonia, the Basque Country, and Galicia to have its own regional-elections, to acquire regional statutes with a constitutional status, and regional powers as broad as the Catalan ones. However, the PSA did not exercise this influence primarily by direct bargaining with central government, as the Catalan CiU or Basque PNV did. Given its size and newness, it had to resort to means of mass mobilization and put pressure on the Andalusian sections of the Spanish parties of the left. As soon as the PSA leadership tried to copy the style which CiU or PNV had used successfully, and to embark on the approach of pacting with the government, it faced severe conflicts with its own 'anti-centralist' base.[29]

Ulrike Liebert

The problem of governability (May 1980–February 1981)

With respect to the endemic problem of stability of the UCD minority governments between 1977 and 1982, the support of regional-nationalist parties in Parliament differed in degree, but none of them entered into government, neither CiU, PNV, nor PSA.

CiU tried deliberately to avoid giving the government 'the security of a numeric majority', but rather exercised pressure effectively by offering its support under conditions which were somewhat different each time.[30] But in contrast to the PNV or PSA, CiU declared from the beginning that it was principally 'obliged to participate in the formation of a stable and progressive majority in the Spanish government and parliament'.[31] Consequently it collaborated in the maintenance of UCD governments, be it by agreeing to abstain in the investiture of the Suarez government in March 1979, be it by supporting it by abstention over the motion of censure, which PSOE proposed in May 1980, be it with support in the motion of confidence, which Suarez introduced in September 1980 – always in exchange for special measures in matters of education, economic, or international affairs.[32] Minoria Catalana was the only nationalist minority which supported Calvo Sotelo in his attempt at forming a government in February 1981.

The five PSA deputies in Madrid showed their willingness to pact with and support the government, but were principally constrained by their Andalusian party members and leadership. Against the 'anti-centralist' and anti-governmental orientation of their party, they voted at least in favour of the investiture of Suarez after the 1979 elections, obtaining from him in exchange their own group status in the legislature. In the motion of censure in May 1980, however, in spite of being inclined to abstain 'in order to maintain a relation with UCD', the PSA group was obliged to cede to the pressures of their party, and had to join the opposition and to vote in favour of the motion. In the motion of confidence, which Suarez put forward in the autumn of 1980, the parliamentary group leadership of the PSA insisted against the external party on voting in favour in order to resolve the blockage of the Andalusian regional process. This 'marriage' with the UCD, whose image had suffered too much during the regional referendum in Andalusia, provoked the final crisis of the party.[33]

The attitude of the Basque parliamentary group towards the government may be considered as the least supportive. The PNV abstained in the investiture of Suarez in 1979. It voted favourably in the motion of censure against him in the spring of 1980 and abstained in the motion of confidence of Suarez in the autumn of the same year. After Suarez's resignation in January 1981, the PNV refused to support Calvo Sotelo as the new head of government in the parliamentary vote a few days before the attempted *coup d'état* – the eight PNV deputies abstained. Sotelo failed to win a majority for his government by lacking only seven votes, against the frontal opposition of Socialists and Communists. The abstention of PNV hence tipped the scale.

Regional-nationalist parties in opposition after 1982

After the shock of the attempted military coup in February 1981, and the disintegration of the UCD, the 1982 elections changed the correlation of forces significantly. The Socialist Party gained an absolute majority and put an end to minority governments which had been obliged to make pacts with differing partners. The regional-nationalist minorities with parliamentary representation lost four of their seats in Congress; but Minoria Catalana and the Grupo Vasco emerged considerably reinforced from the elections. They had to adapt to their new role in opposition.

In this new situation, the Catalan CDC developed the project of a 'state alternative'. This implied 'a theoretical and practical reformulation of the interventionism of CDC in Spanish politics'.[34] Although maintaining the idea of pacts between Convergencia and the state-wide parties, the Catalan moderate nationalists now wanted to participate in Spanish politics directly, passing from a strategy of pressure or collaboration with the governmental party to offering a political alternative. This so-called 'Operacion Roca' consisted of the creation of a new, state-wide party, 'Partido Reformista Democratico', under the Catalan leader Miguel Roca. This party with a centre-right orientation was designed to integrate either regionalist or nationalist groups like Coalicion Galega, and above all the Catalan forces into national politics.[35] The operation failed: in the 1986 elections, PRD obtained not even 1 per cent of the votes, as compared to nearly 10 per cent of its closest competitor, the 'Centro Democratico Social' run by Adolfo Suarez.

With respect to the activities of the Basque and Catalan groups as oppositions in Parliament what is noticeable is that 'Minoria Vasca' abstained completely from active intervention in the legislative process during the constituent and the first legislatures. These 'five years' presence in Parliament without a single legislative initiative . . . might be the expression of political negotiations situated outside the legislative organs of the State and exclusively led by the Basque regional government and central administration'.[36] Only in the second legislature (1982–6) did Minoria Vasca begin to integrate into the Spanish political arena: it presented six bills, one of which was approved.

Very different was the case of Minoria Catalana which 'maintained from the beginning a much more active position in Parliament' (ibid.).

During the first legislature, Minoria Catalana was even more active than Alianza Popular, by tabling fifteen bills, four of which were approved. During the second legislature, their rate of success declined, but the level of activity rose further: from its thirty proposals MC got two approved. One of its principal activities became the presentation of amendments to legislative projects from the government, propositions from parliamentary groups, and decree-laws: during the second legislature, MC tabled more than 3,300 amendments with respect to 92 legislative projects.

The style of MC and 'Grupo Vasco' as part of the opposition in the second and third legislatures differs from that of a (more or less coherently) principled ideological opposition, chosen for instance by a party like 'Coalicion Popular'. Many of their activities concerned primarily the safeguarding of Catalan and Basque regional powers and local interests in ordinary legislation, but also touched on problems of a more general order (minimal pensions with regard to self-employed people, equality of working women with regard to social security, and reform of the military service were among the topics presented by MC during 1982–6). These initiatives drew on the expertise of the regional administrations in support of both parliamentary groups as well as on multiple contacts with local and regional interest groups.

But the parliamentary activity of MC and Grupo Vasco has been confined to that of partial oppositions, not aiming at creating an alternative. What Juan Linz calls the 'task of Spain, and not only of the Spanish Right, to incorporate into central government the modern sectors of the Catalan and Basque Society (if the latter abandons its latent independentism which impedes it)',[37] by no means failed with the electoral defeat of the 'Operacion Roca', given the growing integration of both nationalist minorities into parliamentary work.

Regional-nationalist parties in regional government

The most obvious contribution of most of the regional-nationalist parties and coalitions to the functioning of the new state institutions in Spain has come rather late and consists in their participation in numerous cases in government at the regional level. The opportunities to do so have certainly been limited so far, given that in all regions only two elections have been held, except in the Basque Country where there have been three. While during the first regional legislative terms, only in Catalonia and the Basque Country were CiU and PNV able to form governments, in all other regions Spanish national parties came into government.

The second regional elections, however, reinforced parties of regional ambit in several more cases so as to allow them either to govern with an absolute majority (Catalonia), or from a minority position, supported by political pacts (Basque Country, Aragon), or participate in coalition-government with the Spanish left (Galicia), with the centre-right (Canaries), or with AP (Balearics). Hence by 1987 regional-nationalist parties were governing or participating in government in six regions. In two, Valencia and Navarra, they constituted at least a strong opposition, with some chances of creating an alternative.

The growing and active participation of regionalist or nationalist parties in regional government (with the sole exception of the Basque HB), and especially their collaboration with nation-wide parties in the regional councils and parliaments – most significantly that between PNV and PSOE since the 1986 elections – is without doubt an important indicator of the responsible and constructive relationship emerging between regionalist parties and regional institutions. As far as nationalist parties have consolidated their positions in regional government in at least two cases, have recently entered in regional government in four others, and have a good chance to do so in at least three further regions (Valencia, Navarra, and Cantabria), they confirm one of the striking particularities of the new Spanish democracy, namely its subnational pluralist character.

The emerging subnational party systems: patterns of inter-party relations

Inter-party relations shape the way political conflict is articulated and regulated. Their patterns may be defined by the number of relevant parties and the numerical correlation between them, but they may also differ in the dimensions and intensity of conflict which they express. These relations are crystallized at the regional level in subnational party systems, which may be more or less differentiated from the general party system. By 1987, after at least two regional elections in all regions, we may try to identify the major differences between them, without any illusion about how far they may be considered as consolidated so far. However, this does allow us to draw some tentative conclusions about democratic consolidation.

In his attempt to classify 'five electoral Spains', Josep M. Valles (1987) distinguished between a general model which applies to thirteen regions, and four different models, constituted by Catalonia, Galicia, Navarra, and the Basque Country. His basic criteria in this classification are (1) the level of participation; (2) the orientation of the vote; and (3) the degree of concentration versus fragmentation of political forces, both in general and in regional elections. The level of electoral abstention indicates without doubt something about the type of democratic system being established – whether it is more or less

161

representative. But with respect to democratic consolidation, it appears rather irrelevant, given that average levels of electoral participation in Switzerland, Britain, and Ireland are even lower than in Spain.[38] The same appears true with respect to 'orientation of vote'. Even if the Spanish right still generates – as the data of numerous surveys demonstrate – 'an intense refutation by part of the electorate',[39] it would be wrong to interpret it as an ambiguously anti-system party, and its dominance in some regions as an objective obstacle for democratic consolidation.

In the following discussion we will adopt three premises:

1 that the number of relevant parties and hence the degree of party-political fragmentation may tell us something about the prospects of governability;

2 that the numerical relevance of regionalist or nationalist parties in terms of their strength *vis-à-vis* the nation-wide parties of the left, the centre, and the right, in general and in regional elections may be an indicator of the importance of centre–periphery conflict;

3 that the level of polarization, hence the distance between the parties on both extremes of the scale, but even more, the trend of its development (centrifugal, centripetal), may be a measure of how far conflict is contained and regulated.

Using these three criteria, we will distinguish a number of pure types of subnational party systems, under which we can try to subsume the inter-party relations which have emerged in the regions during the first two legislative terms.

Number of relevant parties

If we count the parties which in the last regional elections gained together around 80 per cent of the votes, we can distinguish between three different situations (see Table 6).

1 *Two-party systems* have crystallized in Catalonia (CiU and PSC); Estremadura (PSOE, AP); Rioja (PSOE, AP); Castilia-La Mancha (PSOE, AP); Madrid (PSOE, AP).

2 *Moderate multi-party systems* (with three or four parties) have emerged in Galicia (AP, PSOE, CG); Aragon (PSOE, PAR, AP); Balearic Islands (AP, PSOE, CDS); Valencia (PSOE, AP, CDS); Cantabria (AP, PSOE, PRC); Andalusia (PSOE, AP, PC); Asturias (PSOE, AP, CDS); Castilia-Leon (PSOE, AP, CDS); Murcia (PSOE, AP, CDS); Canary Islands (PSOE, AIC, CDS, AP).

3 *Extreme multi-party systems* have persisted in the Basque

Country (PNV, PSOE, HB, EA, and EE; if we take HB out, we have to include AP and CDS), and in Navarra (PSOE, UPN, HB, CDS, EA).

These three types may be further differentiated according to the relative importance of nationalist parties and coalitions in them (see Tables 6 and 7).

Table 6: Types of subnational party systems in Spain

Type of party system	Regional-nation- alist majority	Regional-nation- alist minority	Non-regionalist
Two-party	II. Catalunya		IV. Castilia-LM Estremadura Madrid
Moderate multi-party		III. Galacia Aragon Baleares Canaries Cantabria Valencia	V. Andalusia Asturias Castilia-L. Murcia Rioja
Extreme multi-party	I. Basque C. Navarra		

Relevance of regional-nationalist parties

We can further classify subnational party systems according to those in which regional-nationalist parties are dominant, those in which a strong regionalist or nationalist minority has emerged, and those without any relevant regionalist forces. 'Strength' and 'relative importance' of these parties depend, of course, on the correlation of forces existing among them and the major Spanish parties, their ability to intervene in the formation of or to impede certain coalitions. With respect to this criteria, we find the following five types of subnational party systems:

1 *Regional-nationalist extreme multi-party system:* in the two cases of extreme multi-party systems, the various regional-nationalist parties gained together a majority of votes in the last regional elections: in the Basque Country 68 per cent, and in Navarra 55 per cent. These votes did not change considerably with respect to the first autonomic elections in the Basque Country (64 per cent), and in Navarra (43 per cent). In comparison, in the 1986 general elections, the nationalist forces

163

in the Basque Country still obtained 55 per cent of the vote, whereas in Navarra they got only 14 per cent (the UPN did not stand independently). Hence, the latter case differs from the former, in so far as electoral behaviour varies greatly depending on the type of election.

2 *Regional-nationalist two-party system:* this type has emerged in the case of Catalonia, where we find a majoritarian nationalist party (CiU) and a Spanish party in opposition; the Catalan Nationalists have continued to strengthen their position and have improved from gaining 28 per cent of the vote in 1980 to gaining 47 per cent in 1984, so that we may consider them as relatively consolidated. At the same time the Catalan party system experienced an important process of concentration during this first legislature, transforming its initially multi-party system (constituted by the nationalist left, nationalist centre, Spanish left, Spanish centre-left, and Spanish centre-right) into a principally two-party system.

3 *Moderate multi-party systems with regional minorities:* in seven cases regional-nationalist parties have developed some strength with respect to the nation-wide parties, which enables them to participate – actually or potentially – in government; this is the case in Galicia, Aragon, the Balearics, Canaries, but to a minor degree also in Cantabria, Rioja, and Valencia.

In *Galicia*, for example, the system of four major parties (three Spanish, one Galician) which emerged in the 1981 elections had by 1985 become concentrated in a system with only three poles, given the disappearance of the Spanish centrists (UCD) which benefited nearly equally all the other parties, the Spanish right, the Spanish left, as well as the Galician moderate nationalism.

The *Balearic Islands* experienced a substantial decline of regionalist forces, which lost around 6 points from the first to second elections. However, the multi-party system with its three poles, two of which are Spanish, which had emerged by 1983, remained substantially stable during the second elections (as long as we do not consider the strengthening of the CDS as the emergence of a fourth pole).

In *Cantabria* and in *Valencia* regionalist forces gained substantially, rising in the first case from 6.8 per cent in 1983 to 12.8 per cent in 1987, and in the second case to 9.2 per cent. In both cases regionalist parties have come to constitute a potential third pole in the regional party-political landscape, in the absence of the absolute majority of the Spanish right in Cantabria, and of the Socialists in Valencia.

4 *Spanish two-party system:* in three cases (Castilia-La Mancha,

Estremadura, Madrid) we find an essentially two-party system without the presence of any regional-nationalist party.

5 *Moderate multi-party systems without regional minorities:* in the rest of the regions – Andalusia, Asturias, Castilia-Leon, and Murcia – no significant regionalist or nationalist parties have been able to consolidate as part of the moderate multi-party systems which have emerged, and which normally consist of three parties which are nation-wide. The minority share of regionalist forces in these cases was in general stable from the first to the second elections, not altering the correlation of forces, e.g. in *Andalusia* (with a hegemony of PSOE), or declining, as in *Rioja* (AP-majority).

Table 7 Characteristics of subnational party systems in Spain

CA	Relevance of regional parties		Direction and level of nationalist conflict
	% in general elections	% in autonomous elections	
Regional-nationalist, extreme multi-party system			
Basque C.	54.6	67.9	potentially centrifugal highly polarized
Navarra	18.6	55.4	highly polarized
Regional-nationalist two-party system			
Catalonia	34.9	51.4	centripetal moderate
Moderate pluralism with important regionalist minorities			
Aragon	11.0	19.0	)
Balearic I.	2.2	13.9	) secondary,
Canary I.	15.4	27.0	) centripetal
Cantabria	–	12.8	) moderate
Galicia	12.0	22.9	)
Valencia	3.1	9.2	)
Hegemonic party systems without relevant regionalist forces			
Andalusia	2.8	5.9	)
Asturias	–	–	)
Castilla-La M.	–	–	)
Estremadura	2.6	5.7	) non-existent
Madrid	–	–	) or absorbed
Murcia	–	–	) into left-right
Rioja	–	6.5	) conflict
Castilla-Leon	–	–	

Source: Elaboration of data provided by Centro de Investigaciones Sociologicas, Madrid

On the whole, subnational party systems have shown important processes of concentration, due to the suicide of UCD, the crisis of PCE, and the concentration of regional-nationalist votes (except in the Basque Country). Regionalist and nationalist parties have benefited from this redefinition of the political space, and strengthened their position during the first regional legislature(s): mainly in the Basque Country, Navarra, Catalonia, Aragon, Balearic Islands, Canary Islands, Galicia, Cantabria, and Valencia. Hence regionalist or nationalist parties have counted not only in the three 'historical regions', but also, since the first and especially second legislature, in six more regions. In more than half of the Spanish regions, and especially in those with a higher level of economic development, urbanization, and demographic concentration (with the exception of Madrid) regionalist or nationalist forces have contributed to shaping subnational party systems and regional government. What impact this had with respect to conflict regulation remains to be evaluated.

Nature and degree of polarized conflict

The consolidation of democratic institutions presumes some degree of consensus among political forces on the 'rules of the game'. The higher the polarization among parties, and hence the ideological distance between the parties at both extremes of the alternative political scales, the more difficult it is to establish such a basic consensus, especially when anti-system parties are 'game-killers'. A major determinant of democratic consolidation hence lies in the nature, as well as in the level of polarization. Polarized conflict in general is enhanced by a high and increasing level of fragmentation of the political forces. Especially fragmentation of regionalist and nationalist forces may increase the difficulties of channelling and regulating centre–periphery conflict in stable terms. Increasing fragmentation may stimulate centrifugal patterns of competition among regional parties, and it may impede their organizational and programmatic consolidation. In the case of polarized multi-party systems with fundamental oppositions we may distinguish between two different situations: systems in which the centre is incapable of governing; and systems with governable centrist parties.[40] Each of the five types of subnational party systems which we distinguished above develops a particular pattern and dynamics of conflict.

First, conflict in the regional-nationalist, extreme multi-party systems – *Basque Country* and *Navarra* – is highly polarized, primarily according to the centralism-separatism spectrum. In Euskadi, after a period of centripetal dynamics strengthening the moderate nationalism of PNV (1980–4), there has been additional fragmentation recently produced by the schism in the PNV. Profound disagreements persist, e.g. concerning the question of the institutional model to be adopted for the region, the problem of the use of violence, or the question if Navarra should constitute a region by itself or should be incorporated as the fourth province into the Basque Country. While EE gradually participated in the institutional system, HB maintained its extreme positions with respect to the question of Basque independence, and considered institutional participation as 'legitimation of the political reform of the Franco Regime'.[41] In contrast to reformist groups which favour consensus, HB advocates the Utopian ideal of an independent and Socialist Euskadi.[42] There is thus a particularly huge gulf between these Basque extremist, leftist, and independentist forces and the Spanish centralist parties of the right. Within this pattern of polarized, ideological conflict, from 1979 PNV occupied the centre and was the only moderate party able to govern the Basque Country: its electorate placed it on the ten-point left–right scale as a centrist force at 5.8, and on the nationalism scale as a rather moderate nationalist force at 3.7 (PSOE was perceived as much more 'centralist' with 7.1). Hence, at least until the schism of PNV in 1986, we could speak of a centripetal dynamics of polarized conflict in the Basque Country.

Second, the pattern of conflict prevailing in the 'regional-nationalist two-party system' – *Catalonia* – has already historically been very different from the Basque one: Catalan nationalism is less fragmented, is less extremist, shows a lesser degree of polarization, and has a strong centre. A Catalan independence movement exists, but has never found the strength and rarely adopted the violence of Basque Separatism. All the same, the moderate nationalists of 'Convergencia i Unio' – created as a stable coalition of 'Convergencia Democratica de Catalunya' and 'Unio Democratica de Catalunya' in 1979 – have rapidly become the hegemonic force of Catalan nationalism. Without being pressed by separatist extremism, CiU has been much less ambiguous about its desire for regional autonomy within the limits set by the Constitution,[43] and the same was true for ERC. This did not exclude an important degree of penetration achieved by the nation-wide parties, especially PSOE, perhaps due to the greater organizational autonomy which the Catalan branch of PSOE, PSC-PSOE, enjoys compared with Socialist party branches elsewhere, and due to its merging with regional groups, which made them able to mobilize support among Catalan voters. Hence polarization between regional and Spanish parties in Catalonia is much less than in the Basque Country. With respect to regional issues (e.g. the use of Catalan) it is not so much that there are substantial differences but that there are differentiations in symbolic appeals between the two major political forces in the region, and between them and the nation-wide parties. In general, partisan divisions concerning socio-economic issues and ideological tendencies appeared to be more salient than those based on the centre–periphery cleavage.[44]

Third, in the 'moderate-multiparty systems with important regional minorities', a consistent minority of regionalist forces exists, which does not count so much in terms of representation in the Spanish Parliament, but above all in the context of regional politics and coalition-making. Here conflict between regional-nationalism and centralism is less salient, and tends to be monopolized by one of the major Spanish parties, mainly that in opposition. This has been the case in Galicia, Aragon, Balearics, Canaries, and to a minor degree also in Cantabria and Valencia. Regional-nationalism in at least two cases – Galicia and Canaries – has from the beginning been fragmented, extremist, and unstable: the nationalist alternatives being highly diversified, the nationalist political forces underwent permanent crisis, processes of disaggregation and re-articulation, falling in large part 'victim to their political opportunism and to their badly understood pragmatism, which made them reorganize, change image and personnel in order to occupy new political space in view of the elections'.[45] The rise of nationalism to a more important parliamentary position required in these cases the concentration of votes on forces with a more moderate centrist, centre-left, or centre-right orientation, and an ability to enter into coalition with different nation-wide parties (the case of Coalicion Galega, Asamblea Independiente Canaria, Unio Mallorquina, and Partido Aragones Regionalista). This also meant that in the cases where extremist nationalist forces (for instance, the BNPG, or MPAIAC in the Canary Islands) existed, they became progressively isolated and marginalized.

In contrast to the regional-nationalist extreme multi-party systems, there is clearly less distance between parties with respect to both the left–right and the centre–periphery dimension in a moderate multi-party system with regionalist minorities. Above all, they seem to develop a rather centripetal dynamics, which favours the expansion of moderate regionalism with a centralist orientation.

Finally, the two-party and moderate multi-party systems without regionalist minorities are systems in which a regional-nationalist cleavage either does not exist, or has been absorbed into the main pattern of left–right conflict (the case of Castilia La Mancha, Estremadura, Madrid, Andalusia, Asturias, Castilia-Leons, and Murcia). Regionalist or nationalist parties in these cases did not emerge, or were successfully absorbed into nation-wide parties or coalitions. If they acquired a temporary importance with respect to Spanish or regional politics (the case of the Andalusian PSA-PA), they were not able to consolidate. The general pattern of conflict prevailing in this type of system is that of the general Spanish party system: low level of polarization and weak fragmentation.[46]

Subnational and national party systems: segmentation and integration

Although the crucial problem, which is essentially to what extent the party systems with regionalist minorities have consolidated or will do so in the future, remains to be resolved empirically, the principal theoretical question is obvious: what are the conditions which may push towards an increasing segmentation of the national party system by regional subsystems? And, on the other hand, what are the mechanisms which provide integration und unity in spite of diversity?

With regard to the first question, there exists without doubt a disintegrative potential within regional-nationalist multi-party systems, especially those with a centrifugal dynamics and a weakening centre. How far this threat currently exists in the Basque case has to be be left open: PNV and EA after their schism have together gained even slightly more votes in 1986 than in 1984 and PNV has subsequently entered in coalition with PSOE. This experiment may not only make the region governable, but also build a bridge between the Spanish and the Basque party systems. However, only the next elections will show how far the Basque electorate will reward this effort, or how far it will penalize PNV in favour of more extremist nationalist options. Regional-nationalist two-party systems such as the Catalan one, with a nationalist and a Spanish pole, by definition should safeguard the integration of the party system, at least as long as the Spanish part is able to control internal tensions between more nationalist and more centralist tendencies and factions.

On the other hand, we may identify – besides centripetal dynamics and the readiness of moderate nationalist parties to coalesce or compete for alternation with nation-wide parties – a number of other mechanisms which in principle may contribute to the integration of such a subnational pluralist party system. In the first place, it is the level of transference votes between regional and general elections, which may provide a source of integration: for instance in Catalonia, a third of the PSOE voters in the general elections in 1982 gave their votes in the subsequent regional elections to CiU, the same happened to more than half of UCD and AP voters; in the Basque Country, on the contrary, the percentage of transference votes is especially low (only 8 per cent of PSOE, and 4 per cent of UCD-AP-PDP-voters transferred their votes to PNV), while in Galicia nearly half of ex-UCD-voters transferred their vote in the regional elections of 1985 to 'Coalicion Galega'.[47] The transfer of the vote from a nation-wide to a nationalist party – and vice versa – appears to be motivated by rational electoral considerations, in which voters differentiate in a utilitarian manner between the party political alternatives. Only in the Basque Country is transfer relatively low, and hence voting behaviour seems to be based more on party identification than on the result of rational considerations and calculations.

Second, the overall concentration of votes on the Socialist Party since 1982 counterbalances the tendency towards fragmentation produced by the regional-nationalist forces. Although eight regional-nationalist parties gained seats in the 1986 general elections, together they obtained only around 10 per cent of the votes.

Had the 'Proyecto Roca' succeeded in attracting these various regional-nationalist votes, the PRD would have gained nearly 12 per cent of the votes and become the third most important party in Parliament, after PSOE and Coalicion Popular, but before the CDS. This again would have created a multi-party system with many possible alliances and outcomes (leaving aside here the question of how the votes would have been translated into seats). But the failure of this experiment so far, and the lack of coalition-building among the nationalist and the nationwide parties of the centre and right, allows PSOE to govern with the comfort of its relative majority of votes, and absolute majority of seats, without resort to pacts with one or the other of the parliamentary forces.

Most of the regional-nationalist parties we have discussed have made important shifts towards the centre. They are inclined to coalesce, make pacts, or alternate with nation-wide parties. In some cases they have contributed to the isolation, if not the suppression of anti-system forces. They have hence significantly encouraged not only the articulation, but also the regulation of regionalist–nationalist conflict, and hence enhanced the prospects for democratic consolidation. It remains to be evaluated how far these parties have achieved some degree of social penetration and of organizational consolidation which allows us to consider them as relatively stable elements of the Spanish party system.

Party-electorate relations

The stability of the linkages between parties and the electorate is one of the determinants of continuity and change of electoral behaviour, and is hence a condition of consolidation of a given party system.

Spanish electoral behaviour differs from that of other west European countries in that it shows 'a relatively high level of change'. This indicates, hence, 'unstable ties between votes and parties' which may be explained by the relatively shorter history and the weaker roots of parties in Spain, but also by important events like the crisis of UCD and PCE, and frequent internal conflicts and leadership quarrels, especially among the parties of the centre-right and the extreme left.[48] This raises the question about how far regional-nationalist parties have also been affected by this general lack of social penetration and the pattern of internal conflict. Traditionally social penetration and the establishment of links with the electorate have consisted mainly in the organization of the voters and the development of membership-parties.

Membership

Nationalist parties in Spain are particularly difficult to classify with respect to their membership. In some cases their origins in clandestine groups bring them close to the classical 'cadre-party' (HB, EE). In other cases their capacity to mobilize broad mass movements makes them more like movements than political parties (PSA-PA; CiU in its early stages). Their inter-class character and integrative capacity towards different social strata may suggest the classification of a 'catch-all membership-party' (in the case of PNV), whereas their electoral orientation towards a wide electoral basis by means of only very general values communicated by the party leader resemble the 'electoral mass party', as for instance in the case of CiU. Many of the regional-nationalist coalitions which emerged and disappeared (for instance in Galicia and the Canary Islands), however, consisted of not much more than occasional lists around a 'notable', thus did not achieve any deeper penetration of regional society. Although we do not possess reliable information on recent developments of the affiliation rates of the main regional-nationalist parties, we will look at the available data from the early 1980s.[49] We can compare five of the regional-nationalist parties with respect to their member–voter proportion (see Table 8).

Table 8 Member–voter proportion of regional-nationalist and Spanish parties

Party	Members 1980	Voters	Level of organization (%)
PNV	40,000	350,000[a]	11
EE	7,000	90,000[a]	8
CiU	20,000	750,000[a]	3
ERC	7,000	240,000[a]	3
PSA-PA	11,000	327,000[b]	3
PSOE	97,000	5,500,000[b]	2
AP	18,000	1,100,000[b]	1
UCD	144,000	6,300,000[b]	2
PCE	132,000	1,900,000[b]	7

Notes: [a]1980 [b]1979

Soon after 1977 the *Basque* PNV showed an intense capacity to organize and mobilize a large membership, something which the

Socialist Party – which had gained nearly as many votes as the PNV – was not able to realize. With these deep roots in Basque society, PNV conceives itself as both a party and a community (partido-comunidad).[50] By 1981, PNV had around 40,000 members,[51] and organized hence the very high percentage of 11 per cent of its voters (350,000 in 1980). Another measure of the capacity of penetration may be its organizational infrastructure: its important party headquarters at the regional level, and its 250 local offices. Also its close ties with the Basque trade union ELA-STV strengthened its roots in Basque society.

In 1981 Euskadiko Ezkerra claimed that its membership was between 7,000 and 8,000,[52] and that it was thus able to organize about 8 per cent of its electorate. Therefore it can also be considered as a membership-party. A particular resource of EE as of the Basque left in general is the numerous committees organized by it, in favour of amnesty, anti-nuclear groups, and town or village committees which are inspired by assembly-style ideas, and which have perhaps begun to have more importance than the political parties.[53] Herri Batasuna has a weaker organizational basis. But given its links with ETA, its number of activists can be estimated to some degree on the basis of the evidence on ETA activists – in 1978 around 1,000.[54]

The figures on affiliation of the Catalan nationalist forces reveal that their strength is somewhat less than in the case of the Basque parties in their organization of members: in 1981, CDC had around 9,000 members,[55] and CiU about 20,000:[56] with respect to the 750,000 votes received in the 1980 autonomic elections, an organizational level of only 3 per cent. Esquerra Republicana de Catalunya as well as the Andalusian PSA-PA are examples of parties with an organizational level similar to that of CiU – around 3 per cent of their voters in 1979/80 were organized by 1981 – but both, in contrast to CiU, declined. PSA-PA, in spite of its 11,000 members, 150 local offices, and 262 local councillors in 1981, disintegrated after the defeat in the local and general elections in 1982.

The major two coalitions of the regionalist left and centre in the Canary Islands – UPC and PPC – had not more than 2,000 members between them in 1981.[57] Their membership was spread over the various islands and split between the heterogeneous party formations. We lack comparable data in respect of the membership structures of the Galician nationalists – EG, BNG, and CG.

By 1981 at least five of the regionalist and nationalist formations – PNV, EE, CiU, ERC, and PSA – appear to have had relatively solid membership bases. This has not necessarily been an advantage or even a requirement: activists in modern parties may be less important than in earlier times, since electoral mobilization is also influenced by the mass media and by charismatic personalities.[58] Indeed, among the major

Spanish parties, only the PCE has shown a degree of organization similar to that of the Basque parties (7 per cent). The other Spanish parties had much lower levels of organization, even lower than those of the Catalan parties: PSOE and UCD organized in 1981 only 2 per cent of their voters; AP only 1 per cent.

The organizational consolidation of regional-nationalist parties

Not only the nation-wide, but also the nationalist party-political landscape has changed considerably since the first general elections in 1977. It left not even the PNV intact – the party with the longest historical tradition. Even though a 'bitter dispute on how to unite the Basque region politically and territorially' has developed within the party since 1983 (on one side those favouring the power of the provincial councils, on the other the supporters of a stronger regional government), 'the real crisis must rather be found in a personal rivalry between the then two most significant leaders of the party', namely Xabier Arzalluz and Carlos Garaikoetxea – the former controlling the party apparatus, the latter being 'Lehendakari' (president of the Basque autonomous government) since 1980.[59] The leadership quarrel went on and numerous followers of Garaikoetxea were expelled, until the latter created his own party 'Basque Solidarity' shortly before the third regional elections in November 1986. This development demonstrated that the strength of PNV – its deep social roots, its inter-class orientation – was at one and the same time the source of its weakness and all types of centre–periphery and ideological tensions.

Other parties with a historical tradition, for instance the Esquerra Republicana de Catalunya, have become marginal after a promising reorganization and electoral strengthening. A historical nationalist force like 'Partido Galleguista', so successful during the Second Republic, was not even able to reorganize during transition.

Organizational evolution of regional nationalism in the ten years' period from the first general to the second (and third) regional elections in 1987 was most continuous in the case of the Catalan CiU, which transformed itself from a movement-type party, with a strong accent on membership organization and mobilization, to a more and more electoral party with a charismatic leader, Jordi Pujol.

In the other regions, the regionalist and nationalist minorities – Galicia, Canary Islands, Balearic Islands, Aragon, Valencia – showed a more or less pronounced discontinuity and rate of renewal, crisis, and rearticulation of organizational structures, personal and electoral alliances, and tendencies of disaggregation and erosion.[60] The question of how to account for this high degree of fluidity urgently demands an answer when we compare the rise, change, and decline of regional-nationalist forces in many regions, most prominently perhaps in Galicia and the Canary Islands. The lack of organizational consolidation of many of them is certainly one of the major factors delaying, but not impeding democratic consolidation in Spain.

Conclusion

Which of the two scenarios of democratic consolidation with respect to centre–periphery relations identified at the beginning of this chapter, has been more in evidence? The negative – increased fragmentation and polarization produced by subnational parties – or the positive scenario – regional parties providing for participation and responsiveness? Political developments in more than half of the seventeen Spanish regions – not only in Catalonia and the Basque Country – over the past decade have certainly (to say the least) presented a very complex picture. For this reason it is difficult to draw firm generalizations, but all the same certain trends have been visible. These have, by and large, tended to favour the process of democratic consolidation in Spain rather than the opposite. Undoubtedly the regional-nationalist parties have played a crucial role in this respect.

The period of the late 1970s and the early 1980s seems to have been decisive here: it was not only the phase in which centre–periphery relations threatened to disrupt democratization. It also coincides with what is commonly regarded as the move of Spain from transition to the longer process of system consolidation. The conflictive biennial 1979–81 consisted then in a series of crucial tests which the incipient Spanish democracy had to pass. That is, the regional question had the potential, as it were, of preventing this 'shift' in the outcome of political change in Spain, and of impeding its consolidation. It is probably true to say that this question made the early stage of democratic consolidation fraught with difficulties and helped to slow down its achievement. Indeed, in the early years of the period on which this chapter focuses there were several signs pointing to the negative scenario described above.

However, the overall trend has been rather from a centrifugal to a centripetal dynamics with integration rather than segmentation as the outcome. There admittedly remain a number of negative features, of which terrorism must be seen as the most threatening. Also, the developments in the regions have contributed to the Spanish problem of a disunited political opposition on the centre-right. But there are many other findings in this chapter which point in the direction of a constructive role of regional political parties for democratic consolidation. One may mention, for instance, the regulation of centre–periphery and ideological conflict by the parties and the way in which certain regional parties which were previously 'anti-system' have been either neutralized or even integrated in the system; the distinct move by many parties towards centre politics and coalescent behaviour with Spanish parties; and, a characteristic of all these features, the general pattern of pluralism which has emerged in most of the Spanish regions. In terms of the state and inter-party relationships explored by this volume, the outcome has been clearly positive, too: most of the regional-nationalist parties have contributed to the success of the Spanish 'experiment of a nation of nationalities and regions'.[61] The remaining relationship with society has been more difficult because there has persisted strong discontinuity so far as the social bases of many regional parties – with the exception of the Catalan CiU and the Basque PNV and EE – are concerned. But, as Richard Gillespie shows, this is a general problem of the Spanish party system.[62] It perhaps has to do with what Geoffrey Pridham has identified as a general feature of the 'Mediterranean model' of liberal democracy: a gap between political-institutional structures similar to those elsewhere in western Europe, and a political culture lagging behind.[63] Nevertheless, taken as a whole, what differentiates the Spanish party system from those elsewhere in southern and western Europe is the persistent and even growing regional pluralism within the unity of the institutional and party system.

Notes

1. With respect to this definition of the concept of 'democratic consolidation', see L. Morlino, 'Consolidamento democratico: definizione e modelli', *Rivista Italiana di Scienza Politica*, August 1986.
2. R. Gunther, G. Sani, and G. Shabad, *Spain After Franco: The Making of a Competitive Party System*, Berkeley and Los Angeles, University of California Press, 1986, p. 241.
3. P.C. Schmitter, *The Consolidation of Political Democracy in Southern Europe*, Stanford University, Calif., and Istituto Universitario Europeo, June 1988, third revised version.
4. J. Botella, 'The Spanish "new" regions: territorial and political pluralism', *International Political Science Review*, July 1989.
5. Gunther *et al.*, op. cit., p. 241.
6. Extract of an interview by Richard Gunther, cited in G. Shabad, 'Las Elecciones de 1982 y las Autonomias', in *Crisis y Cambio: Electores y Partidos en la Espana de los anos ochenta*, Centro de Estudios Constitucionales, 1986, p. 525.
7. For the subsequent analysis I have used the data on general and regional elections 1977–87 provided by the Centro de Investigaciones Sociologicas, Madrid.
8. J.M. Valles, 'Quante Spagne elettorali? Dimensioni territoriali del fenomeno elettorale nella Spagna odierna', in M. Caciagli and P. Corbetta (eds) *Elezioni Regionali e Sistema Politico Nazionale*, Bologna, Il Mulino, 1987; Valles, 'Wahlverhalten und Wahlentwicklung in Spanien

(1977–1988): Ein überblick', *Zeitschrift für Parlamentsfragen*, 1988, vol. 3.

9. After the 1977 elections, 7 regionalist or nationalist groups from 4 regions held together 24 out of 350 seats in Congress; in the 1979 elections 9 regionalist and nationalist parties and coalitions from 6 different regions won 23 seats; in the 1982 elections, only 4 groups from 2 regions were represented with 27 seats; after the 1986 elections 7 parties from 5 regions obtained 34 mandates.

10. J. Corcuera, 'La configuracion del nacionalismo vasco', in F. Hernandez and F. Mercade (eds) *Estructuras Sociales y Cuestion Nacional en España*, Barcelona, Ariel, 1986, p. 149.

11. D. Della Porta and L. Mattina, 'Political cycles and ethnic mobilization: the Basque case', paper presented at the IPSA World Congress, Paris, July 1985, p. 13.

12. J. Marcet, *Convergencia Democratica de Cataluna*, Madrid, Centro de Investigaciones Sociologicas, 1987, pp. 52ff.

13. J. Marcet and J. Botella, 'Partits, protagonistes de la vida politica', in *Catalunya 1973–1983*, Barcelona, L'Avenc, 1983, p. 74.

14. Centro de Investigaciones Sociologicas (CIS), 'Informe de los Resultados de las encuestas realizadas, entre julio y diciembre de 1978 sobre el referendum constitucional', *Revista de estudios sociologicos*, 1979, vol. 5, p. 288.

15. J.M. Valles, 'Generalitat. Tres etapes d'un projecte inacabat', in *Catalunya 1973–1983*, Barcelona, L'Avenc, 1983, p. 47.

16. Cited after Marcet, op. cit., pp. 296–7.

17. Corcuera, op. cit., p. 147.

18. E. Sevilla Guzman, 'Estructura social e identidad andaluza', in Hernandez and Mercade (eds) op. cit., p. 290.

19. F. Hernandez, 'El nacionalismo catalan', in Hernandez and Mercade (eds) op. cit., pp. 88ff.

20. J. Hernandez Bravo, 'El nacionalismo canario: su entorno social y politico', in Hernandez and Mercade (eds) op. cit., p. 423.

21. J. Linz, 'Conflicto en Euskadi', Madrid, Espasa Calpe, 1986, p. 696.

22. Euskadi, 1982, supplement to 'Egin', p. 103; cited after Della Porta and Mattina, op. cit., p. 28, note 42.

23. J. Corcuera and M.A. Garcia Herrera, 'Sistema de Partidos, Instituciones y Comunidad Nacionalista en Euskadi', *Revista de Politica Comparada*, autumn 1980, no. 2, pp. 172ff.

24. In Galicia as well as in Catalunya, nearly half of the abstentionists in autonomic elections explain their behaviour by 'absence and family problems'; many cases (in Galicia nearly 28 per cent) are attributed to problems of census; a minor share is motivated by 'lack of interests in politics' (less than a third in Catalunya and less than a fifth in Galicia); while only a minority (4 per cent) argue with 'hostility against the democracy'; see R. Lopez Pintor, *La Opinion Publica Española: Del Franquismo a la Democratcia*, Madrid, CIS, 1982, p. 126. For a detailed analysis of the various reasons of abstentionism and the political tendencies of abstentionists see J.R. Montero, 'Niveles, fluctuaciones y tendencias del abstencionismo electoral en Espana y en Europa', *Revista Espanola de*

Investigaciones Sociologicas, 1984, vol. 28, pp. 223–42; Montero, 'La vuelta a las urnas: Participacion, movilizacion y abstencion', in J. Linz and J.R. Montero (eds) *Crisis y Cambio: Electores y partidos en la Espana de los anos ochenta*, Madrid, CIS, 1986.

25. Valles, 1983, op. cit., pp. 46ff.
26. Corcuera, op. cit., p. 151.
27. Forty per cent of the voters abstained, and 8 per cent voted 'no'; see *Boletin Oficial del Estado* (BOE), 9 November 1979.
28. U. Liebert, *Neue Autonomiebewegung und Dezentralisierung in Spanien. Der Fall Andalusien*, Frankfurt am Main, Campus, 1986.
29. M. Jerez Mir, 'Una experiencia de partido regional: el caso del Partido Socialista de Andalucia, Partido Andaluz', *Revista Espanola de Investigaciones Sociologicas*, April–June 1985, pp. 213ff.
30. Marcet, op. cit., p. 298.
31. As for instance, in the electoral programme of CiU of 1979.
32. Marcet, op. cit., p. 299.
33. Jerez Mir, op. cit., pp. 214ff.
34. Marcet, op. cit., p. 336.
35. P. del Castillo and G. Sani, 'Las Elecciones de 1986: Continuidad sin Consolidacion', in Linz and Montero (eds) op. cit., p. 627.
36. J. Subirats and D. Lopez Garrido, 'The Spanish Cortes and democratic consolidation in Spain: relationship between government and parliament (1977–1987)', paper presented at the conference on 'Parliaments and Democratic Consolidation in Southern Europe', Fundacion Jaume Bofill, Barcelona, 29–31 October 1987.
37. Linz, op. cit., p. 655.
38. Montero, 1986, op. cit., p. 77.
39. J. Linz, 'Consideraciones finales', in Linz and Montero (eds) op. cit., p. 653.
40. K. von Beyme, *Parteien in westlichen Demokratien*, München, Piper Verlag, 1982, pp. 312ff.
41. Corcuera, op. cit., p. 152.
42. Herri Batasuna 1983, cited after Corcuera, op. cit., pp. 151–2.
43. Gunther *et al.*, op. cit., p. 348.
44. ibid., p. 349.
45. This description of the Canarian situation finds many parallels also in the Galician case; see Hernandez Bravo, op. cit., pp. 425–6.
46. See among others: A. Bar, 'The emerging Spanish party system: is there a model?', *West European Politics*, 1984, vol. 7, pp. 128–55; Bar, 'Normalidad o excepcionalidad? Para una tipologia del sistema de partidos espanol, 1977–1982', *Sistema 65*, 1985; Linz, op. cit.; Valles 1988, op. cit.; C.R. Aguilera de Prat, 'Balance y transformaciones del sistema de partidos en Espana (1977–1987)', *Revista Espanola de Investigaciones Sociologicas*, April–June 1988, vol. 42, Madrid, CIS.
47. Linz and Montero (eds) op. cit., p. 422.
48. Valles, 1988, op. cit., p. 350; see also Valles, 'Los Partidos Politicos ante la Reforma del Estado: Notas sobre el caso espanol', in J.J. Gonzalez Encinar *et al.*, *Autonomia y Partidos Politicos*, Madrid, Tecnos, 1984.
49. Most of the subsequently quoted quantitative data on party membership are

taken from interviews conducted by Michael Buse with party leaders in his study on the Spanish party system for the German Friedrich Naumann Foundation; see M. Buse, *Die neue spanische Demokratie. Parteiensystem und Wählerorientierungen 1976–1984*, Baden-Baden, Nomos, 1985.

50. Corcuera and Herrera, op. cit., pp. 155–90.
51. Buse, op. cit., p. 231.
52. ibid., p. 233.
53. Corcuera, op. cit., pp. 147–8.
54. A. Munoz Alonso, *El terrorismo en Espana*, Barcelona, Coleccion Tablero, 1982, p. 147.
55. Marcet, op. cit., p. 133.
56. Buse, op. cit., p. 253.
57. ibid., p. 264.
58. K. von Beyme, 'Politische Parteien und die Konsolidierung der neuen Demokratie in Südeuropa', *Journal für Sozialforschung*, 1985, vol. 1, p. 34.
59. F. Reinares, 'The Basque autonomous parliament elections of 1986', *Electoral Studies*, 1987, vol. 6, no. 2, pp. 169–70.
60. R. Maiz, 'El nacionalismo gallego: apuntes para la historia de una hegemonia imposible', in Hernandez and Mercade (eds) op. cit.
61. U. Liebert, 'Spanien, Das Experiment einer spanischen Nation der Nationalitäten und Regionen', *Der Bürger im Staat*, June 1987, vol. 2, pp. 115–23.
62. R. Gillespie, Chapter 6 in this volume.
63. G. Pridham, 'Comparative perspectives on the new Mediterranean democracies: a model of regime transition?', *West European Politics*, special issue on the 'New Mediterranean democracies: regime transition in Spain, Greece and Portugal', April 1984, pp. 26–7.

Chapter eight

Political parties and democratic consolidation in Greece

Kevin Featherstone

The transition to democracy in Spain, Portugal, and Greece in the mid-1970s attracted considerable external attention, and it gave rise to a new 'southern European' profile in political, economic, and military discussions. However, while Greece shares certain social and economic traits with the new Iberian states its political experience has exhibited important differences.[1] The Greek political system has had a longer and more recent experience of liberal democratic rule than either Spain or Portugal, and the Greek transition to democracy in the 1970s has appeared to be a smoother one. To understand the process of consolidation of the new Greek regime after 1974, it is thus necessary to bear in mind the experiences of the previous parliamentary regime as they formed potent legacies affecting subsequent political attitudes.

Concentrating attention on the role played by the political parties in the process of consolidation seems particularly appropriate. While the individual figure of Constantine Karamanlis, albeit aided by a coalition Cabinet, dominated the transition to democracy, the process of consolidation was crucially affected by the major political parties. More particularly, focusing on political parties, as a bridge between state action and wider society, affords the opportunity to highlight important underlying structures of society. Indeed to understand the context in which consolidation was sought presupposes an awareness of the nature of the state and its relations with wider society.

This analysis will thus concentrate on three key themes: party–state relations, relations between the parties themselves, and party–society relations. The analysis begins by discussing the changing nature of state–civil relations, the role of parties in government, incorporatist and clientelistic practices, and their autonomy from the state. Historically, limited industrialization, weak class structures, disorientation from the influx of refugees, and rapid urbanization all delayed the emergence of a strong pluralistic infrastructure. Party structures have been slow to develop; the uses made of the state apparatus are thus of crucial importance.

Attention to these three themes ably demonstrates the progress made towards consolidation of the new regime. Existing literature on regime stability and consolidation has perhaps overly concentrated on the zero-sum issue of whether 'a threatening contingency' is likely to arise, rather than with the deeper, more positive aspects of how a new regime implants itself and of how democratic practices become intensified within it.[2] The new post-1974 regime in Greece has so far passed various 'tests' of consolidation: it has remained intact for some fourteen years; it enjoys a legitimacy probably unprecedented in modern Greek history; it possesses representative institutions and a competitive party system; it has experienced a peaceful alternation of power. Yet assessing the strength or vitality of the new democratic regime would still raise important questions as to the operation of the state apparatus in relation to both collective institutions and the individual citizen, the communication and articulation of interests and the mechanisms for exercising accountability, and the more general content of its political culture. Each of these aspects helps to determine how the democratic process operates in practice, and the health and intensity of its system dynamics. 'Consolidation' could be a misnomer for a process: it must allow for qualitative differences of norms and behaviour developed over time, and for a greater or lesser intensity of those qualities which affect the viability of a new regime.

The nature of the Greek *transition* to democratic processes in 1974 has been well accounted for, as have the events before and after the Colonel's coup in 1967.[3] When considering the political development of Greece, however, reference must be made to earlier experiences which still have an impact: the bloody Civil War (1946-9), the deficiencies of the subsequent parliamentary regime, as well as to the events leading to the military coup (21 April 1967).[4] This chapter will be concerned with developments after the fall of the Colonel's regime (July 1974), when former Premier Constantine Karamanlis was invited to take over the reins of power. Rather than focusing on the immediate transition itself, the perspective will be on the period since 1974.

Parties and the state

State–civil relations have undergone important changes in Greece since 1974, and in particular those involving the relationship between the party in power, the state bureaucracy, and political actors elsewhere in the system. The moves towards consolidation can be examined by reference to two distinct periods: that prior to 1981 when Karamanlis' party New Democracy was in power; and that covering the years since October 1981 when the Socialists (PASOK) were first elected under Andreas Papandreou (see Table 9). Furthermore, certain key developments may

Table 9 Parliamentary election results in Greece, 1974–85

	1974		1977		1981		1985	
	% Vote	Seats	% Vote	Seats	% Vote	Seats	% Vote	Seats
EPEN (National Front)	—	—	6.8	5	—	—	—	—
New Democracy	54.4	220	41.9	171	35.9	113	40.9	126
New Liberal Party	—	—	1.1	2	—	—	—	—
EK-ND (Centre Union)	20.5	60	11.9	16	—	—	—	—
PASOK	13.6	12	25.3	93	48.1	174	45.8	161
United Left	9.5	8	—	—	—	—	—	—
Alliance of progressive and left-wing forces	—	—	2.7	2	—	—	—	—
KKE-es (Communist Party – interior)	—	—	—	—	—	—	1.8	1
KKE (Communist Party)	—	—	9.4	11	10.9	13	9.9	12

Sources: K. Featherstone and D.K. Katsoudas (eds) Political Change in Greece: Before and After the Colonels, London, Croom Helm, 1987; R. Clogg (ed.) Greece in the 1980s, London, Macmillan/CGS, 1983.
Note: Only parties which secured seats in Parliament have been included here.

be highlighted: the abolition of the monarchy and the debate surrounding the new Constitution, the role of the military under the new regime, the break with the old 'exclusivist' practices of the pre-1967 era, and the continuation of clientelistic and incorporatist attitudes by the party in government. These problems will help to clarify how far the two main political parties have sought to revise the state's structures and the consequences such changes have had for the consolidation of the new democratic regime.

The emergence of a new democratic order occurred gradually, under the delicate guidance of Karamanlis. It was not until after fresh parliamentary elections – and indeed the failure of an attempted coup in February 1975 – that the new prime minister tackled the most sensitive issues and dealt with the junta's supporters.[5] While in 1974 Karamanlis' gradualism was praised for its relatively smooth character, by the following year he was being criticized for this very same quality and for the constitutional shape being given to the new regime.

The abolition of the monarchy – a referendum of 8 December 1974 voted 69 per cent against the King's return – facilitated the consolidation and, indeed, the democratization of the new political system. The change is to be explained by the nature of the constituent process underway after Karamanlis' return, but its considerable political significance is to be measured in terms of how far it removed a source of deep-rooted controversy developed over the previous sixty years or more. Karamanlis insisted on his parliamentary supporters maintaining a neutral stance on the question of the King's return, a decision which prevented the monarch's most natural supporters from campaigning on his behalf. By contrast, George Mavros (EK-ND, Centre Union-New Forces) and Andreas Papandreou (PASOK) both declared their party's support for a republic. Karamanlis, despite the initial confidence of conservatives at the time of the transfer of power from the junta, had thus deftly supervised the transition to a republic.

The constitutional procedures undertaken by the new regime were based on some ambiguity. Katsoudas has explained the various stages involved from the first 'Constitutional Act of August 1st' (1974) to the new full-blown Constitution of 11 June 1975.[6] Article I of the first Constitutional Act restored legality in the form of the 1952 Constitution prior to the voting of a new Constitution, with the exception that it did not specify the form of the regime as previously: a 'Crowned Democracy'. Article II provided for this matter to be decided by a referendum: a controversial innovation as, if Greece was being returned to the legality of the 1952 Constitution, it was not for the King as a person to decide 'whether the institution would survive or not'.[7] In any event, the election of a 'revisionary' Parliament to formulate the new Constitution was held on 17 November 1974, the first anniversary of the

Athens Polytechnic uprising. After the question of the monarchy had been settled shortly afterwards, Parliament conducted its debate on the new constitution in less than six months, despite major protests from the opposition parties over some of its provisions.

The constituent process of 1975 was indeed surprisingly conflictual. A lasting source of dispute were the powers granted to the President of the Republic: critics saw them as a 'Gaullist' imposition over and above parliamentary democracy. George Mavros said he would campaign for 'a true parliamentary democracy'. Andreas Papandreou went further: it was 'no better than the constitution of dictator Papadopoulos'; his party, if elected to power, would 'dissolve Parliament and call for the election of a constituent assembly to produce a constitution based on the people's sovereignty'.[8] Karamanlis had said that he wished to avoid 'the fatal weaknesses of the form of government that collapsed'. Katsoudas notes that in formal terms the new powers granted to the Head of State 'exceeded by far . . . those of the monarch under the 1952 Constitution'.[9] Critics focused 'mainly on the President's capacity to either hinder, by-pass, and/or finally dismiss both the Government and Parliament'.[10] Moreover, these exceptional powers were to be possessed by an indirectly elected president, lacking popular legitimacy.

After this initial period of controversy between the parties, criticism of the Constitution's provisions eventually abated. To great public surprise, however, Andreas Papandreou as prime minister announced in March 1985 that his government would not be supporting a renewal of Karamanlis' term of office as president (Karamanlis had moved from being prime minister to president in 1980) and, in addition, PASOK would propose changes to the Constitution to reduce the powers of the head of state. A storm of controversy ensued over both parts of this announcement; Karamanlis, it was later shown, had been badly misled as to PASOK's intentions towards him. The manner in which Karamanlis' successor was elected by Parliament also provoked strong criticism.[11] Katsoudas has argued that the changes passed in 1985 now give autocratic powers to the prime minister: 'a consequence of the absence of the counter-balancing weight of the President, internally-democratic political parties, and the selection of MPs on the parties' electoral lists by the respective party leaders, thus serving to ensure the obedience of the legislators'.[12] The prime minister is now, indisputably, *primus* and none of the major parties has fully developed internal structures to keep the holder of this office accountable. The effective operation of democratic processes in Greece had again thus been shown to be limited, not by constitutional provision, but by the wider weaknesses of political structure and unreformed political behaviour.

Since 1974 both New Democracy and PASOK have, however,

managed largely to consolidate the direction of control and account-ability in government–military relations in favour of democratic rule. After the failure of the February 1975 coup conspiracy, successive governments have remained free of any further attempts at military intervention.[13] Veremis has explained this by reference to a number of developments: the political parties seemed tacitly to agree not to dispute the responsibilities for the past; military officers themselves have abided by western notions of professionalism; a 1977 Act emphasized that the government had sole responsibility for national defence and it abolished the dictatorship's concentration of power in the single post of 'Chief of the Armed Forces'.[14] But, at least as importantly, the climate of tension with Turkey over the Aegean and Cyprus has served to maintain the significance of national defence: Greece devotes the highest proportion of its GNP of any NATO member to military expenditure; a consensus exists between the parties over these defence issues; and the self-esteem of military officers has also improved. During his period of office, Andreas Papandreou has closely identified himself with the national defence issue; indeed until October 1986 he also served as Defence Minister. In the spring of 1987 he threatened war against Turkey if she carried out her threat to start mineral tests in Greek waters; the tension this created over a period of a few days reinforced Papandreou's patriotic image and afforded him political supremacy in the surrounding debate. While the military's interests have been placated, reassurance has been given as to civilian supervision. Thus it may be said that both parties contributed in this crucial respect to democratic consolidation during their respective periods in office.

While the role of the military has changed, the popular legitimacy of the new regime has been consolidated effectively by the moves made to turn away from what Diamandouros has called the 'exclusivist' nature of previous regimes.[15] From 1936 until 1974, successive regimes had consciously sought to exclude liberal and left-wing elements from exercising power and gaining state favours. In a courageous and important initiative, Karamanlis instigated an Act (23 September 1974) to legalize all political parties and to overturn Law 509 of 1948, the 'last major piece of civil war discriminatory legislation'.[16] The legalization of political parties most noticeably involved the Communist Party (KKE), which had been banned since 1947. Prior to 1967, other Civil War legislation had been used to harass known left-wingers: a certificate of 'healthy social views', for example, had been required 'for State employment, for a driver's licence, for a passport and, for a time, for university entrance'.[17] The 1974 Act abolished such discrimination, and the 1975 Constitution safeguarded individual liberties.

The first alternation of power which occurred under the new democratic regime was realized, without disturbance, with the election of PASOK in October 1981. This change of government also served to strengthen the legitimacy of the new order. It did so by meeting the frustrated demands of liberal and left-wing opinion, created amidst earlier bitterness and polarization. Liberal opinion had been inflamed by what they had labelled 'a royal *coup d'état*' in July 1965. The young King Constantine had not only refused a request from the prime minister (George Papandreou), but also tried to split the Centre Union party by establishing a minority government.[18] The political tensions which followed provided the basis for the Colonel's coup. For radical opinion, the abolition of the monarchy in 1974 and the success of PASOK in the 1981 elections thus returned Greece to the course on which it had embarked prior to 1965. This interpretation was further justified in terms of the change it represented to the vengeful outcome of the bloody Civil War. Indeed, PASOK in government carried out its promise to give official recognition to the contribution to Greece's interests made by the national resistance movement, ELAS, during the Second World War; this decision having implications for pension rights and social policy. The final trappings of the old 'exclusivist' and stridently anti-Communist order had thus been abolished and previously alienated social groups reconciled.

The rehabilitation of the Communists is reflected in evidence of public attitudes and the electoral performance of the main party, the KKE, since 1974. A Eurodim survey (Greater Athens only) in 1985 found 46 per cent of respondents blaming 'exclusively or mainly the government forces for the Civil War'; amongst those less than 35 years of age the proportion was 65 per cent.[19] The highest share of the national vote for the KKE was in the 1981 parliamentary elections (10.9 per cent), while in 1985 it slipped to 9.9 per cent. In the municipal elections of 1975, 1978, and 1982 the KKE made a strong showing, and in 1986 it increased the number of municipalities it controls by ten (to 53 out of 303).[20] However, it did badly in the elections in the largest three cities: Athens, Piraeus, Thessaloniki. The 'twilight of the Greek Communist movement' may thus have been reached, as Kapetanyannis suggests.[21] The Communists seem likely to remain a significant minority force – the party has particular influence in public sector unions – but the prospects for the KKE launching itself to a higher level of support must be slim. The KKE has remained marginalized. Allowing it into the legitimate arena has witnessed the limits of its support.

The parties themselves have, however, in certain respects found it difficult to break with the pre-1967 era, or at least with some of the attitudes and behaviour of that period. The initial period of consolidation, up to 1981, provided the main party of the right, New Democracy, with the opportunity to modernize and liberalize the Greek political process. In so far as certain political reforms and initiatives were undertaken, New Democracy made a partial contribution to the attainment of this objective. However, the speed with which the 'new' party broke with the old traditions of the Greek right does not appear to have kept pace with public expectations. The contribution of Karamanlis, and of New Democracy, to the success of the *transition* to a new democratic regime was widely recognized as being of major importance. But New Democracy's leading personnel were associated with the pre-junta period and the party's own ideology and organization were slow to modernize. As Lyrintzis has charged: 'New Democracy remained basically a party of notables which relied on MPs and their clientelistic networks for communicating with the electorate and rallying mass support.'[22] Others have charted its ideological confusion.[23] The party was slow to resolve an emerging debate as to whether to continue with the state paternalism of the past, allowing plenty of scope for clientelistic politics, or to reformulate itself along Thatcherite and neo-liberal lines, something which would represent a major innovation for Greece. New Democracy's failure to adapt meant that it was the election of PASOK in 1981 which prompted the most thorough revision of state–civil relations since the fall of the Colonels.

The election of PASOK brought with it changes of personnel, ideology, and organization. Mouzelis has drawn a historical parallel to portray the significance of the change of personnel:

> in the same way that Venizelism broke the restrictive, oligarchic control that a number of notable families were exercising over the means of domination in nineteenth-century Greece, so PASOK's rise to power has broken the hold that the pre-dictatorial parliamentary elites . . . had on Greek politics. In both cases, one sees the marked entrance of 'new men' into the political arena – 'new' not only, or mainly, in the sense that there was a systematic difference in class origin between the old and the new political elites, but also 'new' in the sense that during the *ancien regime* the latter were political outsiders or were only marginally involved in the political game.[24]

The ideology of PASOK in this context involved a commitment to a decentralization of power from the over-centralized and over-bearing state bureaucracy. The Greek state has had a long tradition of incorporation, undermining the autonomy of non-state political forces. However, as Mouzelis has also commented, PASOK came to power with a unique character: its leadership was substantially less dependent on local party 'bosses' involved in clientelistic networks; yet, at the national level, the party still also lacked effective means to keep the leader accountable and subject to control.[25] This gave the party leader, with his strong charismatic hold over his followers, relatively unrestrained power. Moreover, Mouzelis criticizes PASOK in office, for having adopted the 'typical incorporative tactics' of previous governments, in distributing favours and posts on a partisan basis. The implication is thus that PASOK has superimposed the power of its own leader on the traditional incorporatist and clientelistic character of state–civil society relations. PASOK was an effective vehicle for this: not only did its leader have popular appeal, but also the party had an extensive local organization, a feature unprecedented amongst the non-communist parties. PASOK had not, however, invented dependency, rather its predecessors had failed to erase it before they had left office.

The force of this argument depends on the extent to which PASOK personnel, and particularly its leader, have actually adopted incorporatist and clientelistic practices. While it is clear that they have not totally broken with the past, it may also be too harsh and simplistic to assert that the level of dependency has not lessened. A detailed assessment of this issue is beyond the scope of this chapter, but some general points can be made. On the 'debit' side reference can be made to PASOK's incorporatist policies in relation to trade unions (to be discussed later); to cultural affairs (the continued pro-government bias of state television and radio); and to partisan appointments in public bureaucracies. All three instances are cited by Mouzelis in support of his case. Further evidence might be gleaned from the series of financial scandals which affected a number of PASOK appointees in 1986–7. However, it must also be noted that PASOK has instituted a number of liberal reforms, improved decentralized service structures, and established representative bodies at the local and regional level with responsibilities in specified fields. Moreover, differentiation is necessary – indeed, contrasts must also be noted – not only between individual social groups, but also between urban and rural areas, when assessing the changes to the role of the state under PASOK.

PASOK's 'failures' can be partly related to two of its own characteristics: its over-inflated and ambiguous rhetoric before coming to office, and its own brand of paternalism in its approach to state–civil relations. The former is a consequence of its inexperience and the heterogeneity of the Greek electorate. The latter is of wider relevance to Socialists elsewhere, and it is a particularly important aspect of PASOK's philosophy relevant to the discussion here on state–civil relations in Greece, as it highlights the 'top-down' direction of political power and initiative.

After 1981 PASOK sought to distribute power downwards to a base which was socially and politically weak. Its successful transfer depended, at least partly, on the assertiveness and organization of the intended recipients, overcoming their own inexperience, and a wider climate of controversy and economic constraint. To some extent, the failure to decentralize power and responsibility adequately must therefore be explained in terms of these various systemic pressures and the ambitious objectives which had been laid down. The extension of 'incorporation' under PASOK has had a new character: it has stemmed from 'paternalistic' policies designed to establish channels and structures from the state to social groups previously marginalized. While the intention was to reinforce the self-reliance of the groups involved, the criticism, paradoxically, has been that in practice they have merely been incorporated into a benign state structure.

The tradition of clientelism and of incorporation has wider implications for relations between the state and political parties. Lyrintzis has argued that during the post-war period, but particularly after 1974, Greek governments have undertaken 'an organised expansion of existing posts and departments in the public sector and the addition of new ones in an attempt to secure power and maintain a party's electoral base'.[26] This he terms 'bureaucratic clientelism', and he comments, albeit very briefly, that following such practices weakens both party organization and ideology. The implication is that the ruling party becomes indistinct from the central state bureaucracy: its external organization is weak and subservient, its ideology little more than the pragmatism of government ministries. It is not that there is an inverse relationship between the strength of clientelism and ideology, rather it is a function of how the state mechanisms are used in themselves. It might also be added that this is itself the result of weak social structures independent of the state. The relevance of these social structures to the behaviour of the political parties will be discussed later.

Inter-party relations

Despite the extensive popular legitimacy of the post-1974 regime, relations between the parties continue to exhibit a deep-rooted and emotional polarization between 'left' and 'right'. While, as has already been noted, the new democratic system has turned away from the 'exclusivity' of the past, the divide between the parties remains fuelled by former controversies and images. Consolidation through consensualism or accommodation has not occurred, and the individual voter has supported a party not only (or perhaps mainly) by virtue of his/her membership of a particular socio-economic group, but also by adopting a political identification on either side of the party divide.[27] Traditionally a major determinant of the level of party support has also been the appeal of key personalities – the charisma of Karamanlis, George and Andreas Papandreou, for example – which has promoted some fluidity in voter choices. This 'personalism' has also been reflected in the lack of internal party democracy and the autocracy of the leader. While both these aspects continue to permeate party politics in the 1980s, there is some evidence to suggest a gradual move away from this traditional practice as attention is given to actual policy performance and as the parties seek to assimilate new demands.

One general component of the 'rules of the game' where the parties have been unable to come to a stable consensus, has been the provisions of the electoral law. Prior to 1967, the electoral law was subject to frequent revision, as it was seen as an instrument by which to secure particular political objectives.[28] Indeed the peculiarly Greek phenomenon of 'reinforced proportional representation' – first used in 1951, and then continuously since 1958 with minor changes – was itself born out of the bitterness and discrimination of the Civil War.[29] While New Democracy was in power, PASOK, together with the far left, urged the adoption of a 'simple' or pure version of proportional representation (PR). In office, PASOK introduced two sets of changes. The first (in 1983) abolished the 'preference cross' by which voters could discriminate between candidates of the same party in local multi-member constituencies. The practical effect of this was to increase the power of party leaders, as they now determined the rankings of the candidates offered to the voters. PASOK's second change (in January 1985) was to revise the electoral system: in reality, this was a variant of the old system, in that it gave even greater favour to the first placed party, while also helping third-placed smaller parties. This second change was accepted by both New Democracy and the then President Karamanlis, but the smaller parties accused PASOK of being afraid to lose its overall majority.[30] In 1986 the Communists (KKE) refused to support PASOK-backed candidates in the second round of the municipal elections, partly because of the government's failure to introduce 'simple' PR. Further revisions may be made in the future, but it seems certain that they will be the result of tactical considerations, rather than idealistic principle.

Inside Parliament, party relations have remained conflictual throughout the period under review. Highly charged debates, invoking populist rhetoric, have served to enlarge the differences between the parties in the public mind. Confrontations between the party leaders in parliamentary debates are infrequent and receive major television coverage, focusing attention on their impassioned exchanges. In recent years, Papandreou as prime minister might have held occasional private meetings with other party leaders, on matters of national importance, such as relations with Turkey, but few can doubt the personal animosity that exists between himself and Constantine Mitsotakis of New Democracy.[31] This polarization was reinforced by the demise of the forces of the centre. In 1964 the Centre Union had received almost 53 per cent of the popular vote; in 1974, after its own reformation, it obtained just over 20 per cent, but by 1977 it had collapsed to 12 per cent and by 1981 it had all but disappeared. Politicians of the centre, like their former electors, allied themselves with either one of the two largest parties. To remain in the middle of the divide was to invite political suicide. In the 1981 and 1985 parliamentary elections, the polarization was at its peak, coloured by a language of demonology, indiscriminate images, and the identification of two distinct subcultures. The legacies of earlier confrontations were recalled, a feature which might be seen as being part of a necessary exorcism for the modern polity, but the more immediate consequence was to heighten the political temperature.

From 1977 to 1985 PASOK challenged the right on behalf of all non-right forces – a broadly based rally-cry which maximized its support but left its own ideology somewhat unclear. Not until it was faced with acute domestic economic difficulties in its second term of office did the PASOK leadership turn the full force of its venom on the Communists (KKE). The KKE was now attacked as out-dated and slow to catch up with the spirit of 'glasnost' and 'perestroika' emanating from Moscow. Prior to 1985, the KKE had allied itself with PASOK's campaign for 'change'; in so doing it had contributed to the social integration of the new regime, but now its political stance was being repudiated and its electoral position seemed weak.

For its part, the ideological development of New Democracy after 1974 has appeared confused, unable to clarify its definition of a party of the right. The collapse of the Colonels' regime and the Greek fiasco in Cyprus had left public support for the western alliance at a low ebb and the old anti-Communist fears no longer seemed so potent. With the weakening of these foundations, the pre-1967 ideological framework of the right was at least in part being dismantled. New Democracy found refurbishment difficult: Karamanlis initially disavowed any overt identification with 'left' or 'right'; the old right had been statist and paternalistic to a degree, but the new fashion from abroad was neo-liberalism. After 1981, New Democracy charged PASOK with 'Third World adventurism' and 'totalitarian' instincts. As with PASOK, the two-party polarization enabled New Democracy to hide its ideological ambiguities; strong personality and generational clashes still remained within its ranks.

The spectrum of ideological positions was somewhat revised, however, after PASOK's October 1985 announcement of deflationary economic measures. PASOK dropped some of its earlier 'socialization' rhetoric in favour of a concern with modernization in the face of international competition and the new technologies. Papandreou announced that PASOK's founding charter needed adapting to 'today's realities'. He also proposed the selling of all 'problematic' firms to the private sector: 'fate has had it', he declared, 'that we will be the ones to limit bureaucratic statism in the economy'.[32] Papandreou has thus presented his party as being anti-statist, thereby stealing some of the rhetoric of New Democracy and rekindling PASOK's own decentralist spirit. The move had clearly been prompted by the stale political climate: the government's economic strategy had run into difficulties, and the opinion polls recorded widespread public disenchantment with all the main parties. The domestic ideological debate has thus been revised, although public opinion still appears undecided in its response.

In this atmosphere, to talk of 'normal' electoral swings would seem to be premature. Both parties have now won two successive national elections. Several phases have clearly been completed: the electoral reward for Karamanlis, the demise of the centre parties, the rehabilitation of the Communists, and the establishment of a popular non-Communist left-wing party. In 1981 and 1985 'new' people entered government, overcoming past alienations and frustrations. The post-1985 developments would appear to represent a new stage, but one difficult to predict from the past. Indeed, to some extent, the unpredictability of the present situation stems from the clash of traditional elements with the new, focusing on the relations between the state and the rest of society.

Thus the most salient and constant feature of inter-party relations during the period has been strong polarization – in fact, Greece has probably the highest degree of party-political polarization among west European democracies. While tending to simplify the structure of the party system, this has suggested an instability in political competition, accompanied as seen by some shifting of ideological positions. Given that democratic consolidation involves a lessening of the uncertainties of the transition period, this condition has hardly been favourable to the former or at least it has slowed down its achievement. On the other hand, it is difficult to argue that this intensity of inter-party relations has destabilized the new democratic system; indeed, it may be noted that different and often conflicting political tendencies have been accommodated within it.

Parties and society

The foregoing has already suggested the relative strength of the state over civil society, and the ideological positions of the political parties during the new democratic period have been crucially affected by changing attitudes to the role of the state. An important and illuminatory aspect of the behaviour of parties in a changing society are the relations they have established with other social institutions and movements. In the Greek context, weak social structures have contributed to a lack of authority independent of the state; parties have been both autocratic and interventionist. Such intervention from above is but an extension of how the parties themselves have maintained the power of the leadership over the grass roots in their own internal affairs. Such practices have implications for both horizontal and vertical pluralism in the relations between parties and society, and hence for the nature of democratic consolidation in Greece.

Relations between the state and the Orthodox Church have been relatively stable since the 1950s, though throughout the twentieth century successive governments have established the precedent of intervention in church affairs, with respect to both personnel and property.[33] Until 1987 PASOK followed a low-key approach, but its introduction of a bill in March of that year to transfer some 325,000 acres of forestry and arable land, together with 50,000 acres of much more valuable urban property, from the Church for distribution by the state, unleashed an intense controversy which went to the very heart of the issue of state intervention in society. The Church led a storm of protests at this interference: the relevant government minister was threatened with ex-communication.[34] The Church did not object to redistribution in principle, rather to its being administered by potentially partisan lay-bodies. It was also concerned that, devoid of revenue from the land, it might become more financially dependent on the state, with consequences for its non-party stance. The heat of the controversy eventually led to a compromise agreement between the Papandreou government and the Church before the end of 1987. The party in power had therefore not been able to override the Church. To many, this meant that pluralism had been safeguarded.

In wider society, where interest groups or movements have tried to pursue an autonomous course, their independence has frequently been under attack as a result of both state and party interference. Parties have created their own organizations to represent distinct sectional interests, and these bodies have remained subservient to the party leadership. Nevertheless, part of the post-1974 modernization process has been the emergence of 'new' issues with their own campaign organizations: for the environment, consumer protection, women's rights, peace, and so on. Moreover after the fall of the Colonels, a relative explosion of the democratic spirit led to wider and deeper forms of political involvement. As Fakiolas has noted, PASOK was the first to recognize the growing influence of interest groups: it sought to incorporate them 'into the party mechanism when that was possible' or at least to collaborate with them in order to spread its own influence.[35] This was in keeping with its idea of forging a coalition of the 'underprivileged' and of redistributing power.

The case of the trade union movement is indicative of the more traditional character of state and party involvement in the affairs of interest groups. Katsanevas has outlined the development of a 'paternalistic unionism' dating back to the years of Eleftherios Venizelos.[36] The state was seen as a regulator, but its 'protective disposition encouraged the attitude that the solution of labour problems should come from above – a factor which contributed to the emasculation of the trade unions'.[37] More generally, the weakness of the trade union movement in Greece is, in part, a result of the 'divide-and-rule policy of successive governments utilised for the purpose of controlling the movement from above'.[38] Catephores and Tzannatos have charged that the institutionalization of the labour market and of worker representation was a conscious attempt by the right to weaken the trade union movement.[39] After the fall of the Colonels, interference in the internal affairs of the main trade union confederation, the GSEE, continued. Under New Democracy, 'the Minister of Labour [was] in a position to control the internal power balance of the GSEE – and as a result, he can greatly influence its decision-making'.[40] The minister could exercise his party influence over the majority on the GSEE Executive, otherwise he could press the judicial representative (responsible for conducting the Confederation's elections) to take action resulting in the appointment of a new Executive.

The election of PASOK in 1981 promised the 'Democratization of Trade Unions'; its later Act of that name provided better union protection, introduced proportional representation into union elections, reformed the system for collecting union subscriptions, and eased the conditions on which a strike could be called. To PASOK's supporters, the Act was seen as a major step forward: Apostolidis described it as 'laying . . . the necessary conditions [which] will enable the [labour] movement to overcome [its] organizational, operational weakness'.[41] However, a further law (1365/1983) on the 'socialized' enterprises restricted a legal strike in these firms (Art. 4) to one where '50 per cent plus one' of all registered union members had voted in favour (abstentions thus counting as opposition). Left-wingers, including leading PASOK trade unionists, were strongly critical of this provision.

PASOK also intervened to change the composition of the GSEE Executive. The existing GSEE president and general secretary were replaced, and a new GSEE Council appointed with PASOK supporters in the majority, both changes being the result of two separate Court decisions in December 1981.[42] The changes were attacked from both left and right; a Socialist International delegation also sought an explanation from the prime minister in March 1982.[43] During PASOK's second term of office, its introduction of economic austerity measures led to a further controversy, this time involving a split between the party's own supporters in the GSEE. After October 1985, there were thus two executive committees: one formed by twenty-six members of the old one (seventeen Communists and nine Socialists) who rejected the austerity measures (they constituted the majority), and a second appointed by a Court decision in January 1986.[44] As a result of this split within PASOK, the party expelled seven leading trade unionists because of their disobedience.

Under PASOK, a number of liberalizing reforms had thus passed into statute to help the position of trade unionists, but the party none the less followed earlier practices: in effect, both state and party mechanisms were used to try to maintain ultimate control over union organizations. Opposition to PASOK's actions was constrained: New Democracy was associated with the abuses of the past, and the Communists with the subservience of 'democratic centralism'. An effective and autonomous trade union movement in Greece still remained to be established; political direction came from 'above' from government and parties. To pluralists, democratic consolidation was being limited by such party interference.

A similar theme is also of relevance to the parties' own internal, vertical structures: traditionally direction has come from the top; the social base has been subservient. Since the Colonels' overthrow, the parties have undergone an important, though limited, change with the establishment of their structures to include local branch organizations covering the country. Local politicization has been shown by the slogans daubed across the countryside. PASOK was the first to establish a widely based structure, and after its fall from government in 1981 New Democracy completed its own network.[45] The old, pre-1967 parties composed essentially of local notables (patrons in clientelistic networks) were thus disappearing, though internal democracy was slow to develop in the new parties. It was not until April 1977 that New Democracy held a congress, though this was only of a preliminary nature; it did not elect a party leader nor did it ratify a charter. The party's first full congress was held in May 1979, five years after the restoration of democracy. The delay inside PASOK was even longer: a congress was held in July 1977, but as no votes were held, the party labelled its May 1984 congress its 'first', though this was little more than a rally for the subsequent European elections. A second congress was due to be held in 1988. Both PASOK and New Democracy are dominated by charismatic leaders; personality politics remains important. Both leaders are brokers for patronage and they expect their followers to abide by strong party discipline. In both cases, a Member of Parliament may be expelled following a declaration by the leader that the MP's actions 'have placed him/herself outside of our party'.

Inside Greek political parties, power continues to flow downwards.

This has been affected by the nature of state–civil relations and by the weakness of wider social structures. The parties have integrated their publics into a new legitimate political system, but as vehicles for debate and representation they are still relatively under-developed. The slowness of this change is testimony to the legacy of a system of democratic politics with relatively weak social roots, gradually giving way to more deeply embedded structures along western European lines. Externally the parties claim to be seeking a liberalization of the relations between governments, parties, and interest groups, but again the change appears to be slow, and also controversial. Adapting to a new politics involving autonomy, the toleration of dissent, and effective accountability will thus take time.

Conclusions

It is clear from the foregoing brief survey of developments since 1974 that the analysis of the consolidation of the new Greek regime must have a wide focus, covering developments in the state structure as well as deeper social trends. Focusing on the role played by the political parties offers a single though crucial lens, but it must be turned in various directions and must consider attitudes and emotions beneath the immediate facade. The analysis is thus barely less complex. The foregoing discussion could not hope to cover all the components involved in the process of consolidation. However, three main themes have been highlighted in this survey of the development of the Greek parties and the continuation of the new regime. First, the parties have seen the use of the state apparatus as a means of extending their own hegemony, via intervention and incorporation. State pressures and encroachment have a pervasive effect on civil society. The state tradition has been paternalistic, but also elitist: power has been centralized. Traditionally the parties have been interventionist in civil society, despite the weakness of their own social roots. After 1974, intervention still came from the 'top'; and despite PASOK's decentralist promises, the party found it difficult to break with past practices. In recent years, however, political attitudes have been in the process of a slow revision, not merely by the adoption of 'anti-statism', but as a result of a wider recognition of the need to limit state encroachment on civil society and of alternative means for collective action.

A second, and related, theme has been that the effective operation of democratic processes in civil society has been limited by the weakness of social structures independent of the state and by the maintenance of traditional attitudes and practices. Structures which appear democratic have been undermined by the inability of civil society to develop strong pluralistic forces and by the continuation of illiberal, corrupting social norms and behaviour. Part of this wider social character has been the continuing relevance of personality and of personalism in party politics; traditionally, charisma and clientelism unified when ideologies and collective organization could not.

However, the third point is that the situation is not a vicious circle: indeed, a gradual process of change is in operation, with the traditions of the past on the defensive. This movement is one of 'modernization' and it is one serving to consolidate the post-1974 regime still further. The legacies of past divisions are being seen as less potent, new attitudes to state action are emerging, social change is undermining traditional society, and the continuing viability of the two main parties is establishing them as collective forces with a life of their own. Despite the frenetic tenor of everyday politics, however, change is occurring slowly. Moreover, the demand for change from 'below' remains weak, disparate, and unfocused.

In so far as the democratic course now seems secure in Greece, the new regime can be said to have been 'consolidated' in a minimal sense. The process of change referred to above, however, appears likely to have a momentum which will reconstitute important elements of the political culture; the consolidation will thus be a moving one, with an intensification of democratic norms and practices. It is not helpful to differentiate the structures of state and society in terms of their 'degree' of consolidation; one affects the other, and both seem likely to change in Greece, with the effect that the democratic spirit is reinforced.

The process of consolidating the new democratic regime after 1974 has seen a key role played by the political parties. As the link between state action and wider society, their impact has been of crucial importance, yet the nature of their contribution has been fundamentally shaped by the character of Greek society. Examining their role highlights the relative importance of traditional attitudes and past divisions on the one hand, and new norms and behaviour on the other. For the gradual adoption of the latter to continue will require a response from the main parties; indeed, it will be crucial. Observing the behaviour of Greek political parties will thus remain essential to understanding the progress of the new regime.[46]

Postscript

The above analysis was completed early in 1987. During the next two years Greek politics were turned 'upside-down' as a result of revelations of corruption and maladministration at the very centre of the party–state structure. It is appropriate, then, that this brief note should be added to relate these events to the themes discussed above.

The scandals and controversies of 1988–9 confirm the importance of examining the role and behaviour of political parties in the Greek consolidation process. The revelations concern the relationship between the party in power, its mis-use of state mechanisms, and the impact of what was termed above 'illiberal, corrupting social norms and behaviour'. Few could have predicted what was subsequently revealed, but to some extent established practices and structures made Greek politics vulnerable to such behaviour if the ethical standards of key office-holders were especially low.

A whole series of scandals involving PASOK personnel and PASOK appointees have been alleged.[46] Two major scandals have received widespread attention. The first stemmed from the fraud and embezzlement of the head of the privately-owned Bank of Crete, George Koskotas. Major public undertakings transferred their accounts to his bank for exceptionally low rates of interest. From the profits made, Koskotas alleges that he was obliged to transfer large sums of money to government figures and to PASOK. In addition, it has been alleged that extensive and illegal telephone tapping was undertaken of many individuals of direct personal and political interest to the Prime Minister, a post which carries with it responsibility for the security services. In both cases, Papandreou faces indictment. However, evidence relevant to many of these scandals can be expected to continue to emerge well into 1990, and thus the precise political consequences remain unclear.

In the light of what has become known in the last two years, judgements on the operation of the PASOK Government are obviously likely to be more harsh than that offered above. Evidence has been offered, *inter alia*, of the mis-use of public funds for both personal and party gain, the illegal telephone surveillance of political opponents, and the attempted manipulation of sections of the private news media. The explanation of these incidents must look beyond the behaviour of corrupt individuals to the context in which they were operating. A deeper understanding can be gained by focusing on the clientelism practised by PASOK whilst in power, the inadequate accountability of state bureaucracies, the dependence of groups and bodies in wider society on those in power, and the lack of internal democracy within the party in power. The relevance of these themes is clear from Greek history prior to PASOK's rise to power, and each were highlighted in the preceding discussion.

Against the background of the scandals, the June 1989 elections were held amidst demands for 'Katharsis': a cleansing of public administration.[47] Again, allegations were made of the mis-use of power by PASOK even up to polling day. Large numbers of public sector jobs were apparently offered to wavering supporters, for example. Despite its tribulations, PASOK did not suffer a resounding defeat: indeed, the result was that no party had an overall majority in the unicameral

Parliament. PASOK received 39.2 per cent of the vote (and 125 seats out of 300), New Democracy 44.3 per cent (145 seats), and a centrist breakaway party from New Democracy (DI ANA – Democratic Renewal) 1.0 per cent (one seat).

For the elections, the electoral system was once again changed: another variant of 'reinforced PR' was used. The new system was more generous to the plethora of small parties which usually contest Greek elections. The effect was to deny New Democracy the overall majority it would have secured under the previous system.

With the inconclusive outcome of the elections a further contest was expected before the end of the year. In the interim, New Democracy had agreed to govern with the Communist coalition (Synaspismos) in order to begin the legal action needed to bring about Katharsis. This was a remarkable outcome, given the bitter legacies of the Civil War. This reconciliation was testimony to the continuing process of social integration apparent since 1974. It was also, of course, a strategic move in the self-interest of the parties involved. The viability of PASOK was now very much in question, with its leader facing trial. By contrast, the far left had undergone some transformation: the KKE was finally catching up with Gorbachev and most of the Euro-Communists (KKE-es) had established a new party (the Greek Left) which sought broader support.

Despite the revelations of wrong-doing, the constitutional system survived and the process of Katharsis was set in motion. The prejudices existing between the Communists and the right were overcome. The Greek democratic system had been shaken and shamed, but it came through the crisis without serious challenge. The constitutional structure passed another test: it was even more apparent that the crucial weakness was in the operation of the parties themselves – notably, the particular party in power.

Notes

1. S. Giner, 'Southern European socialism in transition', in G. Pridham (ed.) *The New Mediterranean Democracies: Regime Transition in Spain, Greece and Portugal*, London, Frank Cass, 1984.
2. K.M. Dowding and R. Kimber, 'The meaning and use of "political stability"', *European Journal of Political Research*, September 1983.
3. On the transition, see R. Clogg, *A Short History of Modern Greece*, Cambridge, Cambridge University Press, 1979; P.N. Diamandouros, 'The 1974 transition from authoritarian to democratic rule in Greece ...', Bologna, Johns Hopkins University, occasional paper 37, 1981; Diamandouros, 'Greek political culture in transition ...', in R. Clogg (ed.) *Greece in the 1980s*, London, Macmillan/CGS, 1983; C.M. Woodhouse, *The Rise and Fall of the Greek Colonels*, London, Granada, 1985.

On events before and after the coup, see also R. Clogg and G. Yannopoulos (eds) *Greece under Military Rule*, London, Secker & Warburg, 1972; A. Papandreou, *Democracy at Gunpoint: The Greek Front*, Harmondsworth, Penguin, 1971.

4. See Introduction in K. Featherstone and D.K. Katsoudas (eds) *Political Change in Greece: Before and After the Colonels*, London, Croom Helm, 1987.

5. See P.N. Diamandouros, 'Transition to, and consolidation of, democratic politics in Greece, 1974–1983: a tentative assessment', in Pridham (ed.) op. cit. He notes three key assumptions of the strategy: the most sensitive issues should not be tackled until after new elections had given added legitimacy to the regime, nor before the loyalty of the enforcement agencies had been secured, and in the mean time a thorough purge of the army was impracticable if a fresh coup was to be avoided.

6. See relevant chapter in Featherstone and Katsoudas, op. cit.

7. Featherstone and Katsoudas, op. cit., p. 20.

8. *Keesing's Archives*, 26,894

9. Featherstone and Katsoudas, op. cit., p. 23.

10. ibid., p. 25.

11. Support from PASOK and Communist MPs was insufficient to get their nominee, Christos Sartzetakis, elected on the first and second rounds of voting, but he was successful on the third round (29 March 1985) which required a lower threshold. PASOK had earlier been annoyed at the failure of one or two MPs, who had defected from it after 1981, to support Sartzetakis and pressure was exerted upon PASOK's own doubters before the final vote. When the final vote was held – in the full glare of the television lights – different coloured ballot papers were issued; the effect was to make any disloyalty more obvious. Sartzetakis was eventually elected only by the casting vote of the Speaker, who had become acting president after Karamanlis' resignation, and his participation was itself a controversial act. New Democracy abstained in the presidential votes, and it refused to recognize Sartzetakis until after the elections. Although Sartzetakis' election removed any constitutional requirement for an early election, PASOK decided to go to the polls to seek a renewal of its mandate. It was again victorious, its overall majority intact.

12. Featherstone and Katsoudas, op. cit., p. 28.

13. In February 1975 a plot for a new coup attempt was discovered, with Maj. Gen. Dimitrios Ioannides as its chief instigator. After twenty-three officers were arrested and tried, prosecution witnesses stated that the rebels had claimed the support of defeated Royalist elements, the Primate of the Orthodox Church, and former PM Stefanos Stefanopoulos. The leniency of their sentences caused some surprise. However, Diamandouros, 1984, op. cit., notes that 'in less than six months, the protagonists of the 1967 coup, the leaders of the February 1975 foiled coup, together with the major figures in the suppression of the Polytechnic uprising and in the torturing of prisoners during the seven-year regime, were brought to trial and received sentences varying from life imprisonment for the major figures to lesser sentences for the others'.

14. See his chapter in Featherstone and Katsoudas, op. cit., p. 225.
15. Diamandouros, 1983, op. cit., p. 52.
16. Diamandouros, 1984, op. cit., p. 60.
17. Clogg, 1979, op. cit., p. 168.
18. See chapter by Featherstone in Featherstone and Katsoudas, op. cit., p. 36.
19. P. Dimitras' chapter in Featherstone and Katsoudas, op. cit., p. 82.
20. V. Kapetanyannis in Featherstone and Katsoudas, op. cit., p. 160.
21. ibid., p. 160.
22. C. Lyrintizis, 'Political parties in post-junta Greece: a case of bureaucratic clientelism', in Pridham (ed.) op. cit., p. 106.
23. See J.C. Loulis, 'The Greek Conservative movement in transition: from paternalism to neo-liberalism?', in *The New Liberalism: The Future of Non-Collectivist Institutions in Europe and the USA*, Athens, Centre for Political Research and Information, 1981; and Katsoudas in Featherstone and Katsoudas, op. cit.
24. See Mouzelis in Featherstone and Katsoudas, op. cit., pp. 271–2.
25. ibid., p. 277.
26. Lyrintzis in Pridham, op. cit., pp. 103–4.
27. See K. Featherstone and D. Katsoudas, 'Change and continuity in Greek voting behaviour', *European Journal of Political Research*, March 1985, 13, 1. I am grateful to I. Papadopoulos (Geneva) for having raised this point with me.
28. Until 1926, elections were held on the basis of the simple plurality system in single or multi-member constituencies. Thereafter regular changes occurred: in 1926, 'simple' proportional representation (PR) was used; the plurality system returned in 1928, then simple PR in 1932, plurality in 1933 and 1935, simple PR in 1936, a different version of PR in 1946 and 1950, 'reinforced' PR in 1951, plurality in 1952, mixed plurality and PR in 1956, and finally, since 1958, various forms of reinforced PR. See P. Dimitras, 'Special report on Greek politics', in *Greek Opinion*, Athens, Eurodim, January 1985.
29. See Featherstone and Katsoudas, 1987, op. cit., p. 39.
30. In the 1985 elections, PASOK as the first party received 7.8 per cent more seats in Parliament than its national vote would have warranted under a strictly proportional form of representation, a small decrease in the favour shown to it in 1981 (9.3 per cent).
31. Mitsotakis was one of the renegades from G. Papandreou's Centre Union at the time of the 1965 crisis.
32. See F. Eleftheriou's article in *The Athenian*, October 1987.
33. Article 3 of the 1975 Constitution refers to the Orthodox faith as 'the prevailing religion'. Less than 10 per cent of Greeks have not been raised in the Orthodox faith. Moreover, the Greek state pays the Church an annual allowance to cover the costs of priests' salaries. On past government intervention, see C.A. Frazee's chapter in J.T.A. Koumoulides (ed.) *Greece in Transition: Essays in the History of Modern Greece, 1821–1974*, London, Zeno, 1977.
34. The Church also boycotted the traditional service of Greek Independence Day (25 March), and it organized a number of well-supported demonstrations.
35. See Fakiolas in Featherstone and Katsoudas, 1987, op. cit., pp. 183–4.

36. Th.K. Katsanevas, *Trade Unions in Greece*, Athens, National Centre of Social Research, 1984.
37. ibid., pp. 84–5.
38. ibid., p. 258.
39. See their chapter in Z. Tzannatos (ed.) *Socialism in Greece: The First Four Years*, London, Gower, 1986.
40. Katsanevas, op. cit., p. 233.
41. L.Th. Apostolidis, *Trade Unions and Socialist Transformation,* Athens, Ekdoseis Aichmi, 1984, p. 32 (in Greek).
42. Katsanevas, op. cit., pp. 260–1.
43. ibid., p. 261.
44. Fakiolas in Featherstone and Katsoudas, 1987, op. cit., pp. 175–6.
45. By 1980 PASOK had approximately 75,000 members, but in recent years this has probably fallen. In 1979 ND claimed 100,000 members.
46. See K. Featherstone, 'The party-state in Greece and the fall of Papandreou', *West European Politics*, December 1989.
47. See Featherstone, ibid.

Bibliographical references

Apostolidis, L.Th. (1984) *Trade Unions and Socialist Transformation,* Athens, Ekdoseis Aichmi (in Greek).
Calligas, C. (1987) 'The centre: decline and convergence', in Featherstone and Katsoudas (1987).
Catephores, G. and Tzannatos, Z. (1986) 'Trade unions in Greece: 1949–81 and 1981–83', in Tzannatos (1986).
Clogg, R. (1979) *A Short History of Modern Greece*, Cambridge, Cambridge University Press.
—— (ed.) (1983) *Greece in the 1980s*, London, Macmillan/CGS.
—— (1988) *Parties and Elections in Greece*, London, Hurst.
Clogg, R. and Yannopoulos, G. (eds) (1972) *Greece under Military Rule*, London, Secker & Warburg.
Diamandouros, P.N. (1981) 'The 1974 transition from authoritarian to democratic rule in Greece . . .' Bologna, Johns Hopkins University, occasional paper 37.
—— (1983) 'Greek political culture in transition . . .', in Clogg (1983).
—— (1984) 'Transition to, and consolidation of, democratic politics in Greece, 1974–1983: a tentative assessment', in Pridham (1984).
Dimitras, P. (1985) 'Special report on Greek politics', *Greek Opinion*, January, Athens.
—— (1987) 'Changes in public attitudes', in Featherstone and Katsoudas (1987).
Dowding, K.M. and Kimber, R. (1983) 'The meaning and use of "political stability"', *European Journal of Political Research*.
Eleftheriou, F. (1987) article in *The Athenian*, October, Athens.
Fakiolas, R. (1987) 'Interest groups – an overview', in Featherstone and Katsoudas (1987).

—— (1989) 'The party–state in Greece and the fall of Papandreou', *West European Politics*, December.

Featherstone K. (1987a) 'Introduction', in Featherstone and Katsoudas (1987).

—— (1987b) 'Elections and voting behaviour', in Featherstone and Katsoudas (1987).

—— (1989) 'The party–state in Greece and the fall of Papandreou', *West European Politics*, December.

Featherstone, K. and Katsoudas, D.K. (1985) 'Change and continuity in Greek voting behaviour', *European Journal of Political Research*, March, 13, 1.

—— (eds) (1987) *Political Change in Greece: Before and After the Colonels*, London, Croom Helm.

Frazee, C.A. (1977) 'Church and state in Greece', in Koumoloulides (1977).

Giner, S. (1984) 'Southern European socialism in transition', in Pridham (1984).

Herz, J.H. (1982) *From Dictatorship to Democracy: Coping with the Legacies of Authoritarianism and Totalitarianism*, Westport, Conn., Greenwood Press.

Kapetanyannis, V. (1987) 'The Communists', in Featherstone and Katsoudas (1987).

Katsanevas, Th.K. (1984) *Trade Unions in Greece*, National Centre of Social Research, Athens.

Katsoudas, D.K. (1987a) 'The Conservative movement and New Democracy . . .', in Featherstone and Katsoudas (1987).

—— (1987b) 'The constitutional framework', in Featherstone and Katsoudas (1987).

Koumoulides, J.T.A. (ed.) (1977) *Greece in Transition: Essays in the History of Modern Greece, 1821–1974*, London, Zeno.

Loulis, J.C. (1981a) 'The Greek Conservative movement in transition: from paternalism to neo-liberalism?', in *The New Liberalism: The Future of Non-Collectivist Institutions in Europe and the USA*, Centre for Political Research and Information, Athens.

Lyrintzis, C. (1984) 'Political parties in post-junta Greece: a case of bureaucratic clientelism?' in Pridham (1984).

Mavrogordatos, G.Th. (1983) 'The rise of the green sun: the Greek election of 1981', London, Centre for Contemporary Greek Studies, occasional paper 1.

Mouzelis, N. (1987) 'Continuities and discontinuities in Greek politics: from Eleftherious Veneizelos to Andreas Papandreou', in Featherstone and Katsoudas (1987).

Papandreou, A. (1971) *Democracy at Gunpoint: The Greek Front*, London.

Pridham, G. (ed.) (1984) *The New Mediterranean Democracies: Regime Transition in Spain, Greece and Portugal*, London, Frank Cass.

Tzannatos, Z. (ed.) (1986) *Socialism in Greece: The First Four Years*, London, Gower.

Veremis, Th. (1987) 'The military', in Featherstone and Katsoudas (1987).

Woodhouse, C.M. (1985) *The Rise and Fall of the Greek Colonels*, London, Granada.

Chapter nine

To be or not to be within the European Community: the party debate and democratic consolidation in Greece

Susannah Verney

Democratic consolidation and the Greek transition

Although political scientists are still feeling their way towards an understanding of what constitutes a consolidated democracy, the definitions which they have produced so far indicate that the key lies in the perceptions of the political actors. Thus M. Cotta believes that 'full consolidation' can be regarded as achieved when all the major political forces 'accept the fundamental rules of the democratic game and are confident that each other will comply with them'.[1] The implication would seem to be that democratic consolidation is largely an intellectual process of modifying attitudes to the system until the point where all those involved are prepared to play by its rules.

Meanwhile for Philippe Schmitter, consolidation means 'converting patterns into structures', with the actors coming 'to regard the rules and resources of these emergent structures as given, if not desirable'.[2] This suggests that the establishment of a new democratic system falls into two phases, with consolidation as the period of habituation to the structures set up during the transition from the previous regime.

Geoffrey Pridham has suggested that the shift from the first stage to the second occurs with the 'closing of options' at the first two levels of parliamentary institutionalization. In his three-level model of this process, he defines the 'macro-choice' as the initial decision to adopt a liberal democratic model; the 'meso-choice' concerns whether the system will be presidential or parliamentary and also determines the nature of popular representation through the selection of electoral law; while the last level is the 'micro-choice' rules of the game of the agreed institutional structures.[3]

The Greek transition occurred very rapidly. In the midst of a national crisis with war against Turkey apparently imminent, former Prime Minister Constantine Karamanlis, recalled from his Parisian exile by the political and military leadership, was able to establish a liberal democratic model which marked a major break with the past. While the dictatorship of 1967–74 had assumed a much more oppressive form than its semi-parliamentary predecessor, both these regimes had functioned within a logic shaped by NATO's strategic concerns, which used the spectre of 'Pan-Slav Communism' to identify domestic enemies with Balkan schemes against Greek territorial integrity. Hence Karamanlis' legalization of the Communist parties in September 1974 gave the new parliamentary regime a completely different basis from its 1960s predecessor.

The new system quickly passed its first test with the November 1974 election, widely regarded as the fairest electoral contest to have been held up till then in Greece's post-war history. The meso-level issue of the monarchy was peacefully settled when a majority voted against the return of the King in the December referendum, while the February 1975 discovery of a planned coup attempt left the new regime unshaken. It thus seems reasonable to regard the passage of the Constitution in June 1975 as marking the end of the transition process. While the meso-level issue of the electoral law was not settled, indeed remaining controversial to this day, the 1975 Constitution established the basic form of the system which was to function throughout the following decade. Having acquired legal personality, the new regime was now on course for consolidation.

That it had been possible to complete transition in eleven months was probably largely due to the national crisis which created the perception of a stark choice between 'Karamanlis or the tanks'. However, the process was undoubtedly facilitated by the fact that after the initial 'Government of Seventy Days', which had included centrist personalities, transition had been handled exclusively by one party, New Democracy; indeed, some would say, it had been kept more or less under the firm control of one man, Constantine Karamanlis.

But while this made defining the new political framework easier, it suggested that its consolidation was likely to be highly conflictual. In the parliamentary vote on the Constitution in June 1975, all the opposition parties abstained in protest against the meso-level choice of a President of the Republic with Gaullist powers. But it was another event in the same month, the submission of Greece's formal application for full membership of the European Community, which triggered a debate on the whole question of the regime, including the macro-level choice of a liberal democratic model.

The external factor in the history of the modern Greek state

If it initially appears surprising that the debate on EC membership was so closely connected to the regime question, this can be regarded as the unfortunate consequence of the 'compartmentalization' of political science so deeply regretted by Rosenau.[4] When studying the establishment of new regimes, it is important to avoid an over-narrow focus on domestic institutions, viewed in isolation from the broader system of which they form an integral part.

The implication that national political parties can be regarded as autonomous actors can result in misperceptions of their role, especially in the Greek case. For example, the origins of the 1967–74 junta lay in the nature of the authoritarian parliamentary system, whose position in the international order precluded major liberalization. While the Centre Union was permitted to form an administration, it was rapidly manoeuvred out of government when it attempted to adjust the military–civilian power balance. When the mass popular mobilization of the 1960s indicated that the existing framework could no longer contain the rising demands of the new urban classes created by rapid modernization, the authoritarian right took over with the aim of achieving popular demobilization through military dictatorship. Failure to understand the overall context can lead to the causes of this regime failure being sought at the domestic level in the allegedly irresponsible behaviour of political parties.

The Greeks themselves, however, take for granted an explicit connection between the political regime and its external links. Any foreigner participating in the national sport of talking politics is made rapidly aware of the impossibility of confining discussion to the domestic plane. It often seems as if a considerable proportion of the population views the polity as an only partially autonomous sub-unit of its broader international environment. Long before political scientists recognized the importance of linkages between national and international systems, the Greeks believed that the nature of their regime was largely determined by the 'foreign factor'.

The Greek nation-state had been established in 1833 under an imported Bavarian monarch by agreement between the Ottoman Empire and Britain, France, and Russia. The titles of the original Greek political parties, known as the Russian, French, and English parties after their respective patrons, reflected general recognition of the real power sources in mid-nineteenth-century Greece. Over the ensuing century, the extent of foreign influence varied, according to the role Greece played in the rivalries between these foreign governments. But with the settlement following the Second World War, old-fashioned imperialist spheres of influence were institutionalized into a bipolar bloc system. With Europe split between two hostile camps armed with nuclear weapons and claiming to represent diametrically opposed systems, Greece's front-line position made that country's external orientation a principal determinant of its political and socio-economic structures.

Greece's strategic significance in the anti-Soviet crusade not only impelled the USA to ensure the form of its regime, but also prompted it to intervene regularly during the early post-war years, for example over the meso-level question of the electoral law, with the aim of infusing Greece's parliamentary system with a distinctly anti-Communist content. Thus while Greece's geopolitical orientation determined the general form of its political institutions, its incorporation into the western bloc as a US client-state conditioned the way in which they functioned. The close identification of the post-war regime with US security interests and of the latter with maintaining a politically powerful military as a guarantee against Communism, made it inevitable that the replacement of the controlled parliamentary system by a military dictatorship would be regarded as US-inspired.[5]

When the junta fell as the result of what was widely regarded as a US sell-out over Cyprus,[6] Greece was swept by a tide of vehement anti-Americanism, prompting even the staunch right-wing newspaper, *Akropolis*, to run a four-part series entitled 'How the Americans Cheated Greece'.[7] It had become a universal conviction that the establishment of a democratic regime required a fundamental change in Greece's relationship with the USA. With the withdrawal from the military wing of NATO in August 1974, Greece seemed to be embarking on a major re-evalution of the way it related to the rest of the world.

In a country with such a traditionally tight link between external orientation and domestic political and economic system, the implication was that the latter was also up for re-evaluation; and, as *The Economist* darkly remarked, 'Nobody knows when the repression of a dictatorship is lifted, what forces have been growing unseen beneath it.'[8] But with the application for European Community membership, Karamanlis was able to set the agenda for this debate, keeping the discussion within safe parameters by focusing it around the question of whether Greece was to be or not to be within the EC.

The EC and Greek democracy

In a society so sensitive to the effects of foreign influences on the domestic regime, the relationship with the EC had always been regarded as primarily political. In the Cold War climate of the late 1950s and early 1960s, the association with the Community had been seen as part of the anti-Soviet defence system, with all parties perceiving the EC as an economic adjunct to NATO. The right-wing governing party, the National Radical Union, had expected the 1962 Association Agreement, by strengthening Greece's ties to the west, to reinforce the existing political structures. While the Centre Union also approved the EC link as part of its general support for a western-type system, it seems that some in the party hoped that closer ties with the west European democracies would encourage a liberalization of Greece's authoritarian parliamentarism. Meanwhile the United Democratic Left, which rejected Greece's western orientation, vociferously opposed any kind of link with the European Community, which it believed would intensify US domination and perpetuate what it regarded as the current undemocratic system.[9]

But in the post-1974 era, when Greece was seeking a new direction, the European Community acquired a new significance. The way in which the EC had differentiated its stance towards the dictatorship from that of the USA suggested that the two major components of the western alliance could no longer be regarded as identical. This aroused hopes that accession could change the way in which Greece was incorporated into the western bloc, enhancing its independence from its former patron. For its supporters in Greece, EC membership seemed to hold out the promise that a country which had been an object of superpower politics throughout its modern history could at last become a more autonomous actor on the international and also on the domestic stage.

In addition, the Community's response to the coup had underlined the fact that the EC link had direct implications for the Greek political system. By limiting the Association Agreement to its 'current administration',[10] the Community had made the point that its relationship with Greece depended on the existence of an elected Parliament.[11] During the junta's later years, this encouraged various political personalities, notably J. Pesmazoglu, the chief Greek negotiator of the Association Agreement, to press for a restoration of democracy in order to improve Greece's relations with the Community.[12]

This strengthened a perception, which became universal in Greece after the fall of the dictatorship, that the stabilization of the parliamentary system and accession to the EC were interrelated. It is worth noting that this view was shared by the European Commission, which explicitly linked a favourable response to the Greek, Spanish, and Portuguese applications for full membership with the consolidation of their new democratic regimes.[13] Meanwhile in Greece, both supporters and opponents of accession believed that EC membership would lock Greece into a particular institutional pattern, closely resembling that of the west European liberal democracies.

This would be based on the creation of a permanent relationship. It is in the nature of the integration process that it becomes increasingly irreversible. The legal aspects alone of disengagement from the EC, involving a mountain of complicated issues requiring solution, would be enough to keep any government fully occupied for a considerable time, preventing the implementation of other aspects of its programme.

Meanwhile the economic consequences of trying to disengage from the integration process once it has got under way are incalculable. At the same time, integration is cumulative. Compulsory harmonization of national legislation with that of the EC meant that as the Community extended its responsibilities, there would be more and more areas in which Greek institutional structures would come to resemble those of the other member-states.

Hence in Greece it was believed that EC membership implied a lasting commitment to the current Community definition of a democratic system. Joining the EC would not only help the political system to gel into a particular mould, but would also fix it there, preventing any major deviations either to left or right of the west European norm. Consequently accession was seen as erecting serious obstacles to future attempts to dismantle rather than simply modify the system already set up. With the decision to take Greece into the Community making it potentially impossible to overturn the macro-level choice of a liberal democracy, Karamanlis had found a convincing way to ensure that the system of which he had been the architect was built to last.

The accession debate

This aspect of EC membership was well understood by all the other political forces with the result that one of the major axes of the accession debate was the anticipated consequences for Greek democracy.

New Democracy (ND): Speaking in Parliament about the advantages of EC entry, Prime Minister Karamanlis placed democratic stabilization high on the list of topics for discussion.[14] ND hoped EC membership would improve national security by strengthening Greece in relation to Turkey, and it also expected free trade with western Europe to stimulate Greece's economic development, encouraging the emergence of a modern capitalist state on the EC model. But when the prime minister summoned the Athens ambassadors of the member-states the day the Greek petition was presented in Brussels, he told them that the motivation for the Greek application was 'first and foremost political, as it is concerned with the consolidation of democracy and the future of the nation'.[15]

Through his choice of title for the governing party, Karamanlis had tried to identify democracy with his administration. At the same time, ND's slogan of 'Greece belongs to the west' implied an innate national orientation towards an area which, for many Greeks, represented a more advanced form of democracy. So while also expecting the EC to punish democratic violations with sanctions,[16] ND's main argument was that Greece's democratic institutions would be strengthened 'within the democratic west'.[17] That the concepts of western Europe and democracy had virtually merged in the minds of some ND supporters was suggested when a leading minister, asked to supply a preface to a book on 'Europeanism', chose to write six-and-a-half pages about democracy without a single reference to the mundane reality of the EC.[18]

The traditional Centre: The forces of the traditional centre also closely equated the European Community with democracy, sharing the view implicit in ND's policy that accession to an EC which was gaining increasing autonomy from the superpowers would limit the US potential for intervention and thus set Greek democracy on a firmer basis. But the European Community which provided the Centre's model was not identical to the EC perceived by ND. In economics, the Centre stressed the mixed economies of the EC member-states,[19] while in the political sphere it focused on the social democratic aspects of the west European experience. Believing democracy was not functioning properly under the current government, the Centre hoped EC membership would not only protect parliamentarism, but also stimulate democratic renewal.[20]

But while it expressed serious doubts about ND's democratic credentials and queried its interpretation of democracy, the Centre's differences with the governing party mainly concerned the way the system should be handled in practice. At the conceptual level, there was no fundamental disagreement about the nature of democracy which both parties identified with the west European model of bourgeois liberal parliamentarism. While rather more hostile towards NATO and the USA than ND was, the Centre took Greece's general politico-military orientation for granted, consequently agreeing with the adoption of western structures. Operating within a similar theoretical framework to ND, the Centre could play the role of a 'loyal opposition', contesting the government's interpretation of democracy without challenging the overall system.

PASOK: This was not the case with PASOK, which described its attitude as one of 'structural opposition' towards the regime.[21] Initially seeing the fall of the dictatorship as no more than 'a change of the NATO guard in Athens', party president Andreas Papandreou declared that he had founded PASOK, not as a political party operating within a democratic polity, but as a national liberation movement struggling to free Greece from imperialist control.

The view of Greece's place in the world promoted by PASOK was fundamentally different from that of the right and centre. In line with the dependence theory fashionable among Latin American scholars, the party attributed the frailty of Greek democracy to the country's mode of incorporation into the world capitalist system. It claimed that democracy had to be distorted or suppressed in peripheral countries like Greece to ensure they played their allotted economic role in the service of metropolitan monopoly capital.[22] Rather than expecting accession to improve Greece's democratic prospects by shifting it from the margins to the metropolis of the capitalist system, PASOK maintained that EC entry would make democracy permanently unstable by cementing an unequal relationship. In the party's view the Community, thoroughly penetrated by American monopoly capital and part of 'the same syndicate' as NATO, offered no alternative to US domination. Thus, adopting a slogan of 'Greece for the Greeks', PASOK called for a break with the imperialist system as the only way to achieve a healthy democracy in Greece.

Because of the close link between geopolitical orientation and the political system, PASOK's challenge to the former was generally interpreted as necessarily extending to the latter. But in fact it was never clarified how far the party's emphatic anti-imperialism entailed the rejection of western institutions. The basis of its programme was broad popular participation through decentralized decision-making, while 'socialization', the key to its economic strategy, seemed to mean work-force representation on boards of management. Neither appeared incompatible with western models or EC membership.

KKE: In contrast, the Communist Party of Greece, one of the most orthodox CPs in western Europe, favoured moving towards the political and economic pattern of the opposing military camp. For this party, the Soviet model was the route to Socialism and the latter the only democratic system. Meanwhile the European Community was seen as representing unredeemed capitalism, whose aim of facilitating income transfer from labour to the monopolies could not be achieved under a democratic system. The KKE described EC entry as 'an international act by which Greece would decisively turn its back on the socialist world and socialist ideas'.[23] The party saw accession as designed to perpetuate an imperialist control over Greece which it regarded as totally incompatible with democracy.

Nor did the party agree that accession could provide greater leeway for Greek democracy by increasing the country's autonomy within the imperialist camp. Not only did it see the EC as totally subordinated to US influence, but also the party claimed that even within the Community, inequality between the member-states was safeguarded institutionally.[24] Hence, while the KKE agreed with ND and the Centre that accession would stabilize the current Greek regime, it believed this would prevent Greece becoming democratic.

KKE-Es: The KKE-Esoterikou, formed following the split in the Central Committee of the KKE in January 1968, also defined democracy as Socialist democracy and agreed that the democratic dangers would only disappear with the end of imperialist dependence. But not enjoying the KKE's intimacy with Moscow, this party regarded a move to the Soviet camp as neither feasible nor desirable, meanwhile believing that

PASOK's non-alignment would in practice 'bind the country even more suffocatingly to the US' with deleterious democratic consequences.[25] Like the other Eurocommunist parties, the KKE-Es was thus compelled to base its hopes on a radical change in the international environment, expected to culminate in the dissolution of both the Soviet and the imperialist blocs.

A dynamic assessment of the international situation allowed Eurocommunism to replace a Soviet-style direct assault on the state with revolution by evolution. The assumption that representative institutions could be gradually broadened until they acquired a Socialist content resulted in a perception of the EC's bourgeois democratic framework as providing a favourable environment for the growth of Socialism. Furthermore, the Eurocommunists allocated the EC the major role in triggering the internal transformation of the bipolar system, detecting a growing contradiction between the USA and the European Community which they believed would push the latter's development in an increasingly independent and progressive direction. For the KKE-Es, Greece's long-term democratic prospects were thus inseparably linked to the metamorphosis of the current 'EC of the Monopolies' into a future 'EC of the Working Peoples'.

The implications of the debate

From this brief synopsis of the parties' views, it becomes clear that the accession debate in Greece went far beyond the question of adjustments to trade policy. Indeed when it came to the mechanics of the EC's functioning and their specific sectoral consequences, the Greek political forces displayed varying degrees of ignorance. This reflected a lack of interest stemming from the fact that none of the parties saw this aspect as the major point at issue. With the fall of the dictatorship apparently opening up all kinds of possibilities, Greece had reached a crucial point in its history. The economic details of membership paled into insignificance beside the much broader question of the country's whole future path. The EC debate thus evolved into a major discussion of the basic form to be taken by the new Greek regime following the 'Political Change' of 1974.

The accession debate reveals that none of the parties perceived the Greek democratic problem as a simple question of establishing representative institutions. In their varying ways, all saw democracy in terms of a total system which linked the political and economic levels to the external dimension. The four main political forces thus regarded EC membership as a system-defining choice, determining political and economic structures and fixing geopolitical orientation. While the traditional Centre discerned a continual deepening of democracy within the

Community, it perceived this as occurring within the limits of the social democratic option. For the Centre, as for New Democracy, PASOK, and the KKE, the European Community's general orientation and basic nature were already fixed.

Hence all these parties believed that EC entry would lock Greece into the particular political and economic pattern represented by western Europe. Consequently their acceptance or rejection of EC membership was conditioned by whether or not they wanted to see this kind of 'western' system established in Greece. The KKE-Es had a rather different perspective. While it opposed the EC's present capitalist form, the party's belief in the Community's continual progressive evolution allowed it to accept membership in the expectation of what the EC would become. But like the larger parties, the KKE-Es's attitude to the EC was explicitly related to its hopes for Greece's future political regime.

Underlying the discussion of this question was the major shared assumption that there could be no return to the pre-1967 past: the attention given to the nature of the USA–EC relationship originated in the perception that this was the key to the question whether accession could provide the basis for the new beginning which all regarded as necessary. But if the EC debate illustrates the firm consensus against a restoration of the *ancien régime*, it also shows that its successor had become the epicentre of major conflict. The ideological divisions separating the parties suggested there was little prospect of their co-operating harmoniously within the new political institutions. Political disagreement was not restricted to the 'micro-choice' rules of the game, but covered a range of attitudes, including a direct rejection of the 'macro-choice' of a western-type system.

At times, the EC debate seemed more closely connected with wish-fulfilment than with the realities of the Greek situation. Withdrawal from the western camp, upsetting the settlement following the Second World War and destabilizing the strategically sensitive Balkan-Mediterranean region, was an unlikely prospect. In practice, Greece's choices in 1974 appeared to be limited to the kind of regime that would be compatible with its global orientation: the probable alternative to a western parliamentary system was military dictatorship.

But if objectively the discussion seemed to suffer from a touch of the surreal, at another level the controversy raging around EC membership in the 1970s can be regarded as substituting for the debate which never happened when the fundamental decisions were being made. No public airing of the question where Greece belonged in the post-war world had been possible in the ideological climate of the 1950s, which Constantine Tsoucalas has described as polarized between the 'two opposed and antagonistic, even though essentially different, repressive mechanisms' of the authoritarian regime and the 'intransigent Stalinism' of the KKE.[26]

Thus at the subjective level, the EC debate fulfilled an important need. And democratic consolidation is a subjective process, involving the actors coming to view the existing system as the framework within which they have to operate, regardless of whether their ultimate aim is to maintain it or to change it. In Greece, this entailed all the leading political forces coming to terms with the outcome of the Civil War which had placed Greece in the western camp. As long as major parties refused to accept Greece's global position with its systemic implications, the regime would remain unsettled at a deep and basic level.

PASOK: shifting ground on European policy

In 1974 the new system seemed to be starting life with an impressive initial basis of support. ND and the Centre had gained 75 per cent of the vote between them, suggesting that the alternating roles of government and official opposition could be played by two system-supporting parties. But the 1977 elections, in which EC membership was a major issue, decimated the Centre and reduced ND's majority, while producing a vote of over 40 per cent for the parties which rejected Greece's external orientation. While the share of PASOK and the KKE rose from around 20 per cent to nearly 35 per cent, the far right, a negligible force in 1974, picked up nearly 7 per cent of the vote. The latter was living in a different world from the other parties, hankering for a return to the pre-1974 past. Still identifying democracy with anti-Communism, the far right opposed any modification to the US link, which it regarded as Greece's only protection against the Soviet bloc. Consequently it had some doubts about EC membership, which threatened to stabilize a political system modelled on a western Europe where the development of Eurocommunism seemed to be raising the possibility of Communist participation in government.

While the emergence of a new party on the far right was disquieting for regime supporters, the chief threat appeared to come from the rapid growth of PASOK which had doubled its vote in three years to become the official opposition. Major uncertainty about the future of the system was generated by the prospect of a future electoral victory by a party pledged to rewrite the Constitution and to destabilize Greece's global position by simultaneously claiming greater independence from the USA and blocking Greek entry to the EC.

However, the modifications to PASOK's EC policy as it came closer to assuming government were not only an illustration but also a key element of the party's changing attitude towards the regime. In the 1977

213

election campaign, when it successfully ousted the Centre from the position of official opposition, PASOK was already suggesting that Greece should contract a Norwegian-type agreement with the EC.[27] Norway's trade treaty was soon supplanted as a model for Greek–EC relations by a more comprehensive agreement of the Yugoslav type and subsequently by a 'special relationship', whose main virtue seemed to be that its precise nature could remain usefully ambiguous.

The systemic implications of EC membership gradually disappeared from PASOK's discourse as the nature of its opposition began to shift ground, moving almost imperceptibly from a rejection of Greece's political system to an opposition to New Democracy which could be contained within the framework of the regime. In June 1979 Papandreou handled the ratification of the Accession Treaty as a 'democratic' issue. But the main force of his attack was not turned against the EC and the kind of domestic regime Greece could expect to have if it institutionalized its relationship to a major imperialist centre. Instead he directed the electors' attention to ND's allegedly undemocratic behaviour in not holding a referendum before ceding national sovereignty to supranational EC organs.[28]

That the ratification of the Accession Treaty had a considerable impact on opposition attitudes was demonstrated by the question of institutional participation. Both PASOK and the KKE had previously manifested a total refusal to co-operate or compromise through spectacular boycotts of national parliamentary debates on themes related to EC membership.[29] But now that accession was more or less a *fait accompli*, both parties decided not only to send representatives to the European Parliament, but also to integrate them into the relevant transnational party groups alongside more pro-EC comrades from other member-states.

In the 1981 election, in which PASOK made its successful bid for power, the party gave the issue of Community membership much less prominence than in 1977. The anti-EC polemic was now integrated into an electoral campaign in which Papandreou, eager to attract moderate voters, at one point declared that 'the only thing endangered by the rise of PASOK is the Right's monopoly of power'.[30] The single page the party devoted to the relationship with the Community in its 109-page manifesto was typical in treating the subject as an economic problem.[31] While PASOK promised a referendum, this was constitutionally impossible without the approval of President Karamanlis, who was unlikely to agree. Taken together with the pledge to struggle from within the Community to minimize the negative economic consequences of accession, this in practice implied a tactical acceptance of EC membership.

With his first experience of EC summitry, in London a month after the 18 October electoral victory, Papandreou made the transition from the glorious detachment of opposition, with its attractive but abstract talk of disassociation from the EC, to involvement in the continual process of negotiation, which is the essence of the European Community. Three months later, the submission of the famous Memorandum to the European Commission confirmed that the new government did not intend to overthrow the system set up by ND, but simply to adopt a different approach to administering it. The Memorandum did not ask for a reversal or even a renegotiation of Greek EC membership, instead requesting special treatment for the Greek economy on the grounds of its lower level of development.[32]

Soon PASOK was taking an openly pecuniary approach to EC membership, claiming that the cost of withdrawal exceeded the cost of Greece remaining a member. Meanwhile, the major thrust of its EC policy became the crusade for redistribution from richer to poorer regions within the Community, an idea which can also be found in the thinking of 1950s right-wing governments.[33] While certain issues would undoubtedly have been handled differently by a New Democracy government, PASOK's basic attitude to the Community became more or less similar to that of any member-state government, aiming to get the best deal for its own country. The party's re-election in 1985 and the subsequent adoption of an economic austerity policy supported by a European Community loan were followed by a dramatic change in PASOK's stance, towards what might be described as an increasingly enthusiastic and uncritical Europeanism.

The accommodation with EC membership was greatly helped by the fact that accession, in January 1981, had already been formally accomplished ten months before PASOK formed its administration. The 1981 election showed that the Greek political system of the 1970s, with a different relationship to its international environment from its 1960s predecessor, was flexible enough to allow alternation of government between the two leading parties. This made it possible for a PASOK administration to exist in cohabitation, not only with the 1975 Constitution, but also with the overall domestic and international framework established by Karamanlis. As PASOK's stance consequently shifted from outright opposition to gradual adaptation to EC membership, its supporters slowly came round to accepting Greece's new global position.

In effecting this reconciliation, an important role was played by the rather flamboyant style which the PASOK government frequently adopted, particularly in the context of European political co-operation. For example, the governments of the other member-states were infuriated in 1983 by the controversial Greek refusal to support a strongly worded EC statement, condemning the Soviet Union for shooting down a South Korean civilian jumbo jet which had violated its airspace. But actions like these helped to persuade many Greeks that, despite the new US bases agreement, their country was finally overcoming its legacy of dependence and the national humiliation over Cyprus to establish itself as a proud power with an independent voice in the world. Similarly, *The Times* commented that the excessive fanfare with which Greece assumed the Presidency of the Council of Ministers in July 1983 had made the Greeks 'for the first time in their 155 years of modern statehood . . . feel as equal Europeans'.[34]

Towards consensus

The extent to which Greece's EC membership subsequently ceased to be a controversial issue was demonstrated by the 1984 Euroelections. Unlike the unexciting Second Order elections in the other member-states,[35] the Greek elections turned into a major national contest, involving vast expenditure, the mass mobilization of party supporters, and not inconsiderable violence. But with the main focus of attention directed on the government's record in all sectors, little attention was paid to the EC.

In the rhetoric of the party leaders, the poll was presented as 'the final confrontation between Right and anti-Right',[36] 'a conflict not between two parties, but between two ways of life'.[37] But in a campaign fought 'on all issues' ('εφ όλης της ύλης'), the one issue notable by its absence was the question of Greece's place in the world and the kind of regime it should have. The magic word 'democracy' featured prominently in the discourse of the two main parties. But the ferocity of their exchanges tended to obscure the fact that, rather than supporting different kinds of political system, both PASOK and ND concentrated on casting doubt on the other party's democratic fitness to administer the current regime. Meanwhile the democratic consequences of EC membership were not mentioned at all.

In the 1970s all the Greek political forces had treated EC membership as an intensely political issue – and an issue of macro-politics at that. But in the 1984 Euroelections, the two major parties confined their disagreement to the burning question of which was best able to obtain maximum European Community funding. Meanwhile the UUE also concentrated on promoting itself as the party best able to protect Greek interests within the EC. In all three cases, the line adopted was related less to European considerations than to the party's desire to prove its suitability for government. While PASOK wanted to prevent ND from replacing it in government, the KKE was trying to persuade PASOK to accept it as a coalition partner.[38]

The fact that all three parties treated their prospects of government participation as a purely domestic matter, making no reference to Greece's relationship to the rest of the world, implied that they perceived the post-1974 system as having achieved a considerable degree of autonomy. This was particularly striking in the case of the KKE, as it would imply that the latter apparently did not regard Greece's institutional incorporation into the west as necessarily hindering the inclusion of a Moscow-line Communist Party in government.

However, the KKE's tactical choice not to make disengagement from the EC its central theme in the Euroelections did not imply an alteration in its basic position. The continued commitment to withdrawal was reflected by the steady anti-EC campaign conducted by the party newspaper, *Rizospastis*. Nor did this attitude show any signs of mellowing through participation in the European Parliament (EP), as Kevin Featherstone has suggested occurred for instance in the case of the first British Labour EuroMPs.[39]

The KKE certainly maintained a high profile at Strasbourg. For example, in the parliamentary year beginning in March 1982, it had a higher average number of interventions per EuroMP than any other Greek party.[40] But this active participation, in a European Community institution traditionally noted for a stronger commitment to west European integration than that of the EC member-governments, did not seem to result in the KKE's 'socialization' into a more pro-EC attitude.

An analysis of the KKE's EP interventions by category shows that the party's main form of activity was neither making constructive proposals for resolutions in the plenary sessions nor preparing reports for committees. Instead, it displayed a distinct preference for the parliamentary question, an ideal opposition tool for attacking policy or embarrassing the executive. An examination of their content shows that the KKE was using the EP as a forum from which to denounce all aspects of the EC and oppose any steps towards further integration. The KKE's performance at Strasbourg is an example of the way in which the party functioned within the existing political framework while remaining deeply opposed to it at an ideological level. Thus it seemed that the KKE was able to operate according to the rules of the parliamentary game without inevitably being incorporated into the logic of the system.

However, recently there have been indications that the KKE may be finding this obdurate anti-system position increasingly uncomfortable. Fourteen years after the 'Political Change' and seven after Greek accession to the European Community, both had come to seem facts of life, with a totally negative response becoming increasingly non-viable as a political stance. Certainly it was a serious obstacle to the co-operation with other left-wing forces through which the KKE hoped to break out of the political ghetto to which it had confined itself. Significantly this desire to effect some shift in the party's stance was expressed in the form of an attempt to modify its hard line on the EC.

Presenting the KKE's March 1988 'Theses' on the completion of the EC's internal market,[41] *Rizospastis* director Grigoris Farakos explained, 'While we do not say yes to the EC, at this moment it would not be correct for us simply to say no.' Central Committee member Yannis Dragasakis denied that the call for an alternative economic strategy to face the dangers of 1992 meant an active adaptation to EC membership in contrast to the passive line allegedly being taken by PASOK and ND.[42] But the fact that the party now felt the need to develop more sophisticated policies to deal with the specific sectoral problems which it expected to arise, suggested that the KKE was increasingly being compelled to discuss the agenda being forced on it by the advance of the integration process.

This new ambiguous line on the Community initially appeared as a primarily tactical change. Party speakers continued to stress that, at the strategic level, opposition to EC membership remained a question of fundamental ideological principle for the KKE. However, the December 1988 joint statement with the Greek Left (EAR), one of the parties formed following the 1987 self-dissolution of the KKE-Es, suggests that the KKE may be moving towards a major change in its strategy. New opportunities seemed to have opened up, with the apparently imminent political demise of Papandreou being expected to result in the collapse of PASOK and thus to trigger a major transformation of the party system.

In this changed climate, the KKE seemed to make an explicit turn towards electoralism. The keynote of the joint statement was concern for the preservation of Greece's democratic system. The statement described democracy as the only road to Socialism and suggested that the KKE had come closer to accepting Greece's EC membership than ever before.[43] Should this policy switch prove to be permanent, it will clearly have very significant implications for democratic consolidation.

Democratic consolidation: how far has it been achieved?

After the collapse of the Cold War political system in 1974, Greece suffered a national identity crisis. Disillusion with the USA following the humiliation and shock of the Cyprus invasion resulted in a general rejection of the country's former position as a US client-state. It also activated a hostility towards the west always latent in a society which, prior to the close but unequal relationship of the past 150 years, had followed a separate historical trajectory from its future EC partners. In the mid-1970s, the combination of this emotional anti-westernism with the anti-Americanism of the specific historical moment served to reopen the problem apparently settled by the Civil War: what was Greece and where did it belong?

With the application for EC membership in June 1975, Karamanlis' government hoped to settle the Greek identity problem once and for all. New Democracy believed that by upgrading Greece's international position within a continued close association with the western bloc, it could set the country permanently on a particular political and economic path. Initially the EC choice was only supported by the right and centre, the political forces which were in full agreement with the outcome of the Civil War and the nature of the post-1974 regime.

Then in June 1976 the First Congress of the KKE-Esoterikou voted in favour of a qualified acceptance of EC membership, thus upsetting the automatic equation between leftism and anti-westernism which had traditionally applied in Greece. In suggesting that EC membership was not incompatible with an evolution to the left, the KKE-Es challenged the dogma that the overthrow of the existing system was an essential precondition for radical social change. Promoting the idea that major alterations to the system could be achieved by working within it, the party thus made a more important contribution to regime consolidation than might be implied by its electoral strength. But the key role was played by PASOK, which attracted the majority of the post-dictatorship protest vote. The fact that much of the initial dissent had been channelled through PASOK allowed it to be integrated into the system after the latter formed a government.

Thus, from a focal point of political conflict, the regime and its external links have become the object of growing consensus among the Greek political parties. Of the major political forces, PASOK's change of heart initially left the KKE in glorious isolation. But as we have seen, the latter now seems to be adjusting its views on the EC. The far right also seems to have come round to EC membership, with its main representative, EPEN, adopting a pro-European stance in the 1984 Euroelections. In any case, with its 0.5 per cent in the 1985 general election, the far right's vote dropped to its lowest level since the fall of the dictatorship. Faced with the greater demon of PASOK, the majority of extreme right-wing voters apparently opted for a reconciliation with the system in the form of the lesser evil of New Democracy, which has remained faithful to Karamanlis' views on European policy.

Thus a rendezvous with the reality of Greece's basic global orientation seems to a considerable extent to have been achieved, with important effects for the consolidation of democracy. While there are major programmatic differences between the two largest parties, these are now contained within the limits defined by EC membership, so that their normal alternation in power poses no threat to the political framework.

A question mark still remains concerning the KKE's attitude. Strong forces within the party are clearly opposed to the recent policy changes. Up to now, the problem of a third party committed to an anti-system stance has been handled by means of an electoral law designed to exclude the KKE from government by encouraging the emergence of a two-party system. However, the crisis in PASOK and the possibility of changes to the electoral system raise in immediate form the question whether the end of two-partyism could destabilize the regime.

The international environment, which in the past proved so important in determining Greece's domestic political system, now constitutes a serious obstacle to its destabilization. In an era when the Gorbachev leadership in the Soviet Union is actively seeking better relations with the west, the already unlikely prospects of a major upset of the kind that would be involved by Greece switching blocs have faded even further.

Meanwhile, Greece's accession to the European Community not only has created enormous difficulties for a macro-level shift in the nature of the Greek regime, but also raises impediments to the creation of politico-economic institutions which do not conform to EC models, as the PASOK government discovered when it attempted to nationalize the pharmaceuticals industry. And as the EC's realm of responsibility expands, there will be an increasing number of sectors where member-states will be unable to deviate radically from EC norms.

Thus accession to the European Community seems to have played a significant role in the consolidation of Greece's post-dictatorship political system. It may well be that the country's membership of the EC will continue to act as a stabilizing force, allowing the party system to be reshaped without provoking the collapse of parliamentary democracy.

Meanwhile, an examination of the EC debate in Greece provides a good illustration of the subjective nature of the democratic consolidation process. In the Greek case, coming to terms with the post-1974 political system involved overcoming the cleavages inherited from the Civil War. The changing attitudes of the Greek political parties towards the EC cast considerable light on their growing acceptance of Greece's position in the world and the framework this provides for the domestic political system. Disagreement certainly continues about the content of democracy. This concerns not only the nature of the meso- and micro-level rules of the game, particularly the electoral law, but also whether their administration is undermined by clientelist practices. However, at the basic macro-level, the choice of liberal parliamentarism is now the axis of growing consensus.

While illuminating the role of the political parties, whose shifts of ground contributed to the regime's increasing stabilization, the Greek debate on the EC also indicates the importance of not focusing on the domestic plane in isolation from its international context. In Greece the perceived constraints of the country's external links played a major part in influencing the way the domestic actors saw their situation. The Greek case thus suggests that a fruitful approach to the further study of democratic consolidation might be based on the theory of linkage politics, allowing the interaction between a polity and its environment to be taken into account.

Acknowledgements

The author would like to thank the Leverhulme Foundation for awarding her a Study Abroad Studentship and for so generously extending it. Also many thanks to Geoffrey Pridham for his careful editing, to Mark Mazower for a helpful discussion, to Iakovos Tsalikoglou for a number of stylistic suggestions, and to Fotis Provatas for moral support.

Notes

1. M. Cotta, 'Partyness of government, parliamentarisation of parties and democratic consolidation in Italy after World War II', *EUI Paper*, 1985, quoted in G. Pridham, 'Political parties and democratic consolidation in southern Europe: a comparative approach', paper for panel on *Political Parties and Democratic Consolidation in Southern Europe: Italy, Spain, Greece and Portugal in Comparative Perspective*, PSA Conference, 7–9 April 1987, Aberdeen.
2. P. Schmitter, 'The consolidation of political democracy in southern Europe (and Latin America)', *EUI Paper*, 1985, quoted in Pridham, op. cit.
3. G. Pridham, 'The party-political context of parliamentary institutional-ization in southern Europe: theoretical and empirical perspectives', *Parliaments and Democratic Consolidation in Southern Europe Conference*, Jaume Bofill Foundation–Volkswagen Foundation Conference, 29–31 October 1987, Barcelona, 1987b, as amended by letter to contributors to this volume, 7 December 1987.
4. J. Rosenau, *Linkage Politics: Essays on the Convergence of National and International Systems*, New York, Free Press, 1969.
5. While charges of direct US complicity have never been proved or disproved, extensive US aid and comfort to the junta, including an official visit by Vice-President Agnew, dismayed even former members of right-wing governments which had benefited from the close relationship with the USA.
6. The vast majority of Greeks blame the USA for not acting more effectively to avert the Turkish invasion, while many believe the subsequent partition of the island served US interests. The point at issue here is not what the USA could or should have done, but the perceptions of the Greek people, who felt betrayed.
7. *Akropolis*, 6, 7, 8, and 9 August 1974.
8. *The Economist*, 27 July 1974.

9. On Greek political party attitudes towards the EC 1957–75, see the excellent study by M. Pateras, 'From Association to Accession: Changing Attitudes of Greek Political Parties towards Greek relations with the European Communities, 1957–1975', unpublished Ph.D. thesis, London School of Economics, 1984.

10. On the so-called 'freezing' of the Association Agreement, see G. Yannopoulos, *Greece and the European Communities: The First Decade of a Troubled Association*, London, Sage research paper, 1975; and V. Coufoudakis, 'The European Economic Community and the "freezing" of the Greek Association', *Journal of Common Market Studies* 1977, vol. XVI, no. 2, pp. 114–31.

11. This was not just a matter of ideology. There was also a technical problem involved, as one of the major bodies overseeing the functioning of the Association was the Greece–EC Mixed Parliamentary Committee composed of MPs from the Greek and European Parliaments.

12. This story is told in more detail in S. Verney and P. Tsakaloyannis, 'Linkage politics: the role of the European Community in Greek politics in 1973', *Byzantine and Modern Greek Studies*, 1986, vol. 6.

13. European Commission, *Opinion on Greek Application for Membership*, Bulletin of the European Communities, Supplement 2/76, 1976, p. 7; and *Enlargement of the European Community: General Considerations*, Bulletin of the European Communities, Supplement 1/78, 1978, p. 6.

14. E.g. Karamanlis in *Proceedings of the Greek Parliament*, 12 June 1976.

15. See the Greek press for 13 June 1975.

16. E.g. Kallias in *Proceedings of the Greek Parliament*, 25 June 1979.

17. For some examples, see ND's 'Statement of Principles and Guidelines for Government', *Kathimerini*, 13 October 1977; *Proceedings of the Greek Parliament*, 14 December 1977; ND rapporteur Kallias on the ratification of the Accession Treaty, ibid., 25 June 1979.

18. Prologue by George Rallis in G.E. Stephanakis, Ευρωπαισμός: Μια Καινουρια Πολιτικη Ιδεολογια (*Europeanism: A New Political Ideology*), Dodoni, Athens, 1978. When Karamanlis was elected President of the Republic in 1980, Rallis succeeded him as prime minister.

19. J. Pesmazoglou in *Proceedings of the Greek Parliament*, 13 December 1974.

20. EDIK EOK, ΕΔΗΚ: Η Ενταξη, τα Ελληνικά Συμφεροντακαικαι τα άλλα Κόμματα (The EEC and EDIK: Accession, the Greek Interests and the other Parties), party publication, Athens, 1977.

21. K. Simitis, Η Δομικη Αντιπολιτευση (*Structural Opposition*), Athens, Kastaniotis, 1979.

22. See for example A.G. Papandreou, Ιμπεριαλισμός και Οικονομικγ Αναπτυξη (*Imperialism and Economic Development*), Athens, Nea Synora, 2nd edn, 1975.

23. *Rizospastis*, 30 June 1977.

24. E.g. KKE 'Η Παλη του ΚΚΕ εναντια στην 'Ενταξη της Ελλαδας στην Κοινη Αγορα' ('*The KKE's Struggle Against Greece's Accession to the EEC*'), CC of the KKE, Athens, 1979.

25. KKE-Esoterikou Πρόγραμμα του ΚΚΕ-Εσωτερικού: Για ενα Ελληνικό Δρόμο προς τη Δημοκρατικη Αναγεννηση και το Σοσιαλισμό (*The Programme of the KKE-Esoterikou: For a Greek Road to Democratic Rebirth and Socialism*), KKE-Esoterikou, Athens, 1976.
26. C. Tsoucalas, 'The ideological impact of the Civil War', in J.O. Iatrides, *Greece in the 1940s: A Nation in Crisis*, London, 1981, pp. 339–40.
27. PASOK, Κατεμθμντηριες Γραμμες Κμβερνητικης Πολιτικης Τοη Πανελληντιοη Σοριαλιρτιηση Κινηματος (*Government Policy Guidelines of the Panhellenic Socialist Movement*), party election manifesto, Athens, 1977, p. 19.
28. *Proceedings of the Greek Parliament*, 25 June 1979.
29. Both parties had also withdrawn from the Greece–EC Mixed Parliamentary Committee which administered the Association Agreement.
30. *Vima*, 26 April 1981.
31. PASOK, Το Συμβόλαιο με το Λαό (*The Contract with the People*), party election manifesto, Athens, 1981, p. 62.
32. The text of the memorandum is published in English in *The Greek Review*, 17 July 1982.
33. See S. Verney, 'Greece and the European Community', in K. Featherstone and D. Katsoudas (eds) *Political Change in Greece: Before and After the Colonels*, London, Croom Helm, 1987.
34. *The Times*, 2 July 1983.
35. See K. Reif, 'Ten second-order national elections', in Reif (ed.) *Ten European Elections*, Aldershot, Gower, 1985.
36. Prime Minister Andreas Papandreou in *Exormisi*, 15 June 1984.
37. New Democracy leader Evangelos Averoff in *Akropolis*, 15 June 1984.
38. This emerges particularly clearly from the interview with Secretary-General Harilaos Florakis in *Ta Nea*, 20 and 21 February 1984.
39. K. Featherstone, 'Labour in Europe: the work of a national party delegation', in V. Herman and R. van Lehendebelen (eds) *The European Parliament and the National Parliaments*, London, Saxon House, 1979.
40. Research for the author's Ph.D. thesis.
41. The 'Theses' were published in *Rizospastis*, 24 March 1988. I have discussed them in more detail in S. Verney, 'The New Red Book of the KKE', *Journal of Communist Studies*, December 1988.
42. *Rizospastis*, 24 March 1988.
43. *Rizospastis*, 8 December 1988.

Index